at the Crossroads

Dr. Henry Phung

WESTBOW
PRESS®
A DIVISION OF THOMAS NELSON
& ZONDERVAN

WestBow Press books may be ordered through booksellers or by contacting:

WestBow Press
A Division of Thomas Nelson & Zondervan
1663 Liberty Drive
Bloomington, IN 47403
www.westbowpress.com
1 (866) 928-1240

ISBN: 978-1-5127-5083-6 (sc)
ISBN: 978-1-5127-5082-9 (hc)
ISBN: 978-1-5127-5081-2 (e)

Library of Congress Control Number: 2016911732

Print information available on the last page.

WestBow Press rev. date: 09/28/2016

This book is dedicated to Chhieng Phung, my beloved father, who experienced extensive challenges and learned many lessons in life. He was called to use his personal life and extraordinary experience to enrich both the intellectual and spiritual growths for his family and children so that they can be sanctified by faith and purified by the forgiveness of sin.

Contents

Acknowledgments

Many thanks to all the pastors of Heatherwood Baptist Church and the deacons and elders of the Victory Revival Church in Riverdale, Georgia, for their continuous, persistent prayers and spiritual support. Thanks to so many surgeons, doctors, nurses and hospital staff who provided encouragement, advice and support. Finally, my heartfelt thanks to many of you, who choose to be anonymous but contacted and showed your great love and deep respect to my father during his unforgettable journey, his strong battle against several diseases, and his peaceful departure from this life.

Foreword

In loving memory of my dad, Mr. Chhieng Phung (1921-2015), a survivor from both the Pol-Pot Era (1975-79) and Vietnamese Economic Crisis (1980-81). He is also a survivor from a stroke in 2008 when he was almost completely paralyzed and thought to be dead. He then survived a series of diseases and several remissions of them. Under the grace of our Almighty God, he lived for an additional seven blessed years after the stroke. He indeed is loved and will be forever missed after living a full ninety-four years of age until he was called home by our Lord by leaving a legacy behind so that his children can remember and follow in his footstep. In honoring of the dedication he made for fatherhood and mentorship, I learned the lesson of unselfish devotion and service through humility in my growing-up years. Everyday occurrences and interactions can be as complicated as typhoon, and he taught me how to find peace in the stormy periods even when I was still in my early childhood. When I'm struck by errors, bruised by tragedy and hurt by low spirits, he inspires me to see through role modeling and mental toughness to live my adult life.

Born slightly before the outbreak of a cruel civil war that led to the Cambodian genocide, I have learned and taught how to live through the socialist policies and the propaganda of a better ethnic cleansing. By successfully escape from the bloody war, I learn how to truly appreciate life with the lesson from arbitrary executions, physical tortures, and widespread famines. By living through the communist government and socialist institution in Vietnam, I gradually value more on the notion of human rights and liberty than the idea of segregation and/or revolutionaries combined.

For years, I learned good common sense that says one does not foster a relationship not until mutual trust has developed. Inexplicitly, I always think that a good common sense should be easy to maintain in every walk of life…until common sense turned out to not be so common. Despite cultural differences, I believe that we should live and guide by core value and set of standard that are to do the right thing for others in terms of tolerance and acceptance. As far as I am concerned, the journey of my faith starts out by not following the traditional way or conventional path until series of incidents happen. As a healthcare professional, I acknowledge that the concept of health is a combination of total well-beings in term of body, mind, and spirit. I also acknowledge the greatest wealth on earth is to have good health that can be defined as not being the absence of symptoms or disease but rather the maintenance and achievement of total body function through the state of homeostasis. As a human being, I always have been fascinated by the paradox and interplay between beliefs and rationales. From time to time, I recall that gifting is something that we tend to do day in and night out. It also gives us great skills and advantages to do things that other people are having a hard time to match up with. Time and time again, I learn the reason why each of us can be gifted differently is because God places us with a mission and a vision so that we not only can find our own purpose in life, but we can live our life with a big heart, great passion and extraordinary love. I also happen to believe one amazing, incredible and great understanding of our purpose is to face our challenges from the past and to thus embrace choices from our current situations by focusing on the vision for our future, redefining the passion in our life, and maintaining the spiritual connection so that we can transform our faith and reconnect to the unlimited possibilities leading to a healthier and happier life.

Introduction

The story about to be told details those incredible sufferings from hunger and the dangers he faced in the time of war or political changes. The story also reveals the overcoming of obstacles both in the economic crisis in the Southeast Asia and the recovery from setbacks in due time. This story reflects the sense of personal development in terms of sin, sickness and death from a daily perspective. Despite the need for revolution in culture, tradition, religion and beliefs, this book truly reveals the myth and mystery that the world of science has with recognizing the anomalous events.

This story is written on behalf of a young man who has never finished anything big and hasn't had any great achievement other than standing in the middle of or on the sideline of something but doesn't get a chance to tell people around him that he can make through obstacles and setbacks in this life because of the special encounters and unique connections come from the superb authority or supernatural gifts. This story reflects the struggles and conflicts in terms of spiritual and intellectual mindsets that almost every human beings have by going through different phases of changes in life. This story indeed affects my personal life, my professional life, and even my Christian life to a point that I hardly imagine its turning point when I look back at those journeys. And for the first time, I find myself having a second chance not only in my academic and business settings but also in my very life from war and even to the overwhelming void of sickness and death that my dad has suffered. That little hope and faith have led me to the still water and by His amazing grace, I'm not only saved but gradually I learn how to fully understand and appreciate the facts that His word is perfect and His love remains steadfast.

In fact, each of us is absolutely unique and our experience of life is also extraordinary. Though we can be seen as a separate entity, but we are just a part of a much larger story because we are interconnected in some meaningful ways that allow us all to reveal His intelligence, love and light. I have, from time to time, felt that life can be defined by the evolution of science or conviction from any analytical means. I believe suffering, sinning and dying beliefs are fiction and unreal. I have never learned that death can almost and instantaneously occur on every plane or any phase of existence until the spiritual understanding of life reaches.

Life indeed can come in all forms of storm, hail and lightning, but I'm strongly convinced that God is still the anchor. I believe that there will be a day and time we can inspire others by sharing our story so that we can motivate and encourage others to live and fight through the similar predicaments in term of the deep and thin water of sorrow, failure, brokenness, despair, addictions, sickness and even death. At many levels, I have never thought of healing coming off prayers until I experience heaven is real. By all reasons, I have never seen peace, joy and comfort coming to the dying soul during the very moment until I witness my dad willingly and comfortably surrenders his life when God calls him home peacefully because daddy knows that his mission on this earth has been completed. With no reservation, I truly believe that faith is what we have but strength is what we tend to fall short of and besides, grace is what is given to us so that we not only can claim victory for his Kingdom, but we can assure peace coming from our Almighty God even though we happen to be in the crossroads of financial hardships, storms of sicknesses, drawbacks in relationships, and even at the end of life.

Chapter 1: Wake-up Call

"If I could wake up in a different place, at a different time, could I wake up as a different person?" Chuck Palahniuk

There is always a time for everything as an old proverb proclaims that "not a fallen leaf goes without Her will." Whether it is in motion or not, subconsciously, we might feel that thing seems to move in her way. The sun rises as the day begins when the first dew disappears and the dawn breaks through the clear sky. The sun sets in a golden picturesque landscape over the western horizon to dress in a dark gown. Flowers bloom, rivers flow, and wind blows as the clock ticks. The bird flies, the lion roars, and the snake crawls. Days in and nights out, life begins and ends in the cradle of the universe.

Every life has a story and every story has a line. From the creation of universe to the era of modern science, every life or living creatures begins with a journey. Some life goes through a simple change while others might evolve through a complex or even difficult process. As a human being, we are born, grow up, marry, have kids, get sick, become old, and then die. No one can foresee exactly how this journey will play out. What the future might behold is difficult to imagine because of the myriad infinite possibilities that lie ahead.

Life teems with mystery. The driving desire to find a solution for life's enigmatic situations is woven into our nature. We can't deny the fact that we are curious about what happens in and around us. Relentlessly, we work to find a solution for all that confounds us. From time to time, we question in confusion or frustration and think that life is indeed a conundrum. Do we perceive the incongruity between dream and reality? Do we become aware of the paradox of idealism and the perception between human achievements versus material nothingness? Do we know those who are lost in self-indulgence or addictions are unable to identify the relationship between dream and reality? Do we know who we are and even what we want? Indeed, everyone has a purpose and everyone has an answer. At times, the more we think about what we are going to do, the more confused and frenetic we become. When we look into the mirror of life, our thoughts can become cloudy and what stands in our way is difficult to see. And sometimes when we look at our situations, we can be disconcerted by the sudden attack of our emptiness, especially when we cry out for help and no one answers.

Life begins as a journey. Some journeys turn into an adventure itself. Whether it is by chance or coincidence, we have to understand that any adventure can be complicated if it does not go as planned. Even if it can be planned out in advance, we still can feel that we are somehow off track. For most of the time, we really don't know where we are heading and what awaits us. We see our life can be overwhelming and what we encounter can be frustrating. Imagine that we are driving in circles several times. Many times in our life when we're going to a place that we are familiar with, we still are unable to find a parking lot and are confounded by the one-way streets. We might slow down to look for an intersection, but there is no stopping in the middle of traffic. We try to catch our breath from an open window but soon find the air that we breathe in tends to suck us out. While we wait, we can't help but get bored and might want to jump on to somewhere else.

Indeed, perception is a very strange thing. It is mostly sensual but sometimes can be very hard to fully describe as factual. Our mind or perceptual senses can indeed give us a reflection of what we see, touch, smell or comprehend from environments that we are part of. With the fact that the mind can create an idea or reflection of matter and it gradually transforms into the sentiment of material form known as perceptual sense and therefore develops into the sixth sense. The mind also can trick us with the simplicity of our nature or the obsession from the material world. To a certain limit, there will be few distractions to draw our attention from any conventional programs.

Sometimes the true nature of mind and thought can possibly be understood in form and substance with its divine intervention. Certainly understanding the origin of life can give us great insight to facts and truths so that we can make a distinction of where we stand among the true ideas or the principle of man. In the physical senses, life contains matter, but mind pays tribute to matter. The love of life gives rise to power, wealth, sin, sickness and eventually mortal senses. The love of spiritual gatherings can lead to a calm and quiet life with full godly devotion and seriousness without paying a disrespectful attitude toward any secular authority or cynical world.

Everyone has a life and every life has an expectation. By definition, how do we know that we are living up to our expectations? In fact, no one can possibly argue that life can somehow fill us up with the unexpected. But no one can possibly deny the fact that the unexpected can and will lead us to the unknown. The same principle also can be applied when the unexpected leads to the expected or vice versa.

No one lives without an expectation. Sometimes an expectation, just like a blueprint, is a representation or form made from our desire, and our desire is indirectly affected by our thought process. And over a period of time, this kind of representation can be reinforced and transformed by action or labor, and hence, it becomes the result of performance or workmanship. Whether the expectation is small or large, it is a reflection of hope and desire that are recognized as belonging to us and thus drive us to pursue as that in a dream. For the vast majority of people, our expectation in some fashion allows us to seek the material possession or worldly things with great eagerness and pride.

There are times and circumstances that may cause or turn the expected into the unexpected. From almost all walks of life, you might find out that things can be accomplished by the search of matter, but matter can be scrutinized by substance, mind, or material sense. Every now and then, you might find that many people feel they are successful when they find themselves on the mountaintop of their career, school, business and love. They start to enjoy a little bit more in the provision of wealth, fame and power. There is a time when people somehow forget who they actually are – and some of them hadn't even bothered to figure out how they started in the first place. Gradually they might be trapped or are in the process of being trapped in the trio of addictions, greed or confusion. There seems to be no room left for fear or worries because the mind is driven in the possession of material life. There is no covenant relationship between the spirit and the mind. There also is no connection between the body and soul because enjoyment plays a big factor and it allows the sense of pleasure to be the centerpiece of life.

Certainly, health is the greatest gift one can have. It can be built under the evolutionary theory of day-by-day process and the healing efficacy from natural science. It can be destroyed by corporeal senses in term of guilt, sin and curse. It also can be ruined by the mythological material sense resulting from the disease process, mentally, morally and physically. In fact, the concept and awareness of health can be different from one person to another, culture to culture, and country to country because the difference is enhanced by education levels, family values, religious beliefs, technological innovations and socioeconomic status.

No one really care about their health until they lose it. There are times we are too busy with things around us, and we somehow leave no room for our own health. It is very easy for us to find time shopping on what kind of clothes should be matched up with what type of shoe and then what kind of cologne or makeup we need to put on to best fit in at a certain party, meeting or networking event. We usually don't mind spending hours and even days to figure out what kinds of foods we need to prepare for the family or for some special events. We like to complain of having no time to exercise regularly for ourselves, but we are likely to be too busy talking on the phone, texting, playing video games, watching television, or using social media to exercise. From time to time, we get so frustrated, worn out and upset with our lifestyle, especially our body weight, because we tend to forget health indeed is more than substance and matter combined.

There has never been a time until we create the time. Every day we like to make room for people around us, but we tend to forget about and most likely we tend to not bother to spare some time for ourselves. Every day we spend more time to care for our children, family, friends and pets. Whenever the children cry, we are and will always be there to help care for their needs. We find that it is our responsibility to find out what kinds of friends our kids are hanging out with, what kind of movie or music they like, who they are talking to, and how they do in school or work. We discover that it is a good idea to find out what our friends like, where they are used to hang out, and how they think. Whenever our pets are less active, we kiss and play with them until they get back on their feet. Whenever family members are sick and moan in pain, we become a first responder or advocate so that they can be healthy again. Eventually we stress ourselves out. Our care and love for our loved ones can drive us into a condition that turns out to be more problematic and disappointing than their refusal of our help.

There is nothing more disheartened, disappointing or frustrating than the depressed mind. Certainly caring for others and especially our loved ones always can be a wonderful experience and quite noble. That sense of responsibility can fall upon any one, both men and women. Since the Stone Age, males have served as a provider to both the family and society. Even up to this date, most men believe that they are still the main contributor to the emotional, spiritual, physical, financial and mental well-beings of their family despite the facts that equality and feminism are found in this modern day which seems to be politically incorrect. Even from the Biblical truth, man is the bread winner and protector of his family. He is the laborer and leader in the marketplace. He should be responsible for what is happening in and around his family in term of marriage, parenting, discipline, and activity level. Women by nature are caregivers and helpers. She is honored and respected by the sacrifice and passion she has for her family and children. She also is commemorated by the value and love she shares responsibility with her beloved in term of what is in and out of the family. Sometimes this role can be interchanged and interdependent in term of society, cultures, religion, beliefs, class and ethnicity.

For years, I have sought a purpose in my life and have repeatedly asked myself why I am here on this earth. Oftentimes, I love waking up each morning knowing that I have one thought in place but not too many loosen things to catch up with. Sometimes I wake up in the middle of the night and also before dawn, and I love sitting up in the center of bed without lights on or music, just my listening to my breathing and to my heart beat without any interruptions. I love to feel whatever comes into my mind. I want to live my life the way that all of us know that we should. But in reality, we usually don't and we always can't. In some strange ways, I know that I am running at a great speed. I gear up very high to chase for my dream. I think the blueprint and expression of success are the measurement in term of money and the ownership in term of property, fame and power. From months to years, I seem to not understand what I look for and surely enough I fail to find out why I am still running after. I even write down what I plan to do hoping to see from what I want. From time to time, I go over my to-do-list in comparison to my result list. Regardless of how much energy I spend, how much time I put into, and how much works I do, I always find out that they are not aligned with my goal, value and mission. With endless nights, I find myself in tears when I try to connect them with my purpose.

Perhaps stepping out of the box, telling the truth, and living out loud are ways to rediscover myself. The possibilities for reaching out and making a difference in other people's lives are not in my textbook at a time when I don't understand the relationships between what it is that really holds my life together and what propels me forward. I learn the fundamental drive in human existence lies in the need to find meaning in life but I never come close to learn self-fulfillment emphasizing on individualism that eventually drive me off from serving others as well as myself until I take a close-up look at my family.

What draws me into this is the concerned response I get when seeing my dad seriously ill for the first time. In retrospect, I see that my dad has been living his life in taking care of his family. He puts all his time in the nurture and growth of his children. I always remember what he used to say – that every seed needs to be grown in a good environment. To have a fruitful result, a plant needs to undergo careful irrigation, trimming, and cultivation because storm, wind, mold and locusts can threaten and disrupt growth. The same theory can apply to mankind as well. With strong family values and a good, nurturing environment, a child can and will develop strong character and good physical and intellectual health, as he or she grows older.

There has never been a day that my dad led his life without showing his passion and concern to the ones he loved and so to the people he associated with. Ever since I was a kid, dad always told me that a man needs to stand by his words, to work hard at all times, and by all means to complete his responsibility and his God-given assignment. On any given day or occasion, people happen to forget who you really are and what you actually do, but they won't necessarily forget what you do to them and what you speak to them with little to no objection or rejection at the time.

The only reason for that is no one knows how far reaching those words can be and what can those words and deeds do to influence people's mind and thus to change their attitude and behavior. Sometimes, even a simple word or phrase might mean nothing to you at the time, but it can turn out to be a significant factor in another people's life. Dad also reminded us that we shouldn't count on having family, except in memories, unless we truly show them our true heart.

As an entrepreneur, dad worked very hard every day to support his family. He usually left home shortly after dawn and then came home late after dark. When he was in the store, he made sure that every customer got his or her merchandise at a reasonable price. When the store ran out of things that customers needed, dad would personally go out to other suppliers or factory where he could stock up on the merchandise. He never would charge his clients additional charges or take their tips for special services. He always said that customers are a part of his family and they should be treated with respect, honesty and love. He also told us that customers give us good opportunity to enhance the quality of our service and provide us a chance to improve our personalities in term of attitude, thought, and discipline, not to mention our reputation and integrity.

As a master and keeper of the house, dad showed us the great wisdom and love he had for the family. As always, dad was a good chef, and he was very picky in the use of ingredients, preparation and taste of food. Since teenagers and up to the recent days, we usually saw him sticking around the kitchen with mom to ensure the dishes were perfectly prepared before serve. Dad used to say, "Food is one of the best gifts God gives us to enrich and nourish our flesh, and it should be fully enjoyed in our labor or leisure and by the art of fine cooking as well." We found that is absolutely true, especially during holidays, birthdays, and special events because daddy always was there to show us the secret of fine cooking or culinary art. In addition to that, our family was blessed to have a wonderful dad who constantly reminded us children to study hard and master the skills or knowledge we have. Dad always reminded us of his favorite phrase "to first work hard and then desire more." Dad constantly encouraged us to set school as our priority because a higher education and training will better prepare us for good career and future so that we won't need to make our living with the way he did it, through physical labor. From time to time,

7

he made sure that we children had completed our homework assignments before dinner was served. If anyone of us was caught in idleness or cheated in school, he or she would be reprimanded and not allowed to eat dinner. He or she was then sent to their room to reconsider or figure out what he or she had done wrong. This helped us to remember his teaching, and it indeed triggered in our thoughts about our own actions in term of shame, guilt and redemption. Further, it alerted us to the need to change for goodness sake!

Growing up in a middle-class family, dad had built himself a strong sense of independence after undergoing the devastation of war and economic turmoil from the Great Depression in Asia. He demonstrated to us the life of his strong will, belief and devotion to foster a family with happiness despite of his lack of a higher education or college degree. Though he has lived a tremendously busy life in work, dad never failed to show us the better way to achieve a healthy life. With serious planning and preparation of a better future for his children, dad constantly feeds us with tough questions and proper solutions to the challenging problems we face.

His health was derived in part from nutritional supplements, vitamins, herbs and exercises. Since I was a kid, I seldom saw dad taking drugs or medications, unless he was at least moderately ill. Pain killers, muscle relaxers, and non-steroidal anti-inflammatory drugs (NSAIDs) would be seen as unnecessary in his daily conditions. He frequently told us that there should be an alternative way to the taking of a pill. He believed that the prevention of disease should focus on a day-by-day process, but it did not mean the reluctance or stupidity of not seeking care in any episodic events. He always stated that there was no reason for us not to ask if we didn't know an answer or were in doubt, and there also was no justification for us if we do not search for an answer unless we truly know what it is. From time to time, we remember what dad once told us that things usually would not be changed a lot unless we acted upon them.

As far as I can remember, dad liked to add herbs into his daily cooking. He often put Chinese herbs and medicinal black mushrooms in selective dishes so that more flavors would be found in meats and vegetables. That preparation not only became tastier, but it tended to increase the nutritional level. Due to his being highly active in outdoor activities such as mountain hiking, bicycle riding, jogging, spinal hygiene exercise, gardening and vegetable planting, we usually saw dad takes zinc, Ginseng and herbal teas. Dad explained to us that those products were important and necessary for our health because they helped to improve our energy in term of "Chi," which can form the foundation for good circulation and joint movement. They can also provide us with pure and natural supplements to maintain Yin and Yang balances that can eventually lead to strong immunity, productivity and detoxification. Furthermore, they can help the body to develop natural harmony through duality and enhance strength, vitality and youth for a healthier life.

No one knows how important one's health can be until he or she loses it or is at the brink of losing it. Whether we care or not, health does mean something very significant and sometimes can cost us dearly. To some younger individuals, getting sick may mean discomfort, high fever, bruising, or a cut. They usually carry a take-it-easy attitude because they simply believe a pill or bandage can help to cover the problem and recovery is just a "couple of days away" process. To some middle-aged individuals, getting sick may suggest some kinds of pain, dysfunction, illness, weakness or disruption to the normal process of their physical, psychosocial and even sexual activities. Most of the time, these people will initiate a more aggressive, direct, honest and straightforward approach because they strongly believe that seeking a cure can help to eliminate the "stressful tomorrow." To the elderly, getting ill may not only mean the loss or deprivation of health and painful symptoms, but it may also suggest prolonged suffering or distress and perhaps long-term disability. In general, the elderly believe treatments are indispensable, and that process indeed can go beyond a pill or bandage.

In retirement, dad usually started his day by drinking his favorite French-style coffee mixed with condensed milk going through the filtering drip. Then he did some simple laundry. He liked to keep the house clean at all times whether it was the floor, sofa, kitchen, bedroom, bathroom or garage. Dad always reminded us of his commitment to love, his devotion to work, and his dedication to serve. Dad always pointed out that if a person did not know how to work or to put his or her heart out in every small thing, he or she would have tougher times and bigger challenges dealing with any larger, more complicated problem. As time goes on, we found that is absolutely true, as dad became physically weak to a point that he was incapable of doing things he was used to do since he suffered from hypertension and diabetes.

One early morning before daybreak, my mom called me into dad's bedroom. As I rushed to the room, my sisters told me that dad felt very sick. Suddenly he became chilled and pale, his pulse weakened, his breathing turned shallow, and he was in pain. After knowing dad recently took some prescriptions for cold, sinus, and loss of appetite, I immediately call his doctor's office to see if dad can be seen in his office at the first hour in the morning. The answering service from the doctor's office advised us to immediately take him to the hospital if we felt the illness was life-threatening.

After a few hours of waiting in the local hospital and series of medical procedures, the medical staff and physician from the emergency room told us that dad was scheduled for hospital stay. Due to the nature of his illness, possibly related to his past medical history, the admitting physician advised us that it was beneficial for dad to have good medical attention so that the attending physician and staff could find out the cause of the illness. For the next few hours, our heart sunk deep while we saw dad became weak and even speechless. We thought about how he might not even really know what was going on.

Imagining how life can turn out to be if you are seriously ill sometimes is harsh. Perhaps what worried us most at that time was not the physical condition of dad's illness but rather, that might be the effect from his past medical history accompanied by the incompatibility of senility, as facing the disease process. By the evening, we found that dad was scheduled to be placed in the intensive care unit (ICU) because his blood pressure kept dropping, his vitals were unstable, and he was unlikely to know where he was. Meanwhile, my family and I felt very depressed.

For a while, we seemed to find ourselves, as if in the midst of a storm. Minute by minute and hour by hour, we searched for new inspiration to sustain our hope amid the drop of intravenous (IV) fluid and the beeping of the heart monitor. Day in and day out, we continued searching for miracles in the examination reports from physicians, nurses and clinicians who provided us with good signs and good news since dad had slipped into a coma. We were hopeful but not overly optimistic that dad would soon open his eyes.

For the past few days, dad had been unresponsive to our call and talk since he went into coma. The physician team told us that dad suffered from severe infection and dehydration that had eventually shut off the kidney function. Because dad was over eighty, slow recovery seemed to be a normal process despite that he was given adequate and sufficient medications and care from the ICU staff. Laboratory work, vital monitoring, examinations, follow-ups and imaging studies became a routine protocol during this period, and even the refill of saline plus other medications to control blood pressure and infection through the intravenous drips turned out to be vital.

Given the fact that dad was physically weak and very sick, waking up became a problem. Every day, doctors and nurses told us that the outcome assessments looked promising and dad just needed some time for his body to fight off the severe infection. Once the infection was clear or reduced, dad would slowly get himself back. As time went on, we put our focus and hope into every lab report to ensure that the high level of white blood cells, blood urea nitrogen, sodium, low level of potassium and hematocrit were monitored along with the irregular heartbeats and the fluctuated vitals. We believed that once the symptoms and contents were under control, dad would have a greater chance of waking up regardless any key issue from his chronic renal failure. Meanwhile, we also were greatly concerned about how dad might progress to another journey because the sense of suffering can hit really hard and close to home at any time.

What bothers us most during that moment was not the condition of dad's health and the status of when he would awaken but rather, the thought or worries about factors we could not control. Certainly no one can tell how things will turn out. And no one likes to see the pain and suffering his or her loved ones going through. Certainly no one would expect to see anything worse happened to their beloved especially when they are lying on the hospital bed or intensive care unit. For a while, my family and I felt lost and remained silent. We really did not know what we are going to do, how we are going to do, and why dad was still sleeping. Every now and then, we wondered and questioned how dad became so unconcerned that he did not even think about us and his friends anymore. Did that mean dad no longer cared about the Ginseng chicken soup he used to eat, the spectacular relaxation over South Beach he enjoyed, or the long hike over the Great Wall or the Eiffel Tower that he planned?

Without knowing what the future might hold, we wondered if there actually was a future behind those busy days and sleepless nights. But in our world, there seems to be an untouchable cliché and a boundless disappointment that root into every segment of our thought and every corner of our life as soon as my family and I put ourselves into the shoes of our dad to understand the fact that he has to live with the affliction. Even though we were strongly supported by our friends and were highly convinced by the scientific evidence and test result, we somehow find ourselves dying for the fountain of hope and showers of blessings, as Dr. Yohannan, who is the founder and president of Gospel for Asia, once said, to enlighten and guide our path.

For the next few days, my family and I diligently and patiently are in and out of the hospital to stay side by side with dad, as we have never been before. We feel crushed. Emotionally, we are somehow not much different from the leafless, yellowish and dried-up plant. Where and how can we find the emotional nutrients to sustain life at this moment? Perhaps, the best therapy to our despair lies in the idea of spiritual love. Day by day, ministers, deacons, elders and members of our church visit us both in the hospital and at home more often than they used to. They spend time sharing gospels and praying with us so that we may be able to find strength and comfort in the Lord. Throughout that time, we truly feel the seed of Biblical truth and the moments of brotherly love provide a great blueprint for us to understand promises from the Bible and the healing from Christian Science turns out to be the one and only source leading to a strong foundation of life.

I am surprised and thrilled when my family and I slowly experience the solitude. Indeed, we see anxiety, sorrow and pain growing out of the elderly ill. The shadow of wreck seems to have disappeared and it begins to rip apart in search of the divine presence. This incidence may be the beginning of a good transitional period to secure our faith and to broaden our knowledge into divine authority and intervention. With limited knowledge on how the manifestation of faith plays out in our health and our beliefs in material life, science and intelligence can be confusing and misleading. Sometimes they can even grow worse at every step or stage of process. What really drives us closer to the divine nature is not the presence of fellowship and the devotion of stewardship through compassion but rather, the connection of the invincible touch. It feels like the warmth of a hot spring. It nourishes the cells and rejuvenates the vitality of life.

Late one afternoon, two of my sisters check into the hospital to stay with dad. For the past two hours, they become bored with the normal hospital routines and medical procedures when doctors come in to auscultate dad's chest and lungs and then they also wiggle or tap on dad's toes for responses. Nothing indeed happens because dad is still in a coma. The doctor smiles and then walks away to write his report. The cleanup crew comes in to pick up trash, do the housekeeping, and clean the bathroom. The nurse also comes in and out to update vitals, refill saline and medications. Nothing seems to change dad's conditions. By the fifth hour there, my sister Kim jumps on her feet and shouts that dad just moved the fingers of his right-hand. Then she runs out of the room and straight to the nurse station to inform the nurse and staff that dad might have been awoken. Then the attending nurse comes, the charged nurse comes, and the nurse technician also comes in. Some of them make phone calls to the unit and also report to the physician on call. All of a sudden, our tiny room becomes crowded and an implicit joy is found from those desperate eyes.

"He'll be all right," the nurse says.

The nurse opens his eyelids and shines the light on to dad's pupils. Shortly after that, dad moves his arms, and his eyes are gradually opened despite the fact that he is still too weak to talk.

"Hi…dad," Kim says.

"It is ok, dad," says Helen, my other sister, when she notices daddy is looking around the room.

"It is not so easy to see and imagine what dad goes through and how he feels," says Kim.

"It is ok Kim…I'm going to suggest that we move on," says Helen.

From those moments on, the world seemed to turn her light back on by giving dad another chance to write his story and to make his legacy. Sometimes I just wonder what if I had been born in a different family and lived in a different country, would I have had a different experience? Perhaps I would, but overall I don't believe there would be any major differences when I tried to deal with how I feel about my responsibility to take care of my loved ones. I also found myself questioning about what this experience means for me in my life when I put my toes into the water of the experience that my dad was having.

A day later, my family and I decide to tell dad the whole truth of what he has been through. We believe that there is nothing for us to hide and that the best part of being a family is to set forth our honesty, trust, support or forgiveness to where, when and how we need them the most. Looking at dad, we see the weeping tears from his eyes, and we feel that he fights off a wave of emotions. It touches my heart when daddy knows what he has and he probably figures out how he does. Needless to say, we believe that daddy has faced tortures from this terrible disease. We believe that family is bound by laughter, tear and companionship and further, it should not be kept in any deepest and darkest secrets. We see what worries him in comparison to what surprises us is that we truly don't know how dad feels about himself. Indeed we can't keep on worrying about something that we can't completely keep under control. We are absolutely convinced that the best healing in this world belongs to those who give all their hearts out to the sick, who wrap their hands around the wounded, and who have their fingers reaching across to those in need at a time when friends or families may eventually give up on them or when the world might literally provide them with no real answer...

Chapter 2: The Tsunami of Life

Though the waters thereof roar and be troubled...God is in the midst of river...He still commands that be still and know that I am God (Psalm 46).

L ife is continuous, adventurous and unpredictable. Everyone has a life and every life has a form. A form can be circular, rectangular or zigzag in shape. A form also can be filled with colors, pictures or even with nothing in background. Still a form can reveal the remark and character with its own content inside. Perhaps a form is just a form and it should not be compared to that of a book. And besides, a form should be kept as simple as possible so that it can be built in or stands out on its own away from that of the corners or construction.

Life can be defined as an encyclopedia, but at some point life seems to be more than a collection of records. Every life is a written book of its own, recording, reflecting and revealing the uniqueness of experience that a person progresses through from chapter to chapter of a journey. Some journeys reveal warm sunshine while others are filled with thorns on one side of the road and potholes on the other. Some lives require high maintenance while others turn out to be low key. Perhaps with little to no preservation possible, life can reflect an endless story in the conviction of any physical, intellectual and spiritual senses.

Storms are a part of realities of life. From some perspectives, the storm is universal and can be somehow identical despite of size, shape and time and besides, it can occur at any place. The idea of waving in the storm can be found in all races and cultures across the boundary of religions, educations, and beliefs despite the experience might vary. To a certain degree, a storm is almost impossible to avoid or stop from any happenings based on our intuition or ability. One way to be brought less destruction to things or to people surrounding us, to some extent, is to expect less and get assistance from resources we have. And if God wants a storm to hit our life, it can certainly hit us at any time.

Perhaps the idea of chasing a storm and the notion of surviving a storm can become a critical turning point in our thinking. What one experiences during and after the storm can be a crucial, heartbreaking, life-changing event. There is absolutely no "right" or "wrong" answer to what we must do at the time. There is no doubt in our mind, and there is no justification for why the metaphorical storm exists in the first place. Certainly, the stakes will be too high and too risky for any individuals to do nothing if they see what is coming with the storm, even though it can be a very small one. The idea of fighting about why and what a storm is would be unwise, and it can make anyone frustrated or even cynical about the gloomy phase of life, the moaning stage of pain, and the shadow of death, if they don't seriously take action before the storm hits. And there is absolutely no penalty for any individuals deciding to do nothing at the time – except remorse, guilt and despair when they look back at the event.

Right or wrong and act or not act tend to be a dilemma of decision-making and the movement of a thought process. Whether rooted good or bad, every decision we make reflects the journey of perseverance, confidence, fear and struggle. There always will be some rooms for improvement in term of expectation and desire. There also will be some rooms for suggestion and correction even if the outcome is at its worst or the plan might mismatch the reality. Typically, people are convinced that a detailed, step-by-step approach turns out to be an effective solution and that perception can help provide clues for any further damage.

To some individuals, a storm can come as a nightmare that threatens to steal what they have or what they've built, whether that could be a relationship, wealth, health or family. And certainly that nightmare not only can turn all life upside down, and it also can disrupt what people hold or stand for. To other individuals, a storm can come in a form of a flood that helps to wash away sin, wickedness, lust or addictions. Perhaps the purpose of a flood is not to destroy what people are entitled to but rather to take away all that does not belong to them.

There also are times when a storm becomes necessary to sharpen our faith. When people are in the middle of storm, they have a hard time figuring out how they want to get out of it, as they are holding on to terrible grief, anger and brokenness. Indeed, a storm can drive people to different beliefs. Only those who have survived from a storm restore their pride and confidence in life. In general, no one can possibly imagine what can be left behind if people are so caught up in the wave rather than the storm itself. No one knows how long they can recover from the emotional toll and physical damage, and only God knows how long it would take to get to the peaceful state.

What occurred during the storm sometimes becomes a challenge for people to remember. One reason for that is the fear and worry about how to reduce damage in term of physical toll. Another reason for that is the psychosocial loss, isolation or disconnection from friends, relatives and loved ones. A storm can present life-threatening events that lead to suffering, affliction and condemnation. And it often is tremendously stressful, and perhaps heartbreaking, for those who lived through the tragedy or devastation to share their experience and their real story unless they are not parts of storm victims or survivors from any natural disasters.

There are myths associated with storms, especially hurricanes. Those who live by water, a coastline, or a sea know that a hurricane can come in different sizes, shapes and forms. In general a hurricane even can be categorized in terms of wind, speed and geography. Far more than that, each of them can be driven by the changes in pressure, degrees of moisture, and the directional force of the earth. Each storm can consist of episodes and be followed by others. Usually, one storm tends to lead to another and it tends to be greater, highly destructive and more powerful than the previous episode.

Illness, which is similar to a storm, sometimes occurs in series, episodes or patterns. Illness can be caused by material sense and mortal mind. Illness can lead the body into destructible form, and it can exist if we embrace all thoughts of disease, sin and belief in mortality. As a matter of fact, illness can affect all ages, race, colors and genders, and it can also change one's life regardless of social status, economic or financial background, and religious beliefs. Whether you like it or not, illness can come in different forms, beliefs or theories, and it has no mercy on anyone and certainly requires no permission from anyone to carry out its manifestation.

Yet, illness also is a disease process that tends to accumulate from a disruptive life or a form of reckless living. Obviously there are some sign and symptom before an illness or disease strikes. Sometimes some sign comes in short duration that we might or might not be aware of it while others may exist a little longer than expected. Illness often tends to present itself in some strange way such as storm or hurricane that can't be added up or measured from a normal standpoint. Far more than that, illness can happen by accidents, at any times, for whatsoever reason and with all costs because it is perplexing, complicated and possibly endless as of nature, definition and measure.

For the first few weeks after dad was discharged from the hospital, he was completely loved and surrounded by friends, family, children and grandchildren. Wherever he went, dad was impressed by the loud, deep sound of his voice, the attitude of diligence, and the sense of seriousness he kept because he was reminded by people of his loving kindness, sincerity and friendliness that fostered good relationship. As for the family, dad was highly respected by his passion for love, his devotion to perfection, and his consistency in parenting. Now and then, we were reminded of his slogan to "not mix business with pleasure" if we want to secure our highest priority of life and the greatest success of all times.

Perhaps the feeling of comfort, joy and sweetness lies in the sense of belonging, which family is all about. For my dad, family was the heart and soul of his life. On any given days, dad would do anything to protect it from lack of organization and from falling apart. Despite the fact that dad was on his way to recover from chronic renal failure, our family worked very hard and followed closely with the doctor's recommendation to accommodate and assist dad for a better transition to home so that he would be healthy and safe enough to take care of himself again.

Taking care of other people is not always easy. Whether the caring of an individual is for physical, social, mental or spiritual needs, it can become a challenge or tough assignment. It also can turn out to be the most rewarding work if one knows how. Time and time, only the true caregiver sees through the needs of the ill or disabled and until then, life will ease its way through. Otherwise, it will be no much different from nightmares, earthquakes, lightning, storms and thunders that can reproduce the percussion of damage and catastrophe in a matter of time.

With great support coming from family and friends along with the care from the home health nurses, dad began to show some signs of recovery. He took small walks, talked on the phone, and took baths with assistance. He started to laugh, pray, tell stories and even stop his grandchildren from fooling around or gossiping too much in the house. He began to eat again, but the amount of what he put in turned out to be less than before. He also began to complain about the taste and the quality of foods that did not live up to his standards. Sometimes he complained about the loss of appetite when we gave him the liquid diet or some thickened formula as prescribed. As the days went on, we became worried and concerned about his health, his ability to stay on the path of recovery, and his ability to fight disease.

There is not a day we don't think about how to implement and improve dad's living conditions since he came back home. Everyone and almost all in our family helped to maintain a rotational schedule so that we had at least one person remaining in the house at any time to take care of our parents' needs. The rest of family members should be ready to standby in case of the other caregiver is down or sick. No one is complaining or questioning of the roles they play in this rehabilitation and recovery process. We all believe that our consistency and determination to stand by our dad during this moment are significant and mandatory because, if we don't back him up in this battle, he will have terrible time to face it alone and who will he possibly turn to for help?

Life was good for dad during his stay at home. He enjoyed family time with his daughter and son in-laws with chats about life's changes and the world they were used to live in. He also liked to have good time with his grandchildren and hear their comments on TV shows, movies series, and the daily news. He usually didn't like noises or loud speaking when watching TV or movies. Dad also enjoyed quality time with his friends when they visited him. He did not care much about gifts people might or might not bring for him but rather, the heart they have for him during the visit. As dad always said, the heart is where things are put in order and come together for a good reason. Dad also pointed out that if people showed you or gave you things but did not show you where their hearts are, then you would be better off taking things from no one.

With all the good things given to dad, we truly believe that he should recover as expected. However, the reality turned out to be overwhelming and almost took all of our breaths away. The incident happened on one late afternoon in the fall when the weather finally cooled off a little bit with a mixture of clouds and raindrops. Dad was taking an afternoon nap in his bedroom upstairs. He looked so calm and peaceful. As he slept, the world seems to have slept with him as well. And almost everything around him turned out to be quiet and motionless except some snoring.

No one knows exactly how long dad was asleep. Perhaps it was a half hour, one hour or two. Then a noise suddenly comes from upstairs. It sounds like a thunder blasting through the silent night. My sister immediately ran upstairs to find out what is going on. She couldn't believe her eyes and then she screamed. Mom also ran upstairs, and they see that dad is lying on the floor on the side of bed and is moaning in pain. Thereafter, the rest of the family members received calls and soon after that, we all rush home from work. By the time we all got home, we see that dad is no longer screaming for pain but instead he seems to complain of having pain and tenderness in his arm, jaw and legs that make moving difficult. No bleeding, no numbness, no facial paralysis or atrophy, and no loss of consciousness found, though. There was some level of confusion and difficulty speaking. Dad was scared, disoriented and shivered. Deep inside our hearts, we think that there is something going on inside of him, and we are not sure of what it could be except the fact that we are told dad is trying to get off the bed and fell before he got to the bathroom by himself. When I got close to dad and checked out his conditions, I initially found nothing wrong beside the obvious signs of disorientation and pain after the slip and fall injury. Until then, I'm surprised to hear some kind of roaring or pounding sounds coming not from his heart but around his ear. I begin to worry and tell my family that we need to take dad to the local hospital as soon as possible before it could be too late. In my mind, I keep checking the time because I know that if dad happens to have a mini stroke or transient ischemic attack (TIA), lucky enough my family and I still have few more minutes to an hour of waiting to observe any changes before dad started to experience more complicated symptoms such as numbness, facial paralysis, slurred speech, and weakness before a stroke arrives. Meanwhile, I truly believe that we are waging in the storm of some horrible and life-threatening disease. In the back of my mind, I could see and smell what is coming in my way and I almost can envision the life of my dad might be in serious trouble or danger if my family can't come to the final consent at any time soon so that we can rush dad to the emergency room (ER) for a detailed evaluation.

On our way to the local hospital, dad's conditions gradually worsened and he turned out to be more confused and had hard time holding on to himself. By the time he got off the ambulance and was transported through the back door of the emergency room, he immediately received medical attention. All of a sudden, we were circled by physicians, nurses, technicians, and administrators. History, vitals, examination, lab work, and IV fluid were performed. An electrocardiogram (EKG) was taken and then X-rays are also ordered. Physicians and medical staff applaud us for doing the right thing. A few hours later, the attending E.R. physician returns to the room telling us that the preliminary test results are negative for stroke but won't rule out the possibility because dad has a few signs of stroke. Besides, the ER physician also is concerned about the lab values, which are all against dad, and the state of his consciousness. The E.R. physician then ordered and recommends dad to stay in the ICU for cardiovascular care. The physician stated the hospital stay will allow other doctors, specialists, nurses and staff to have sufficient time monitored closely with any stroke-related issues dad happens to have.

Life in the ICU was not something new and unfamiliar for us since dad's last admission. What differed from the last encounter was that our dad will be treated for cardiovascular and stroke-related conditions instead. With our previous experience from the unit, this admission seemed to be slightly less stressful even though dad was in a semi-conscious state. With the friendliness, courtesy and passion from those familiar staff and medical personnel, we felt comfortable because we know our dad would pull himself through. With the care he was receiving, we knew our dad would be in good hands for a while.

With a close look at patients in other rooms, we found that most of them have been admitted for a while for hypertension or heart disease. Along with the prevalent cause for the hospitalization, I gradually found the conditions of diabetes, cardiovascular diseases, pulmonary diseases, malignancies, overweight issues, infections, and traumas tend to be higher and more predominant in the elderly seeking immediate medical intervention. And among those incidences, slip and fall become one of the major causes leading to stroke, fracture, and long-term disability.

Aging indeed was a normal degeneration or progressive process in the body. Aging is not synonymous with diseases, but diseases can become more common as age progresses. Usually the diseases are present with non-specific and multiple symptoms that involve many organs. Increasing age in the elderly tends to be associated or linked closely with higher morbidity and frequent use of healthcare services. The prevalence of slip and fall in the elderly also becomes a gloomy implication for long-term care or permanent disability that requires highly on both assisted living facilities and home health agencies in addition to medications or surgery. For us, we are glad our dad was fortunate enough to have a wonderful team and talented groups of medical staff, technicians, therapists, nurses and physicians including the family medicine, internal medicine, cardiologist and neurologist who work around the clock striving for excellent care and recovery for their patients even though dad was in and out from his conscious state.

During the second day in the ICU, dad became very weak and finally went into coma. The bedside monitor revealed signs of low blood pressure, fluctuated arrhythmia, and both the CO_2 level per respiration and SpO2 saturation per pulsation were also below average. Vital assessments were done every 30 minutes to ensure the body stayed in the optimal range. Oxygen was transported through the nose to maintain a critical level, which was usually above 95%, helping to circulate in the bloodstream, brain and heart. Oxygen was also used to further assist and meet the body's need for respiration. Intravenous fluids and the administration of potassium and sodium were transported through the vein into the body to maintain water balance, to increase the intravascular volume for raising blood pressure, and further to help keep vital organs from dehydration. Medications were mostly transported through the IV fluid.

During the second day after dad went into coma, he had changed very little with his status remaining the same. Looking around the ICU, people came in and left. Family and close friends stuck around with their loved ones. In almost every corner of the unit, I could hear the soft flap of shoes scratching on the tile floor as nurses, technicians, therapists, physicians, medical personnel and staff passed through the door and down the hallway, the *ding* from elevator doors opening and closing, the smell of fresh brewed coffee, the cranking of soda can tops, the sharp smell of antiseptic that never really covered the strong odor of sickness.

For the past two nights, the weather turned out to be cooler with moisture and high pressure moving from the Atlantic. Watching the heavy rain fall and wind blow on the window, I wondered if there would be a sunny day tomorrow. With the weather forecast coming from the local TV news, I questioned the accuracy of events and nature of things that might be changed, notwithstanding the unknowns or incidents. With my sentiment can be as worst as the weather at the time, I hoped this weather forecast could be true because I was tired of learning the coming of this storm. Subconsciously, I felt the dark clouds racing across heavens such as a curtain pulled across the sky, the strong wind soaked to my skin, the distant sound of thunder echoed over the ceiling, and all the different pressures and unbearable humidity come to show off the savage beauty. I had nothing to say against the storm and its raging force. In the meantime, I didn't really care about its stinking sense or stinky smell. But I was more looking forward to see that my dad would be awakened and recovered again just like what I was expecting something good coming off this stormy rain.

With the heavy rain knocking on the window, the night seemed to last longer than usual. The tall street lights seemed to stand beside those lonely nights, and they were looking to shine on those empty hearts. Along with the appearance of drizzles and fogs, this late evening became harder for anyone to look further ahead. This experience is not any difference from me despite of the fact that I was familiar with the environment; however, the sense of acknowledgment and recognition could somehow turn out to be obscure, ambiguous and questionable in terms of affliction and despair. In a global sense, whether the view was for our daily existence or state of mind, we demand to see it and expect to know it, for our own good and for the sake of people and things around us. Given the fact that such an unpleasant view was in place, we could possibly relate our life to be absolutely true and find moving on difficult if we couldn't get to see through to the bottom of things, even if we would agree to give it our all.

Hours went by, and the rain started to slow and might even have stopped at some point, but the fog wore on, heavily covering the trees, buildings and roads. They were just like demigods who come to engulf the simplicity, serenity and beauty of life with complexity, disturbance and ugliness so that life could be treacherous, paradoxical and mysterious. Across my windows, I see the dark shadiness from the crisscross of fog layers, but I can't see what was covered ahead of the fog, and I dare not imagine what kind of life could be if lies behind the fog. On a separate thought, I think that life can be born in the middle of rainstorm, thunder, lightning or shadiness. For the entire night, the nightingales were the presentation of guardian angels who come to ease the suffering and to soothe the grief for those who were in pain, distress and sickness. These guardian angels didn't stop working hard to take care of the sick and the needed, and they also didn't mind consoling their families during those long and sleepless nights. They gave their hearts out and shared their life in the tears and joys of the less fortunate. Then the concrete voices, the constant steps, and the tireless works of both the nurse and technician broke through the silence and loneliness of night and gave way to a new yearning day. Looking from my windows, I felt the world was shutting me out by all the messed-up views and unknown diseases. In deep thought, I could hardly know how to make the right decision because any small mistaken move could lead to chaos into my life and to those around me.

By the morning, our room became crowded again. The attending physician came in to evaluate dad's conditions, review his chart, and auscultate his heart and lungs. The physician told me that dad's lab report revealed signs of elevated white blood cells, calcium and creatine phosphokinase (CPK), low iron, and decreasing hematocrit. He was going to refer to physicians from the internal medicine and infections for a second opinion. He orders the continuation of IV fluids, medications, blood chemistry work, and information update from nurses at each shift. By the afternoon, physician from the infectious diseases come. He evaluates dad's heart and lungs and takes a reading of his urine. The physician then went over his chart, made some notes and left the room. Later, another physician from the internal medicine came in. He performed an exam on dad's eyes, feet and toes for signs of responses. He also evaluated dad's heart and lungs. Then he told me that he was going to order the

CT (Computerized Tomography) scan on dad's brain to find any sign of hemorrhage or relationship between stroke and coma. By the evening, staff from the radiology department had come and they transported dad downstairs for his CT scan.

A few minutes later, dad was back to his room where he was wired and reconnected with all the necessary medical devices. Dad remained sleeping and seemed to enjoy a little more rest from his coma and shock. The medical professionals and staff encouraged us to stay strong because dad looked very promising from the test results and reports despite the fact that he was unable to get himself up. When visiting hours arrived, children and grandchildren came and stayed with dad. Some of his close friends and long-time business associates also came by to cheer up dad despite that he had no knowledge of their presence. Some of them brought flowers while others brought fruits and baskets during their visits. Though dad did not know exactly who visited him, we knew he would be pleased to find out who had after he woke up.

By the late evening, when all the visitors were gone, dad's conditions remained the same. His breathing continued to be shallow, his arms and legs were not moving, but his heart was still beating. No one could possibly tell how long this journey would last and where it would lead. But in the midst of this unexpected incident, we were glad to see that dad was living up to his calmness and was still fighting for his unknown destiny. Along with prayers, as pure and selfless as they are, we were grateful by the fact that dad turned out to be stronger in his daily encounter with diseases, pains and even complications. Looking at the little to almost no response from dad, we truly believed that no words, tone or expression could possibly describe the distress and anguish we face and on the other hand, we constantly felt the storm of emotions hit us at the all-time height. We truly wanted to let them settle and we desperately needed to keep them from rocking our world. In spite of all that had been done for dad, I still hope that my prayer requests to the national televised Christian media networks and churches would bring in some miracles in days ahead.

Tonight was the same as any other night. The attending physician comes by around midnight for the re-evaluation. He finds out and was aware of the fact that dad had moderate swellings over his arms and ankles. He told me not to worry too much about it and he would take care of the swellings. He was going to order dad a set of chest X-rays to find out the relationship of wheezing and crackle he finds from the lung auscultation before he returns tomorrow morning for the follow-up. For the entire evening, our room became busier than before as the nurse was in and out of the room to refill saline and medications. The certified nurse assistant (CNA) also comes by every one to two hours for the vital signs, urine output from the Foley catheter and manages urine disposal as necessary and then records that on dad's chart.

Around 3 a.m., a radiology technician came by with the portable X-ray machine. After verifying the correct information from the patient's arm band, she made a few exposure of chest film on dad and then leaves. Around 5 a.m. or perhaps slightly before dawn, the phlebotomist comes in and draws some blood to prepare for laboratory test by 8 o'clock the next morning. Shortly after daybreak, the housekeeping crews begin to kick off the day with a fresh makeup of the environment. Some of them cleans and waxes the floor of hallway with the use of heavy machine. Some others come in to pick up dirty bedsheets, used towels, and disposable needles or hazard containers with the overhauling buggy. Still other came in to clean bathroom, empty trash, and mop floors with full energy and good spirit. With all the noises given from human conversation and machine work, I'm perplexed by the fact that my dad still sleeps so well and became unaffected.

By 7 a.m., the night shift ended, and the day shift staff and personnel took over. Nurses briefed one another on the patients' cases. This ICU floor allowed every nurse to take care two patients or three the most in their twelve-hour shift. Personnel and medical staff were exchanged their duty and assignment on patient file, flow of hospital beds, and paging system. By 8 o'clock, most physicians were reading their patients' charts and ready to make rounds. Around 9 a.m., the attending physician, who was accompanied by the day shift nurse, came in to do a follow-up and evaluation on dad. The doctor told me that the result from the CT scan shows no signs of clots in vessels or brain damage in term of stroke or TIA, and he was still waiting for reports from other team professionals. He also told me the chest X-rays shown that dad suffers from pneumonia. He would put in some new medications and order oxygen therapy for every eight hours to help treat pneumonia. Hopefully by the time dad wakes up for the next few days, he would then monitor the treatment unless new condition arises.

No one exactly knew how much time dad needed to overcome his sleep hunger or coma in other sense. We believe that dad should not miss out the opportunity of seeing what was happening around him for the past few days. Even though he indeed might need some additional time to sleep, but he at least should wake up first and tell us what or how he feels so that a better care or new treatment could be formed to shorten the pain and suffering. To dad, this might be one way to get rid of his lifetime stress and workload. Perhaps these coma and shock might be the break he mentioned a few years ago when he was asked about longevity and seclusion in terms of life and death issues.

Movement was always a key issue during the time of dad's coma. Movement indeed was the proof of life, and it helped to sustain force or activity within an organelle. As doctors pointed out, sometimes going into coma might not necessarily be a bad thing because it helped the body to overcome some kind of infection, unknown toxic level or malignant condition in the system. But as long as the body could still maintain good vital signs, productive respiration, and a heartbeat at the optimal level, it would be all right for the patient. Even the doctor from internal medicine told us that edema on dad's extremities could be related to the immobility from prolonged lying in the bed, as fluids eventually accumulate over time. It also could be caused by some kind of cardiac and pulmonary problems. He was working closely with the doctor in family medicine on the medications and also instructed the nurses to work on the body and bed repositioning to minimize the swellings. In the meantime, he agreed with other doctors to monitor dad's progress through daily lab results to ensure the levels of high sodium, low chloride, high calcium and low hematocrit staying at the physiological range.

By the early evening, the church elders and ministers come by to visit dad. They spent time with us and consoled the family during this depressing period. This revealed a remarkable truth of God's unforsaken love and reaffirmed Christ's commitment to enrich peace and security for those who acknowledge their hunger for His touch and for those who turn to God for His refuge. With the guidance from our senior pastor, we begin to worship God through the reading of scripture and the singing of hymns. We didn't know how long the time had passed and perhaps, some of us might be exhausted and thirsty, but somehow we felt a strong energy forming in the room. Everyone started to pray. We pray, the elders pray, and our senior pastor also prays with his hand laying on dad's hands and forehead. Our prayers become stronger and louder and eventually they could be heard in the next room. We felt we were drawn close and near to God by the cleansing from His holy blood. We were justified by the content of His righteousness. We were moved by the binding of His anointing and Holy Spirit. We also believe that healing takes place and abides from divine law.

Night came and the street became quiet again. Lights in the ICU's hallway were turned down, and visitors were finally asked to leave patients' rooms. All of a sudden, the prayers stopped, and the separation of divine power and church gave way to nursing care. Every now and then, both the nurse and nurse tech came in to keep an eye on dad. Throughout the whole night, dad turned out to be calmer and more stable than the previous night, even though he was still in a coma.

From some people's perspectives, there were no firm absolutes in the health profession's approach to healing. In general, the concept of having "no significant change" does not mean the total failure in procedures or policies from the practice management standpoint. It was a far more time-consuming process that helped to test the effectiveness of procedures, information and technologies. It also was a time-based issue that demands our patience, faith, and belief in the superiority or supernatural beyond our systemic thinking and intelligence.

The attending physician had performed a follow-up on dad just a few hours or few days ago, I couldn't remember at the time which was true. We really lose track of that. But we had not seen any sign of him waking up, and from the depth of our hearts, we noticed that almost every day since our last prayer, the elders and our church ministers come to constantly pray with and pray for dad during each of their visits despite the fact that daddy is undergoing excellent medical treatment. And in the midst of our confusion and distress, one day we found dad finally awake. The team doctors then come by to further evaluate dad's complaint of dryness in mouth, burning sensation in the extremities, and difficulty swallowing.

With the best procedures and tests possible being done on dad, doctors still had a difficult time figuring out the cause for his dysphasia or difficulty swallowing. They recommend a temporary feeding tube to be directly inserted from the nose into stomach to maintain good nutrition and balanced fluids for the body. In the meantime, they told us to wait until dad recovered from his cardiovascular and pulmonary conditions. Only by the time dad was able to recover from his coma would the physicians come up with some plan for speech therapy or a swallowing test to see how those muscles in the tongue work in terms of muscle strength and function.

For the first few days after he woke up from coma, dad seemed to have lost his memory. Every now and then, we found he was having difficulties telling us what he wanted, to remind mom of clearing up dirty laundry every morning, and to turn on his favorite movie channels. Even more than that, dad also had a hard time to identify people and things he knows. Sometimes he was wrong on the date, time and place when we asked him. He was not in the mood of making conversation as he was used to be. He doesn't laugh, yell or joke. He just remained on the hospital bed quietly.

Perhaps one of the most painful experiences we feel in life is not the pain itself but rather the helplessness of it. With all that happened during this incident and the thrilling recovery from dad's last admission, we had a difficult time imagining how he might survive and overcome the odds. With dad's past medical history plus the recent health concerns, we have a good reason to believe his emotional change was a natural adjustment from depression arriving from a severe sickness. Listening to the hoarseness of his voice, his difficulty in speech, and the loss of connection between his thought and conversation, we felt desperate and lost. But we happened to accept that even the diagnosis of Alzheimer's would not be a surprise given his age. For many days and nights, as taking a close look at dad's impartial and almost speechless expression, we wondered if there was anything we could or might do to help change this outcome.

In fact, persistent and continual medical services were indispensable and family counseling was necessary to ease affliction and distress. A good balance between all these treatments was to enhance speech therapy in addition to the nasally-inserted feeding tube from the intravenous pump that provided nutrition and fluid into the body. The feeding procedure helped to feed those who were unable to chew and swallow food, and it further helped to increase the quality of life and to thus maintain appropriate weight and nutritional requirements. Perhaps, the one possible best treatment dad had so far might not necessary be the medication, the IV fluids, advanced imaging study, nursing care but rather, the blending of all other health professionals, the availability and accessibility of care from the health system this great country provides.

With the progress he makes through the critical care, dad eventually was transferred to the cardiovascular unit. Looking at the promising results dad received from the medical care and the tough journeys he was on, we become silent during the adversities to hold back our deep emotions from the ill. I had no doubt in my mind that dad was indeed lucky to get away from stroke or TIA because hypertension and diabetes were a part of his extensive medical histories. In fact, statistics show approximately six percent of United States populations had some form of diabetes, and more than five millions people worldwide were actually suffering from high blood pressure. High blood pressure or hypertension tends to have a strong correlation with diabetes and was a leading cause for chronic kidney failure, prevalent in the elderly. Statistics also reveal that people with high blood pressure could have five times higher risk of having stroke and two times higher to have heart attack in a given year. Hypertension also became one of the risk factors for heart failure, arterial aneurysm or any heart diseases. According to the Merck manual, five to ten percent of those people who had high blood pressure related to kidney disease; people with poor diabetes control could be more susceptible to infections or many serious long-term complications, of which heart attacks and stroke tend to be more common. With the awareness and acknowledgment dad had for all those factors that work against him, I was truly thankful that disease and sickness don't play the devil's advocate to further ruin his health. But this journey doesn't stop there, it somehow makes its way to open up another journey that requires us to look for and look out to God and his intervention into daddy's health.

Late one afternoon on a day that was not much different from any other, two of my sisters went to visit and stay with dad. What shocked them and the medical staff were not the agitation and depression from a seriously ill old man who was pacified by sedation, pain-killers and anti-inflammatory drugs but rather his calmness and passion. What caught their eyes were the smile and laughter from a friendly individual who says "thanks" to his visitors and caregivers. He seemed to have forgotten the pain he had, and there were no tears found over his wrinkled eyes and pale skin. Instead, the sense of comfort and joy appeared on his face. He began to ask why he was being treated so long in the hospital and when he could go home.

As my sisters spoke with dad, they slowly found out something actually happened during our last prayer session. Up to that point, we didn't know what was physically happening to dad at that time, but we were aware of the changes being made to justify our curiosity and quest for divine presence and the cleansing process. It was not a coincidence that divine healing takes place beyond the form of scientific myths and that miracles exist beyond all shadows of doubt. We were anticipating the question of "where is God now, and why did God do what He did?" because the Scriptures tell us that his omnipresence could always be found in any gathering of more than three people who shout out the name of Jesus the Lord and that He would come to their rescue.

Living in this secular world, our nature is to believe in what we can see and touch. Getting our hands and fingers across anything that we had no clue about is almost impossible. Just as in the Biblical days, we were no different from some of His early disciples or many followers who happened to believe only what they could see or touch. In reality, we were honored to have a life experience and testimony that depicted how an action was done and to further learn from what God wanted to teach us in the process. However, the grace of God tended to bless those who believed without seeing or touching it because Christ the Lord could break through all barriers of impossibility and invisibility to show us the truth and if necessary, He could use all his creations to demonstrate us of his supremacy.

Dad said during his previous coma, he was actually traveling instead of sleeping. He told us that he went through places, saw lots of things, and was greeted by so many people whom he'd never met before. He walked, swam, and sometimes flew during those journeys. He recalled passing through some high mountain with green vegetation, a still river without fish, a garden with beautiful flowers behind a gorgeous river, and a narrow pathway with dead bodies and flies. For most of the time, dad said that he was traveling by himself, but strangely enough, he didn't remember being asked to pay for those trips.

Recalling the first trip, dad said that he was invited to a mountain hike from a strange lady, who bore long beautiful silver hair and spoke in a light and decent voice. During that trip, dad didn't get a chance to see her face at all. On his way to the mountain top, dad was exhausted, bruised, cut, hurt and almost passed out. One reason this trip was so different from any others he'd been on was because he was the only hiker in the midst of road, rain, snow, cold and heat. There were no flowers, animals or other human beings along the way. Winds stirred the trees, birds sang and grasses withered. When he was alone on the mountain, dad clearly heard everything in his surroundings with no distractions at all. By the time he reached a big round surface from a steep wall, he saw a stream of water and lake flowing calmly underneath and then he was led by a teenage girl in front of a gorgeous lady who dressed in a shiny white gown and with a golden band over her head, like that of an angel. The lady showed dad a beautiful view of a great plantation, its farmland and vineyard on the east side of the mountain where people worked, danced and sang with joy and smile on their faces. She also showed dad another magnificent picture of a cosmopolitan city on the west side of the mountain where people were killing, crying and moaning for help despite they actually dressed in beautiful colorful robes. She then told dad that she was looking for individuals to wade through the killing field to lead those people back to this mountain top.

Moments later, the lady grazed dad's hands and their feet rose off the ground. Dad began to fly; his body turned out to be shivering; his eyes were swollen and red that he could barely see anything ahead; his legs felt like being caught on fire. He didn't know how he ended up flying and why he had to travel with this lady. Subconsciously, he was shocked, frightened and almost passed out. Suddenly he heard a voice that said, "Do not afraid for I was with you." As soon as he opened his eyes, dad found himself above the clouds. All the trees and buildings were below him. By the time they flew a little higher, dad could see the moon and stars close-up. Suddenly, they flew faster against some lightning and passed a dome-shaped entrance, and then they landed in front of a gigantic tall building that was made up as that of the centuries-old European castle.

Not knowing where he was or what he needed to do, dad was instructed to enter a beautiful arched door. Behind it was a fountain; a small passage underneath the fountain to another end of the building. The lady told dad to follow her closely and to not speak a word once they move into the fountain and beyond. Despite the coldness of spring water watering through his body, dad didn't feel a single drop of water fall on his body. Instead, the feeling of warmth and cleanliness accompanied the brightness and reflection of a silver star, whose light covered his body. Then they took a pathway on the right side where they were approached by the fresh smell of herbs, the blooming of flowers, and the colorfulness of fruits. As soon as they got into the garden and vineyard, they were greeted by angels dressed in silky white garments. Some angels danced while others sang. Still other angels played musical instruments. There was no interruption to the harmony of music performed by the angels. There was also no disruption to the serenity and beauty. Everything was in perfect rhythm and order. The air was fresh, the wind was soft, and the sun was warm. Birds hummed and animals rested. But there were hardly any signs of human beings.

By the time dad reached the center of the garden, the lady reminded him to not touch anything on his own. In the middle of the garden stood a tall beautiful tree surrounded by a couple of smaller trees. Both were filled with lovely and colorful fruits. This lady angel explained to dad that the biggest and tallest tree was of life and the one surrounding her was of knowledge. The fruit on those trees included that of the healing, prosperity, jealousy, emotions, health, wealth, disobedience, vengeance and sickness. He who touches or eats fruits from them would reap the results of his own. She also added that the Master of the garden would be disappointed and upset if his people failed to keep and follow his law. Before leaving the garden, dad wondered if there was any relationship between human existence and the garden. The lady told him that one day man would come before the Master to be reaffirmed and assigned a role in the Armageddon where his final destination would be set forever and thereafter.

The second journey was a fishing trip by a lake or river in the country side. Dad told us that it was the most embarrassing and frustrated experience at an outdoor activity he'd ever had. He could hardly imagine an amazing fishing trip would turn out to be somewhat disappointing. Certainly he did not regret taking that trip at an elder's invitation. In fact, dad was looking forward to catch big fish, but he caught nothing. The good part for that trip was that dad found himself from being lost, and he started to learn how to let go his ego and to thus go forward for the fishing of humanity.

Remembering the recent trip spent at the lake with this stranger, dad insists that he didn't know this man whose eyes were like burning flames and whose hair was like long furrow. Dad explained the reason why he was up to fishing was because he had nothing to do while walking by the lake on a sunny afternoon. Due to the sincerity, hospitality and loneliness of the old man, dad agreed to join him for the fishing down the road. And for the first few hours, nothing seem to happen under the Tuscan sun. Despite the wonderful bait lures dad places under the hook and the good techniques such as casting, spinning, drifting, lining, dragging, and jigging were used, there were no fish being caught. Without seeing any fish from the stream, the old man suddenly hands dad few big fish he gets from a simple catch and release. With a good smile and friendly look, this old man continued to tell dad that he was still searching for individuals who would like to become a good fisherman for the lost souls in this life.

Indeed, life was full of interruptions, confusion and complications. Sometimes, we felt that our lives were dry as a desert waiting for rain to turn us around. On the other hand, we sometimes wondered why our lives were no different than a peelable onion with the mysterious tastes of bitterness, spice, and tear. Looking at the ways dad described his incredible journeys and the attitudes he carried even in this current illness, without a doubt his recovery revealed God's breakthrough over impossibilities. It indeed was an effectual working of his grace, power and healing over the threats of infirmities or physical illness.

Before we try to figure out his status and progress report the next day, dad speaks to us with tears about the astonishing and fearful journey he was on. Unlike several past dreams, this story catches all of our attention. Dad said that it happened late one afternoon when he rested in front of a lovely fireplace in a room filled with lights, decorations, flowers and fragrances. He reclined there so relaxed while listening to the music. Suddenly two big, strong, and ugly men came in and dragged him out of the house. They took him into a vehicle and drove off. As they moved into the traffic, all the building and people were also moved with them along with time. Perhaps, it might be a split of a second, a minute, or one hour, but they stop and get off the vehicle into a quiet street, poor neighborhood, and old ragged building.

As they get into the building, the moisture, chill and darkness overwhelmed dad. Dad said he felt so heavy in his head that he was physically spinning in between compartments, noises and cries but could hardly see anyone or touch anything. It seemed like he was passing through graveyard. It also seemed like that he was crossing some cold stone walls where he began to travel upside down against a violent current that sucked him into some unknown, looping holes. During the spinning and tossing, dad felt chillier than before as they traveled longer and deeper into the passages. Suddenly, they stopped and a voice whispered over dad's ears saying, "Open your eyes."

As soon as dad opened his eyes, he could hardly imagine and believe the place where he had set his feet. The first stop was a magnificent ballroom with beautiful hallways, colorful lights, and loud music where people were dressing in spectacular costumes and crowned with stylish masks and make-ups. Some people was busy drinking, dancing and smoking while others were indulged in drugs, fighting and chasing one another. No one seemed to really care for others in term of brotherly love. Everyone seemed to be complacent in his or her own form of abuse or lust regardless of what circumstances or condition would be.

A second stop was a party house in the basement. There was a long and wide hallway on each side of the aisle with odd pictures on the wall. There was a big center stage with numerous flashing lights and balconies surrounding the platform. On his way to the entrance, dad saw lots of people being tied up by rods and iron chains along the hallway. Some people were bleeding while others were hanging upside down. People were moaning and yelling for help all over the hallway. As soon as dad got closer to the center stage, he sees a pool of sulfur, a stream of buffer, a lake of fire, a river of blood, and a volcano of erupted foul odor that mixes with multiple colors. The chamber was filled with darkness, fear, scream and horror. People were gradually brought to and in front of a big, long and deep furnace-like opening where bodies were tossed. Different colors were

35

generated during each burning in addition to the terrible sharp moaning and yelling. Before a burning sacrifice was initiated, there would be a loud noise coming from the back of the room and that noise seemed to finalize the judgment call. If there was no interruption or objection from the room, a small dance would be carried out before each of the burning performance. During the burning sacrifice, the image of body reflects and circles along the flames into the sky or open space. Then the ghost spirit continued to echo throughout the room even after the body had been fully executed.

With so many scary and horrible events happened on the floor, dad was completely frightened and perplexed by the reason and the location he was set in. With curiosity and determination, dad confronts the two big, muscular and ugly men who escort him by asking "why do you take me here since I do nothing wrong?"

The two guards don't answer him.

Dad continued, "Perhaps I guess you guys might be mistaken me with somebody else...you knew I don't live here, ok?"

The two sentinels were still silent.

For a while, dad turned out to be frightened when he looked around the big pool of people lined up and stood side by side with him in front of the hot sizzling platform. Names were called, and row by row, people were executed and disappeared. As he got closer and closer to categorizing the non-human intelligence, dad began to virtually denote to what exactly constitutes sentience and how it principally was recognized as life in contrast with death, and he also began to question why and to what degree he might have a life after this death.

In his unspoken fear, dad turned to one of the guards and said, "Sir, would you tell me that this was not real nor true...This was not for me and I'm just visiting, right?"

"You knew what...I was just like you...pretty scary when I first get here...I was told to bring you here," one of the guards says.

Without knowing what might happen next to him, dad hardly imagined the misery of trick or treat coming out of this demonic world filled with a strong sense of sin and death. Deep down in his heart, dad knew that it was neither the time nor the season for trick or treat. He had a hard time to believe in the truth from the demonic world that focuses on death as the centerpiece of all massacres and the devil also emphasizes physical torture as a ransom to sin. What bothered dad most during this non-invitational trip was not about the fearful journey to hell itself but rather, it was the confrontational issue of death that could trigger at the shortest time of his life. Screaming, tearing, kicking, fighting, pushing and bleeding were echoed all over the chamber. And perhaps the most imminent threat to dad's life at this moment was to figure out a solution or alternative that could possibly help to delay the process. Before dad gave another thought on how to avoid the penalty, he hears his name was called and before he knows, his body was lifted into the air heading toward the dazzling fires.

While he was carried over the open space, dad felt that his body temperature rises above 135 degrees Fahrenheit and his heart beats faster. Eventually the beating turned out to be remarkably fast to a point that he could hardly breathe, especially when dad was brought next to a big round and deep fireplace. His physical body was carried horizontally by six muscular people, and they begin to dance through the crowd, smoke, crying, hot springs, rock and combustion. Without knowing how long the process would take, they eventually reached the top of the platform where the combination of heat and stench of blood was so strong and heavy that dad found catching his own breath tremendously difficult.

By the time those people started to release their hands, suddenly a clear and loud voice broke through the noisy crowd saying "Behold, Beelzebub! All of you Succubus and Amon stay back...let go that body and put it on to the floor." For less than a minute, a group of angels picked up dad and covered him with a lovely white garment flowing with golden bright lights and the beautiful smell of flowers. Gradually they begin to lift, bound, and move away from the crowd, and then a soft harmonized music left behind the moaning field as they took off.

With tears on his eyes and unspoken joy on his face, dad turned to us children and said, "Kids! I was glad to be back." With the acknowledgment of all the pains that dad had suffered, words can't be indescribable and even become emotional. In the light of what had happened to dad, we believed that dad indeed had an amazing and outstanding journey to wade through the thin and thick of life while it turned out to be significantly impossible for many others to do so. Of course, we believed that if it was not by the grace of God, dad won't be able to overcome his afflictions and he would surely have hard time to turn all the calamities into his favor, not mentioning the death and hell-like lesson.

For the next few weeks, dad spent most of his time in the course of treatment and rehabilitation. The attending physician and team physicians worked very closely with other healthcare professionals to come up with good assessment during each of their evaluations. They tried to co-manage with speech therapist, dietician and physical therapist to figure out whether dad still had the ability to swallow, eat, drink and walk normally on a daily basis and to determine whether dad was able to recover on a timely manner.

Physical therapy was ordered and used to help restore, maintain and promote overall health. It was implemented for dad to improve mobility, increase strength, prevent or limit permanent physical disabilities so that he won't be bedridden for so long and further to help improve his ability by performing easy daily tasks at home to expedite his recovery. Meanwhile, speech therapy was ordered to assess his progress and to help guide dad for better eating, chewing and swallowing. It provided him with good information and techniques on proper eating. It was done to prevent dad from aspiration or choking and also tended to provide him with good instruction and monitoring on diet in term of adequate nutrition. Still, the intense program of rehabilitation therapy was not an easy adjustment for dad.

For the next few weeks, dad showed some signs of recovery. Everyday dad tried and worked very hard to adjust to his new life. Dad began to eat again, though just a small meal. What worried us most was not about how long dad could fully recover but rather how long he could go back to his regular diet. With the fact that he didn't get sufficient nutrition from his diet, the team physicians recommended dad to have a temporary feeding tube placed inside his body. Being told about the procedure and its safety issue, dad was furious and he refused to have it placed inside his stomach. Despite encouragement from the medical staff and support from the family and friends, dad still insisted on not taking the recommendation.

About two days after the gastroenterologist's recommendation, dad was briefed from his lab report that he had an extraordinary high calcium level in his blood stream and a white focal density in his lumbar x-rays after he was stressed from his physical therapy session. A follow-up with the cardiovascular specialist was scheduled to review his chart. A day later, dad was also evaluated by the oncologist. Out of the blue, we were stunned by the change and big surprise when life plays one of its mysterious tricks on the ill. Gradually, we begin to see the preliminary test, lab and assessment were taken in consideration and precautions were taken for the possible malignancy issue. Then an MRI study was performed in the lumbar spine to rule out diagnosis and prognosis of malignancy prior to the recommendation for biopsy and spinal tap. For my family, this study indeed came at a bad time, and the recommendation for aggressive procedures would be slightly more than what dad could possibly handle at the time, especially after what had been happened to him. On the contrary, I personally welcomed the study as a good way to root out the chronic disease that was once affecting dad in term of cardiac and pulmonary functions. Certainly no one in our family expected a diagnosis of cancer, but at its worst, we were not saying anything or mentioning it to anyone while all diagnostic tests were still ongoing.

Dad had been losing weight during the past few months since he'd become sick. During a few of his early hospitalizations, dad showed the total loss of 20-plus pounds or about 20% of his total body weight with no intention of losing them even he was not obese at all. Along with the medical history of diabetes, multiple severe infections, and cardiovascular disease, I would say that dad might or might not have the malignant disease. Despite cancer could be very common in the elderly, it tends to be the accidental finding for the elders. I was totally convinced and remain hopeful that if dad happens to have cancer, it shouldn't be the end of world for him compared to what was actually affecting him at the first place. Even if tests confirmed the presence of cancer, dad might have lived with it all through his life. That was indeed a blessing if dad happened to have cancer without having sign and symptom since its beginning. I still believed that dad was in good position according to the progressive treatment protocol and the advanced medical technology our country has. As the days went on, my heart was hardened and bombarded by the threat of cancer, and I begin to read more from cancer researches and stories from the national cancer survivors. Mentally, I continued my aggressive prayer to the Almighty and made my covenant with Him that I would testify his love and healing power if my dad found to be negative for malignancy and cancer-free from test results.

Since the days I started my holy sacrament with God, I turned out to be more spiritual and affirmative – in terms of principle, truth, dogmatism and evangelism – than just believing in a religion that focuses on the revelation of Christ the Lord and the Trinity. I refused to accept any religious practice and priesthood brought on by the curse of Babylon, the false system in Ancient Persia, the Messianic Kingdom, the preempted pseudoscience from the Judeo-Christian heritage, the secular humanism or cynicism without the presence of the Holy Spirit, the baptism and taking of the Holy Cross, and the sanctification and justification of the Holy Blood. I denied the presence of cancer and rejected the spread of malignancy in my dad's body when I made my prayer request to the Lord because I believed in the divine healing by commanding and taking authority over sickness, curses, and evil spirits. Every night I read the Bible, although I seemed to not quite understand all that was meant in the Scriptures in comparison to the literature and research from science and health that I was familiar with. Yet, I found healing to be occurring at all places and at all times when we decide and are willing to seek the truth for our loved ones. Strangely enough, my days began to draw me closer to God because of my unyielding faith, my unfinished business of prayer, and my constant search for His words that continue wrestling over my spiritual darkness and fear to a point that I cordially and selfishly ask God to forgive, deliver and heal my dad. In spite of my absence from church gatherings and my naïve regarding Christian Science, I was blessed to see the problems of my life narrow when I focused my mind and prioritized my time on His words.

With great anticipation, I walked into the hospital and stayed with my dad every night, waiting to see a miracle from the Lord. I lost count of the days spent with dad. I literally could see and feel the long-range impact of this mission, which was greater and larger than my life and the sacrificial lifestyle combined. I knew all of these problems could be over once the findings and reports rectify. Without changing my belief and shaking up my faith, the test results came slower than I hoped for. I could sense the clock was ticking and time seemed to be running out. I wish they came in next morning and said dad didn't have cancer. If he did, I would go straight to my family and remind them of this beacon of hope that gives us strength and courage to communicate gospels and words against the shadow of sickness and the curse of devils.

Dealing with adversity requires an extraordinary impersonal character to pull plug against the feelings of inadequacy. It was not about how and when to catch the first wave of sickness but the strategy and emotion to make room for the unexpected disease as if the healing had been done. Though we had no rights to be a victim of a disease, we could manage it by staying proactive. Despite that we might not have had all the correct answers for why things happen in life, we could choose to live a less stressful and painful one by denying or rejecting its devastating effect on our bodies, minds and souls. We need our faith and courage to lay the constant, juggling emotions completely onto the cross with Christ so that we could get some rest in between our conflicting minds and crazy thoughts.

In the midst of chaos, fear and confusion, we fortunately were able to find peace and comfort. Literally every perceived stumbling block and difficulty in the medical settings fired our passion and commitment to make a quantum change in our unyielding battle for a better tomorrow. The day finally came when the advanced imaging studies and lab results showed no cancer, and I slowly started to catch my breath. Meanwhile, my family and I were joyful to find our dad off the hook from this terrible disease. Compared to other patients and their families, we were truly blessed by the amazing grace from the Almighty. For us to understand the purpose of His Kingdom was a humbling experience, and we looked forward to receiving the blessings He brings to all who support Him and are obedient in their faith.

A few days later, dad was released from the hospital, and his home health nurses followed up to ensure the consistent and continual care. During the first week of staying home, dad was alert and consumed meals at his normal pace. He took small bites, soft foods and liquid diets every 4-5 hours along with medications. Then dad was scheduled with physical therapists who worked with him at home to evaluate and assist his development of mobility. It was to his advantage that dad continues to catch up with his treatments and therapies in a duration and frequency he could be comfortable with. He also continued to closely follow his care plans so that his health conditions could be monitored.

Life, in other words, could be seen as a change of weather. As ever, there were good and bad days. There seemed to be no absolute prediction of what the weather would be on any given day. Sometimes it might be a beautiful sunny day in the morning and then suddenly turned stormy in the afternoon. Life indeed could be not much different from that of weather because numerous unexpected and unknown elements move cohesively along with the mystery of universe. It was a hard, argumentative truth that health could be the same as that of weather because we might not necessarily know what could possibly happen to our body a few hours or days from the moment we left our thought, heart and emotion behind. Though we could possibly let our emotions and feelings flying high, but they could lead us to nowhere.

There is an old Chinese verse, "Always prepare for rain even it was in a good day." Certainly, it doesn't mean all good days should be followed by bad days; however, the meditation and preparation for the worst should not be disregarded. What most excites us during the home health service was the success from the therapy that offers us a break from the sickness, and it gradually gives us confidence to celebrate dad's minor recovery from his illness. Unfortunately, a good thing doesn't always last long. One sad thing during this comfortable moment was dad's vomiting and fever that came in the middle of one night. The symptoms were like some kind of viral infection. Hours later, dad turned out to be very weak and sick. He began to experience difficulties in eating and drinking and only a small amount of food and water had been taken during the past 24 hours. This condition, which came as a nightmare, was like a sudden blow to the head for each of us. We felt shaken up, disoriented and speechless especially during the Thanksgiving holiday when good things were supposed to simulate and add up by glorifying and honoring God's presence and blessing into our lives. It turned out to be something haunting us with a vicious relapse of sickness and disease combined…and the possibility of death.

Chapter 3: End Road or Crossroad...
But Heaven was real

Though I walk through the valley of the shadow of death, I would fear no evil for thou art with me; thy rod and thy staff comfort me. (Psalm 23:4)

Thanksgiving Day is a special day for Christians to commemorate the grace and to appreciate the blessings of the Almighty. It was also a meaningful day for us to celebrate our achievements, possessions and gifts from the Holy One in terms of the wealth, health, peace and love that we have. Certainly, everyone wants and expects to spend that particular time with his or her family, beloved, and special ones. No one likes to have a special time that makes them feeling awful, painful, pitiful and miserable. And in fact, no one like to trade in or exchange the sense of pleasure and family fun on that special day for the sense of pain and moaning of sickness.

Generally speaking, Thanksgiving Day and the ensuing weekend should be filled with joy, comfort and love. Personally, I believe in holiday miracles, stories of angels, and the true meaning of giving. That Thanksgiving holiday no longer was simplistic, pure and beautiful as that of the fairy tales, kid books and comedies, as it used to be, and instead it was replaced by stress, distress and agony since dad was admitted to the ICU. All wonderful plans for the Thanksgiving celebration and party at home were suddenly cancelled. We were just like millions of sick people and families across the States being invited to a party of disease and needed to deal with unknown illnesses. We didn't know what would be on the menu, and almost none of us dared to challenge the smoking heat, stinky smell and precipice. To varying degrees, we seemed to be randomly picked out by the devil to participate in the event that promotes the flavor of sickness and the taste of suffering.

Perhaps one of the saddest feelings for anyone to experience during this kind of holiday is the feeling of anonymous fear. Sometimes it comes in the form of resentment or of annoyance – or even both. The reason for that was because you never knew what you were going to get. For us, we found that this unfriendly invitation and ongoing infliction were bigger and more complicated than the formality of celebration itself. Gradually, they begin to take over our thought and time. On the other hand, the recurrence of sickness in our dad had gradually turned out to be some kind of fatal toxin that began to infect our bodies, minds and souls in some very strange way. Perhaps this illness could be an infectious outbreak that began to spread through his heart, stomach and blood vessels that the team physicians were having a difficult time explaining. The medical staff began to ask whether dad was having advanced directive or living will (LW) at the time and whether we want them to resuscitate him if he happened to be at his last minute.

To some extent, the concept of having a living will or an advanced directive is a challenging choice that sometimes is misunderstood, and certainly we were no exception. To the people of the West, a living will (LW) represents a legal document or inherent right of the sick, terminally-ill or near-death individuals who happen to appoint their healthcare agent or legal team to make significant healthcare decisions about the end of their lives that were based on the consents or to abide by the terms and conditions in the living will drafted. One part of a LW helped to keep the treating doctors, nurses or healthcare facilities from any liability issues or for any ethical violation from occurring. Another part of the LW allows the dying person's wishes to be honored. Usually a living will could be prepared at the time of the terminal illness of any kinds or prior to sickness. To Easterners, the draft of a living will would mean that the ill could be on their way to death with no chance for recovery. Usually Easterners don't like or are unwilling to have their living will done because they think of it as a bad luck or curse for the living ones, notwithstanding of any pre-arranged funeral service. Another concern in drafting the living will was to spare our loved ones from the agony of indecision or emotional breakdown of choice relating the natural or artificial conclusion of life. It was obvious that death could be imminent, gradual and inevitable. Therefore, no reason or decision could save us from the final moment and also no one could stop us from making the decision best fit for our need or want. Personally, I strongly believe in letting nature take her course is preferable to reverse the natural process of dying. Though modern life in North America focuses remarkably on the pursuit of perpetual youth, liberty and everlasting life, but at the end of the day, none of us were immortal. My only agenda to that was because, even if we could seek successfully ridiculous life-extending measures, the actual life or living condition might be worsened in term of the vegetative state. With some random thought, living in a constant pain and torture could be as bad as dying. If it was irreversible, why bother to live a low quality of life? Since my principle and conceptual sense regarding the end of life decision was similar to that of my dad, he empowered me to facilitate and act on his behalf if necessary.

Looking at his calmness and paleness, I had unspoken words for the ill. As soon as I saw the services and care he was receiving, I felt relief to see dad surrounded by skillful medical staff and professional physicians who worked tirelessly and around-the-clock to save his life. On a second thought, I was having an uneasy feeling when I found dad in severe respiratory distress. Dad had very weak and almost absent pulse except for the femoral one during this E.R. admission. The E.R. physician had to cut a small opening off dad's right anterior thigh region to set up the IV fluid transport into his body. As time went on and for the next 24 hours, time became very crucial because the lab work, breathing treatment, vital check and imaging study were used to closely monitor and assess the conditions.

In less than a day, dad was admitted to the ICU with life support devices and a heart monitor to the side of his bed. The goal of this mechanical ventilation was to prolong life for those who had long-term neuromuscular diseases or life-threatening health conditions impairing their ability to breathe normally. The device was set up by endotracheal tube inserted into the mouth where oxygen-enriched air was delivered to the body and carbon dioxide was removed. The device provided a built-in alarm system to alert the caregivers and to thus record the patient's respiratory data directly connected to the nurse station. The process was aimed to promote patient comfort with necessary ventilator support to aid recovery.

In other words, the device helped to push air into the patient's lungs in form of inspiration and at a time it allows the lungs to empty air out in form of expiration. The device was used to help monitor the heart and lung functions to a point that it could restore, revitalize, and reconstruct most of the capacity to match up with what my dad needed for his breathing. The device eventually was set up to monitor and prevent a coma or any long-term damage to the brain.

Perhaps dad was really tired this time, as he seemed to need few more days of rest so that he could get over his bitterness. With dad still falling in his world of unknown sleep and also due to his past history of comas, the team of physicians realized that it could take more than a couple days of intensive treatments and ongoing therapies to help him recover. All they did was to keep track of any complicated factors that might worsen the conditions. Certainly the imminent procedures they recommended were to monitor the daily results from lab works, vitals, and imaging studies. On the other hand, they also advised us to consider the placement of long-term life support devices if dad failed further to recover on his own.

Hour after hour and day after day, our minds and thoughts were lost in space and the unreality of being. We were frightened and began to worry how long dad needed to overcome his coma. My sister, brother-in-law and their family came home for the Thanksgiving holiday, and they were somehow stuck and trapped in the trio of sickness, life and death that our dad was still fought on the line. The timing was bad, especially when fear took over everything we believe. It also caused us to sweat over any decision that literally made a difference in the outcome of his recovery.

The concept of being together over the holiday was indeed a blessing and tradition in our family. That year, we felt uneasy sharing dual responsibilities of taking care of our dad but shared with one another our appreciation that we had stuck together as a family. We celebrated that Thanksgiving holiday by sharing stories of the past year and by making plans for future get-togethers. We made sure the details we shared with one another were richer. We also ensured the unique experience from our siblings became the mirror for others in terms of intellectual and spiritual lessons we learned. And unlike before, we celebrated that year's Thanksgiving by commemorating our dad's overcoming of sickness and death during his last couple of hospitalizations.

One precious moment in life was to have friends and families around during the celebration of a holiday. The time could be disappointing to not fully and physically enjoy the holiday with our loved ones as we had to witness the struggles our beloved father was going through. It was also quite a long and hard journey we had to go through, especially when we faced the illnesses and infirmities that threatened the well-being of a disrupted and damaged system. Instead of dwelling on the grief and anguish dad lived with, we truly believed both the combination and complication of symptoms tended to be the cause of his sufferings. We learned sin and sickness were not the qualities of soul or life itself but rather became a part of the fear, heredity, contagion, inflammation and injury that could induce disease. We also came to our senses that lamentation was worthless, needless and causeless. We pulled ourselves together to stand with our dad to fight off the coma and disease.

A couple of days after dad was under the radar of intensive medical care, we found out how fragile human body can be in terms of hygiene, drugs or willpower. Certainly no one knew what kinds of pathways or systems that our body utilizes to balance between sickness, life and death. It was obvious that no one knew what was going to happen in the matrix of self-destruction and recuperation within the body itself when science revealed life was not exactly the opposite of death and life should not be at the mercy of death. Besides, sickness should not be thought as coming at a loose end of health. On the same token, no one could cheat on death unless the one who saves the life and dares to revive for the dead one. If not, otherwise, life is just what seems to be the cell theory in term of viability, regeneration, structure and function in all living organisms.

Looking at the beeping on the heart monitor and listening to the rumbling on the ventilation device, we found that time moved very slow against the possible progression and complication of disease. Deep down in our minds, we seem to be not much different from a pregnant woman who was trapped in the triage or trimester of temperament, depression and melancholy. In addition to stress, we craved the snoring, grunt and cooking dad showed us in his pre-comatose life. We expected the day when dad would get over his debilitating conditions. We also cried out loud for the peaceful delivery of a healthy father who struggles through and bounces back from the incredible underlying diseases.

Days went by and there were no signs of significant improvement. We began to worry because we truly didn't know what kind of problem dad suffered. The hospital then arranged a meeting with our family to discuss the situation. By the time my sister Miley and I get to the meeting that day, we were surprised by the information putting forward from the medical team, dietician, pathologist, nurse, and staff including both the social service and family counseling departments. It indeed was a formal discussion panel that focused on transparency and openness to allow family members and caregivers to gather sufficient and accurate information on the patient's status. It tends to help family members making the correct decision and choice for their loved ones.

The purpose of this doctor and family meeting was to discuss treatment options and to develop an open dialogue between the doctors, administrator, patient, family members and caregiver. The focus of our discussion was that dad had a long and extensive medical history of hypertension, diabetes, cardiovascular disease, TIA, kidney stone, chronic obstructive pulmonary disease, chronic renal failure, anemia and severe infections complicated by aging, the physicians team came to their consent and recommended that it was beneficial for dad to have life support if dad fails further in his respiratory treatment. Hospice care was recommended if dad came close to the end of his life. But if dad recovered from his respiratory distress, then the question would shift to address his long-term problem. The doctor and hospital recommended a temporary feeding tube known as percutaneous endoscopic gastrostomy (PEG) tube to help provide dad with adequate nutrition and to prolong his life while additional treatment options were still searching.

With acknowledgment of the severity of the problem and the management team's professionalism, we came to a consensus to follow dad's wishes. I remember dad telling me that he would rather pass away naturally if the medical doctors' procedures, assessments and treatments weren't curing him. Dad also insisted on not living in nursing home or having any major surgery done on him without his consent. He insisted on having a peaceful journey during his last moment and to not carry out a major intervention and interruption to the natural way of life set forth by our Almighty God.

With what the medical profession told us about dad's condition and with what dad also had instructed us to do in case of his failure with treatment, we found ourselves caught up in a dilemma that made for a tough decision. Certainly, we didn't want to rush through everything by coming up with something that might be regretted for the rest of our lives. Even more than that, we found making the right assessment without mentioning the difficulty of reaching any decision was awfully stressful. And in-between those uncertainty and desperation, we requested to buy some time for dad's treatment so that my sister Miley and I could have few days to discuss dad's health problems in detail with the rest of the family.

Back from the meeting, our minds were totally lost, as if we'd fallen into some unknown and weird space. And almost for the entire day, we were disturbed and overwhelmed. Our whole family started to fall off the tracks. At some point, I saw our emotions could be bigger than the problem, as our mentality and faith were shipwrecked, our thoughts were hit into the iceberg of unreasoning, and our energy sunk to the bottom of ocean floor. Hypothetically speaking, we don't know what could happen to dad for the next few days or even the next few hours. One thing we could be assured of was that we didn't want to see dad having poor quality care despite that his life was not good at the time. We reminded ourselves that dad actually took more than three days to overcome his coma in the last few episode, and certainly during this time, we see dad might not be any different or any easy than before. In other words, what we pondered and worried about was not about how much time to get him off his coma but rather what was the likelihood and possibility that dad could come out strong from his coma.

To some people, every day might be a new day filled with great expectations. To our family, every day unfortunately seemed to be a nightmare. Every day seemed to unveil some unfinished business and an untold story of new tests results. And for those few days, it seemed not so easy for all of us since we found that we need to get our fingers across some tough issues to come up with a decision before something worst might happen to dad. Certainly we didn't expect that could be true for our dad. Deep down in our hearts, we didn't give up our hope to look for something bigger and more refreshing.

As usual, my sister and niece stayed with dad in their daytime rotation until I checked in at 8 p.m. to relieve them. In the daytime, friends came to visit dad between the stops by familiar medical staffs. The church elders and our senior pastor came to visit dad and pray for him, as usual. They, especially our senior pastor, always reminded us to put all of our faith unto God, who specialized in all that was impossible to mankind, and who would bless us according to the riches in glory Christ has. The senior pastor continued to console our family and told us that this incident perhaps was a good test God had for dad and our family because God wants to show His children the loving kindness, tender mercy, and awesome healing He restores for them. And it was always by His grace that the sick heal, the deaf hear, the paralyzed walk, the lost are found, and even the dead rise.

As before, spending the night in the hospital was not always a pleasant experience. Whenever dad was hospitalized, I also happened to live in the hospital with him. Beyond those sleepless nights, I begin to question the true value of health, especially when I witnessed the agony my beloved father suffered in his advanced age. My heart also went out to those who struggled with their sickness or injuries. I found the most fearful threat to the sick might not necessarily be the journey of experiencing the pain, the battle for a deadly or life-threatening disease, and the road to live through the unknown future but instead, it was the lack of support or eye contact from their loved ones. No one enjoyed the feeling of loneliness, the sense of emptiness, or the thought of rejection. The fact of the matter was that I truly believed our nature demanded to know a little about a lot rather than a lot about a little regarding to our health conditions. If we didn't put one foot out of our comfort zone to test our desire and to explore the terrain regarding to our illnesses, we would never be able to find out the truth and we would never be going to get close to the kinds of relationships we expect, not to mention the passion and thoughtfulness to share with someone who we love dearly.

Amid the night's silence and serenity, I could sense her light whisper through my ears and her warm touch on my face. Despite the tranquil surroundings, I could hear every moaning and crying from the sick in addition to the steady steps of nurses and the medical staff. In spite of all the things happening within our family on the top of what was actually taking place in and around patient rooms in the unit, I wasn't stopped from seeking God for his peace, love and comfort through the reading of his words and the intimate relationship in prayer. To me, this serenity gave me some deep thoughts and wonderful time to reflect upon the past, cherish the present, and look forward to the future.

Late one night during my stay with dad, I overheard a voice calling my name. Jumping to my feet, I ran to dad but was disappointed to find the voice did not come from him because he was still in his coma. I looked around the room but saw no one. I immediately opened the door but saw no one in the hallway either. I began to question my own alertness and subconsciously felt some chills in my bones but couldn't believe my sense of being stressed and hysterical that led me to fantasize about hearing voices or even hallucinating. Then I returned to my folding chair and heard the calling of my name twice again. Due to the fact that the voice was so loud and clear that I came to my senses realizing the calling was real and not in dream. With astonishment, fear and curiosity, I quickly covered my mouth with both hands. I was frightened, scared and freaked out. My body shook as I prayed from my chair. I didn't know how long and why I had been that way. All I could remember was that I screamed, kicked, cried and then fell into a deep sleep, which I had never had for quite some time. In that sleep, I found myself traveling – though perhaps traveling – was not quite the right word. I found myself going somewhere, but became clueless about where I might be going, and perhaps I was taken to some part of the world even I myself could hardly know or recognize...

Indeed, living in the name of faith according to Christian principles and divine law can be very difficult in this cynical world. From time to time, I don't believe that I happen to have wicked fingers twisted in my prayers. Notwithstanding the fact that it became even more difficult to believe in the possibility of balancing any reality in the theory and practice that reveal from a dream. The fact of the matter was that the mortal thought and mind don't build in and live up with the higher learning from any spiritual apprehension in forms of sin, sickness and even death. Sometimes that became a factor for me to overcome the shadow of doubt while, on the other hand, it also gave me an excuse to look closely at what was revealed from the dream. I could be a fool to believe such a small incident could stop me from seeking the true power.

Deep in my heart, remembering my dreams were not among my daily practices. I truly didn't remember the last time I'd had a dream. That could be fairly true from what my family and friends comment about my practice of dream because I have nothing to look back and fewer things to look forward to. The memory of my past and the reality of my present somehow had tangled to a point that I almost forgot there was a time in-between. One fascinating feeling during the fearful prayer that night was neither about the search for peace nor the comfort for good sleep but that I'd been given a chance to discover a biblical truth, a time to meet my soul creator, and finally a lesson to learn for life.

The occurrence took place between a cool late evening and an early morning. Due to the moisture and a drop in temperature from the stormy weather, the morning turned out to be a little bit chilly. With the unexpected voice and a name being called out of nowhere – not mentioning the fact that I was lying next to someone who was in a coma, as if he were dead – it turned out to be scarier and even chillier than it could be. In the dream, I walked out of a patient's room under the guidance of some kind of light, passed through a wide double door, and climbed a long stair. At last, I came to the end of a narrow hallway. I saw no one along the way and the voice still echoed in the air. With curiosity, I opened the single door where I was caught by four beautiful angels. Suddenly, my heart was almost fallen out because I realized I was somehow standing on the shaky wooden stair that kept my body from falling down to the street. And in front of my eyes, all I could see was an open space, indefinite boundary, and a breathtaking turbulence. As I took a quick look at my surroundings, I found that I was indeed standing at the top of some kind of a tall building, which I neither recalled visiting nor I had seen anywhere, not mentioning the fact that it was totally different from the building I went to and stayed in every night.

Without knowing what could happen next, I found this journey to be the most stupid idea I had ever had. Before I attempted to take a step back from where I stood, I heard another voice saying, "My child, why do you fear?" All of a sudden, my eyes open up widely and subconsciously, I found those words to be familiar. I knew what I see, read, and hear that before, but I just can't tell where I did see, read, and hear about it at the moment. By the time I tried to speak it out, my mouth turned out to be so stiff that I become speechless.

I don't know how long I had been standing there against the strong wind, but I remember that I stood there until my body grew extremely chilled. It could have been just a minute or maybe a few hours. By the time I learned how to ask the angels of why and where I had to go with them, I saw a shiny pathway from the clouds that begin to form like some kind of arching and expanding structure with rails; initially, it looked like some kind of stairs, but slowly it turned out to be a bridge. The bridge turned out to be bright, wide and long, and was covered with numerous golden chains reflecting from the loose, dark but semi-silver clouds. The surface of the bridge was formed by star-like sapphire, and the stairs were decorated with ruby in a crossbeam arrangement. I didn't see any arch-like cable-supporting suspension with modern steel. I didn't see any cement concrete pavement, but the footing drain system, which was connecting through thick clouds, was built to sustain pressure from storm and wind loading. I saw shiny beam retrofit railing mounted at each curb across the bridge so that I could see where I was about to head.

By the time the bridge was completely formed, I could hardly see any human beings walking on it. Instead, I was completely amazed by the almost instant formation from a magnificent architecture that neither Philips Johnson and Richard Rogers nor Alberti Leon Battisa and Bramante Donato could possibly have designed in just a few minutes. I was totally moved by the fact that there was no defects found within each block or connection, and that every large or small construction was somehow put together as a masterpiece from the fine art. I was also grateful for the fact that I was chosen to witness this awesome process from the beginning to the end. To me, this formation was the most intelligent creation of forms, shapes and decorations in any cultures. And the construction revealed the most advanced, sophisticated and profound works of architectural designs that embed more highly perfect than the medieval arts, Renaissance, and monumental palaces or fortresses combined.

Despite that the bridge was fully and beautifully built, I was unconvinced that it would be safe for me or anyone to walk on. The bridge could possibly be unsafe; the reason that no one was able to come close or pass through the bridge was possibly because it had not yet been fully tested. Perhaps it was not in our best interest or benefit so that no one was intended to bypass or drive through it. From some random thought, I didn't find the construction to be as dissimilar from that on our world other than God was not in the middle of the way. On second thought, I truly believed that Jesus came to this world not only to fish mankind for God's Kingdom but to also build bridges among people of different religious backgrounds and interfaith practices so that they could embrace harmony and unity within God's standards.

For most of our time, whatever we knew in life seemed to serve us less well than those we don't know some time. To some people, life could be full of surprises, and curiosity could drive us to break through the boundaries of beliefs and barriers of differences. To others, life could be full of tricks, and even the idea of insanity could derail us from our focus and could even send us into the ditch. Certainly, the new road might never exist not until we agree to give up the old path. On the other hand, the road could become narrower if we always limited ourselves; otherwise, we won't be able to cross the bridges of impossibilities.

During the time flying in the open space, I found myself being caught up in strange feelings and thoughts since the appearance of this wonderful structure. I had a difficult time distancing myself from what had been happened to me and what was heading in my way. I truly didn't know how I was going to do with it or if I should be doing something instead of holding and hanging up there by the doorway. Surprisingly enough, Michael, the Archangel, tapped my shoulder and told me to step forward.

"Oh no...Me?"

"Yes...you," Michael says.

I turn to him. "No! I can't jump that."

"Who told you to jump?" He stretched out his hands and wings.

"Me...No! I can't. You really mean that...flying...like what a bird was doing?"

"Right! What...you're scared?" Said Michael.

"No, Sir! You probably don't understand. I don't fly...I only walk."

"How do you know that you can't fly? Have you ever tried before?"

"No...But I don't believe I can."

Michael then turned to the other angels standing in front of my eyes. "Gabriel and Anthriel would show you how."

A few seconds later, I was instructed to stretch out my arms, turn my head forward, and put my feet up and out. All of a sudden, I felt my body hopping, rising and spinning in the air. I also found myself falling from a hundred feet tall building and was then picked up by guardian angels. Then we broke through the clouds and out of the open sky. Viewing from the above, I felt life was indeed a motion or movement that was developed and enhanced by a living mechanism. Without vitality, our body was not different from a living creature that contains neither sparkle nor wellspring. When we move, the spirit moves, and all other creatures also move with us like the flashes of lightning.

I don't remember how long we had been flying or how far we had gone. But I recall we were in and out of the streets, parks, cities, villages and farms. We cut and chased in the thin air and also in a dark cloud without assistance, approval and navigation from the air traffic control crews. The longer we flew, the colder we got, and the more turbulence we faced. Somehow, I believed that we reached the stratosphere or even the exosphere where no clear boundary of space could be seen. Gradually, I realized that the reason I couldn't see clearly was because of my own sin and disobedience, and eventually I had to trust God and his Words to lighten my path. Finally, out of nowhere, we landed in front of a cone-shaped gate under a magnificent construction and the beautiful bridge that I had seen earlier in my trip.

By the time we passed through the bridge's entrance, I saw there were no security guards or workers around. And not too far from where I stood, I saw the quietness of the street and heard the soft serenity by a planet as if the spaceship taking off into space. The street was a one-way something I knew despite that I had not seen any moving vehicles. To my surprise, one of the angels, Anthriel, reached into her pocket and took out a small metal-like device and pressed a switch. Within a few second, we were approached by an Amtrak-like spaceship that was stylish and elegant standing next to a beautiful one-way sign built in a diamond-cut arrow that was placed on the right side of the entrance. Upon closer inspection, I found the spaceship was built with a state-of-art design and equipment. By the time we boarded, I'd never been so anxious and frightened in my life – not because my life was in the hands of an auto-pilot system but because I was told my next stop was in Third Heaven.

There were several meanings to the word heaven that was mentioned in the Bible. Taking root from both Hebrew "Shamyim" and Greek "Ouranos," the word "heaven" refers to God's dwelling place. The Holy Scripture revealed "the Lord had prepared or established his throne in heaven, and his kingdom rules over all" (Psalm 109:19), and it was also written as "the heaven was my throne and the earth was my footstool" (Isaiah 66:1). Heaven was a part of God's creations since he creates this universe and sets forth creatures in order. Among them, God names the atmosphere that surrounds the earth as the filament (Genesis 1:7-8). Heaven was also a real place for spiritual and physical dwelling and as the Bible said that "in my Father's house were many mansions: if it were not so, I would have told you. I go to prepare a place for you. And if I go and prepare a place for you, I would come again and receive you unto myself; that where I am, there you may be also (John 14:2-3)." Clearly the concept of heaven was something real and this journey to heaven began to open up a new chapter in my spiritual life as much meaningful as that of my earthly living as well.

We move undisturbed toward our destination. The road was smooth and soft as that of a silk cloth. We traveled at the steady speed, feeling as if we are surrounded with love, and we press on as if we are enlightened with some new discovery about life. I felt the trip to be amazingly comfortable and pleasurable, despite that I didn't find any information or travel guide like I had on previous cross country tours or overseas trips. There were neither television commercials nor travel magazines to be read. There weren't stewards, stewardesses or conductors to serve my needs except the two angels who were with me all along. As our journey continued to move forward, the open space from the sky seemed to be smaller and narrower. Eventually, we passed through a steep mountain then through stormy rain and warm sun. Suddenly, we stopped in front of a tall waterfall, and I could look from my spaceship into the area around the waterfall. Anthriel pressed her remote control button, and at the twinkle of an eye, the water from the fall began to move way, yielding a passageway for our spaceship. By the time we passed through the fall, I couldn't even believe my eyes anymore because everything I saw was spectacularly beautiful. I couldn't imagine how my simple but perplexing life ended up in this fairy tale-like world of reality.

Anthriel, the rest of the angels, and I stepped into a glassy compartment. After a few seconds later, I was given new clothes and shoes and was instructed to put them on. Before we split up from there, another angel, Ambriel, reminded me that "you are allowed to travel anywhere in the West side of land. Do not go close to the waterfall at any time."

"You really mean that...but why?" I ask.

"You'll know and would be directed to the East side when time was appropriate," said Ambriel.

For a while, I become totally confused about the instructions I heard and began to wonder the reason behind them.

"You should not touch things in the West side, especially those build in silver and gold," Michael said. "Trust me, you don't want to be caught up there..."

For the rest of the night and few nights after that, I had almost exactly the same dream, vividly revealing the fundamental truth that all creations were made possible by the hands of God. In those dreams, I found myself being brought into the glass house. Then I was somehow transformed before I toured the paradise. Throughout the places I visited in that wonderful land, I didn't find any torment, anguish, cry or suffering. But instead, I was totally amazed and jealous about the peace, joy, serenity and security that people had in their lives notwithstanding the beautiful scenery, fruitful life and wonderful smile from their faces. One disappointing thing was that I don't know or recognize what languages they were speaking and what planet they were coming from and so I was unable to fully communicate with them.

During my first journey in the Third Heaven, I had that privilege of visiting the West side of the land where the living condition and all constructions immeasurably surpass the wisdom and knowledge of man. All things and matter that I got in touch with were directly communicated from one to another perfectly. There were strong moving forces among the body, object or activities that formed as both a perfect obscurity to be seen by the naked eyes and sensual arcana to be incomprehensibly describable by words, tone or expression. There was literally nothing that could impede or slow down the activities or movement of life. Everything that appeared before my eyes revealed a correspondence with and a cohesiveness from divine power, and that was why it was so different from the kind of popular science we believe or live in. I happened to notice that the stone, wall, garden, river, and even the sky were a reflection of God's creation. Nature itself reflected the artistry of God and left no room for me to question the presence of a deity.

Certainly no one knew the reasons why I was in the Land, and even I myself still wonder about the fact why I was chosen to visit the Third

Heaven. Perhaps, those citizens in the Kingdom really don't care about it at all except the ones who brought me into the Land. Sometimes that turned out to be bothering me quite a bit when I look into their eyes. But deep down in my heart, I believe it was not a coincidence that the Angels had me in the Heaven, and according to the Bible, it was to God's grace that we, and especially I today, were able to enter the Kingdom of God. I truly don't believe that neither my works nor faith could credit me to this Land. According to the Scripture, we were saved because Christ had paid for our sin in full due to the blood he shed over the Calvary, and those who believed in Him were forgiven for their sin and were given a ticket to the Heaven when they die or sleep in other senses. Literally, I believe my presence in the Heaven might be related to my death. But how could I be dead if I was young, healthy and with no history of trauma, injury or sickness unless I was knocked out by something unknown and perhaps, some mysterious or supernatural power?

Walking in human flesh, I was honored and humbled to be transformed with the Holy Spirit and spiritual seal, as I continued to grow accustomed to the life in the Western Horizon. I felt morally obligated to walk in the direction toward what my eyes saw, my ears heard, and where my heart belonged. I truly believed in the will or inspiration coming from above, not from beneath or from within. From the vineyard to the building of a golden palace, I began to realize God's plan was in every step of the way. My eyes opened to a point that I had never been before in the acknowledgment of error, evil, right, wrong, sin, sickness and death. I found sinful motives and false beliefs trying to eat me alive, but they couldn't stop me from enjoying the fruits of the spirit. I eventually saw spiritual powers breaking through the atmosphere, and I also saw the glory of God shining through every corner of darkness to capture the healing and teaching without exploiting other theologies.

When I step back into the glass house, the evil spirit and Satan begin to twist every fact that I knew. But deep down in my mind, I realized this experience was a great process for me to understand and trust in God's powers reigning over any subtle degree of evil and deception that Lucifer and his team attempted to blast the moral sense, mortal mind, corporeal life and material remedy. I also realized that all conscientious or mental malpractice could arise from weakness, ignorance, conviction and contemplation with mistaken or wicked purpose that the devil tended to pull us away from God's presence. By the same token, I truly believed the fundamentalism of Christianity or Christian Science proved the omnipotence, deity and divinity from creation of the world. Hence, God's presence revealed the principle of infinity, dogmatism and spiritualism that states evil disappears from the reality of good and the world of darkness also vanishes before the sun of righteousness.

During my stay in the Western Horizon, I was perplexed over how heaven was a literal, spatial place. Indeed, heaven contains millions of planets, stars and galaxies extending in all directions that can't be seen clearly even with telescopes, and as the Bible said, "when I consider your heavens, the works of your fingers, the moon and the stars, which you had set in place" (Psalm 8:3). During my second visit to the West side of the Third Heaven, or paradise in other writings, I was overwhelmed by the fact that the angel Gabriel told me of her existence going far beyond the other sides of heaven. Gradually, the further I travel over the Northern sky, the more difficult I could see the boundary of our earth, and the more curious I became about the mystery of life. A few times, I wondered what if I happened to be a scientist, could I fully capture all the details and calculate all the facts and theories? Without any imagination, I found myself not knowing the clouds or stars at all. I didn't recognize all of the myriad of cultures from all walks of life. I didn't even live through the broken promise of my time while staying at the Third Heaven. I never saw any tears or sorrow in the eyes of those citizens, and I did not hear any complaints by or setbacks in the life of those who lived under the shadow and provision of the Almighty. Deep in my heart, I was thrilled to be a part of this incredible journey; it was the story of a lifetime that provided me with the greatest uplifting moment for my Christian faith. I also was inspired by the perfection and completion of love that play a significant role in the lives of those who dream big to be Christ's followers and aim high toward the Kingdom of God. Besides, I truly believed that if I was apart from Christ – or in another words, if I couldn't be with Him – I would rather be drifting in another space.

As I continued to chase through the wind, the up and down through clouds, I began to find that greatness rests in God alone. I had not found any sunrise or sunset in the Northern sky, and I also had not seen any day and night over the Western Horizon. When I was tired and fatigued, I just rested in the earthy grass, without worrying of being killed or ran over. There were no Boy Scouts, nannies, police or security guards, but I felt safe to go anywhere I want. There were no killing, yelling, fighting or pushing around. There were no dirty talk, loud noise, bad joke or cries even though I happen to not all understand. There were no separation in colors, types and settings. Everything seemed to work under a smooth and cohesive system. If everything stopped for one moment, I could definitely tell you that it was the divine existence and intervention. I could also tell you that as soon as I turn away from matters, I immediately turn myself into the things of spirit with the fact that immersion and prayer were steps leading to a transforming faith and life only God could provide.

There wasn't a moment I didn't enjoy my exploration of the West Land. No one knew how far I had been gone and how long I had been lost. No one could get in the way to find out how I felt at the time since I started exploring the West Land. And in midst of all the frustration and cynicism, I heard my name being called from the trumpet of angels, and I knew that was my new destiny. I also knew my time had come to enter the East firmament of heaven. By the time I got to the East gate, I was totally amazed to see the construction that was once in both the Palace and Renaissance forms reincarnating in the modern art. No one claimed to be the builder, designer, architecture and developer of these elegant and stylish designs. Seeing two tall beautiful trees standing among the colorful flowers, fruitful plants and blooming garden where a small river ran diagonally across the Land was fascinating. Colorful fish were seen all over the warm river flow. Upon the river were fountains with a long and narrow bridge extending from the embankment into a magnificent tall castle-like mansion.

When I entered the mansion, I was completely stunned. The floor was covered by gem stones, the ceiling was filled with silver, the wall was put together by sapphires, and the pillars were formed by rubies. The foundations of mansion and wall were built with precious stones. There were a total of twelve different precious stones crafted for twelve different gates. The first course of stones was jasper, the second sapphire, the third chalcedony, the fourth emerald, the fifth sardonyx, the sixth carnelian, the seventh chrysotile, the eighth beryl, the ninth topaz, the tenth chrysoprase, the eleventh hyacinth, and the twelfth amethyst. Each of the twelve gates was covered and made from a beautiful single pearl that stood out on its own. There was one big chair and twelve small chairs on each of the two sides of the podium where the elders and angels were sitting in front of the gates. They were dressing in shiny pure white garments down to their feet and were wearing golden crowns over their heads. There were another four angels, who stood on the four corners of the room, dress in feathered suits and play in lutes, bagpipes, trumpets and horns. There was one person sitting on the big chair and throne in front of the seven golden candlesticks and a silver-like water-glass mirror. His hair was snow white, slightly wavy and long, his beard was brown, his fingers were long, his hands were soft and delicate, his forehead was open and serene, his nose prominent, his face oval, blemished and somewhat ruddy, his eyes were shiny and flame-like, and his mouth is prominent but slightly oval. These scenes that vividly appeared in front of my eyes were exactly the same description from what the prophet Micaiah said, "I saw the Lord sitting upon his throne, and all the host of heaven standing on his right and left hands" (II Chronicles 18:18).

As soon as I was brought into the big hall, I was also told to bow down and kneel before the presence of God. The two angels who walked me into this hall were directed to speak with the fourth elder and angel sitting on the left side of the podium before he was asked to leave the hall. By the time the exchange of information passed to the center of the podium, I began to cry out loud and to shiver and tremble, as if a drunkard. Then I heard voices speaking through my ears. In the beginning, I don't quite understand what they were until a silk-like air blew into my ear and nose. They gradually grew louder over time and finally I overhear a deep voice speaking through the water-glass mirror but it was the softest and warmest tone I had ever heard in my entire life.

"Why were you crying, my child?" Said the voice.

"Who are you?" I shout. "Oh no! Am I dead?" By the time I see what were all around me, I was frightened by begging them "please...please let me go."

"Fear not, my child, for I am the Lord."

"Your cries and prayers for your dying father had heard and echoed all over this chamber," said the voice. "Do you know the reasons why you were here?"

"No...my Lord!" I reply. "Am I dead already, my Lord...because the Bible said that only the ones reborn would see the Kingdom of God."

"Verily I say unto you...it was your faith that brought you here. Remember the prayer requests you give from your leisure, work time, and restless night. You search for your spirit and you cry out and cry aloud to the Lord, and because your requests echo with prayers from your families and churches, it was I who deliver you off your distress by offering you this trip so that you could see all the great things the Lord had done for you."

"But I don't know...how?"

"He was the jealous, righteous and justified God," the voice speaks. "It was your heart and soul that I'm going to bless to those whom you get in touch with. You were here because you had been praying for it."

"How could I do that while my father is still in coma and remained very sick?"

"My Child! Let not your heart be bothering for that," said the Lord of the host, "do not worry about what you should or should not do for tomorrow because tomorrow would take care of herself. You see that in birds, animals, mankind and even the farthest of the sky and the deepest in the ocean floor. Every things fall into a plan."

"How could I know your plan, my Lord...I mean your plan for my dad?"

"You believe in my son Jesus...certainly you'll know His way and plan." He seemed to know what I was about to say. "When the time comes, you would find the signs I had for you and you would have the comforts I give you." That man then turned to his elders and angels. "Gabriel and Pravuil! Come on up and bring forth the Book."

Suddenly my eyes opened, as if I was about to be caught up with some kinds of treasures never seen before. A wide screen of encrypted words and symbols sprung from the thick, heavy and gold-bound book, which I guessed to be the Lamb's Book of Life, reflected over the shiny ceiling. A few minutes later, I saw a new but familiar face coming out of the right hand of the one whom I had a privilege to speak with earlier. This person had a long curly brown hair, thin and golden beard, spotless and wrinkle-free cheeks, and grayish-blue piercing eyes. He dresses in a white robe reaching down to the feet, his voice sounds like thunder and rushing waters, his right hand holds on to seven stars, and out of his mouth came a sharp double-edged sword.

"My child! Do not fear...for I was your God," said the voice, "your faith and obedience had saved him, your father, to experience another chapter of life. Take a look at this." The Lord points to his left side of the ceiling.

As soon as I started to move my head toward God's direction, I see my father dressing in a grayish sleeping gown, a hospital gown, and he was sick and lies in the bed. Then I also see that my father was walking as if he was lost...No! He was actually spinning within and in between some kinds of whirlpool, current or wind. Gradually I was exposed to a life that was committed no murder but exorcism, idolatry, witches, vandalism, sorcery, palm reading, tribal god and evil spirits that my dad had participated, delivered, and worshiped, individually or collectively. Before I speak out to the mediator of false teachings, the pernicious ways of transgressions and the tribulation of sin dad leads his life, I see the Lord uses his right hand to wipe out what was coding on the ceiling and in my father's life. In return, an empty page appears. Suddenly the image of my father disappears in front of my eyes.

"How should I know my dad was all right and he lives again?"

"Remember this, my child! Your consistent prayer, persistent faith, and unyielding spirit that challenge you to commit one-tenth of your lifetime to serve the Lord and Christianity in response to the truths of spiritual healing cause him to earn a new life." He continues "do not tell anyone...I mean anyone and even your family about this. Take this as my covenant with you and remember to keep prayer with closed door at all times. By Wednesday night there would be a sweep of cold air coming in from the Northwest and for those rooms that fall short of prayer, moaning and torment would come to them by dawn."

"You know my dad had lots of illnesses and diseases being diagnosed and he also had hard time to get foods into his digestive system," I said. "Can you or would you please do something to that as well?"

"Do not let Satan plant the seed of doubt and suspicion in you," He said. "You should know your Lord was a justified and almighty God, and He would not fail you because his promises had never changed."

"So, how should I go from here, my Lord?" I ask. "How should I tell my family about it?"

"Don't be afraid because I would send you the signs and the comforters. You should testify me in front of millions of people."

"How should I know your plan?" I asked.

"Grace would be with you, my child! The presence of the Lord and His wisdom would shine on you. By that time, you would find the truth and door of Heaven would open to those who were hungry and thirst for His words and so, salvation and revival would come to heal the lost, ill-faith, disbelieved, broken and sick."

"My Lord! You think I could do that....But you probably don't know because I've never done that before."

"Be strong and courageous! You would be a good ambassador for my Kingdom."

"But how could I do...fulfill your plan?"

"Go in peace, my child, for I would be with you," said the Lord. "Do remember the covenant I had for you. Now and until then, do not drink wine or other caffeinated drinks and do not eat anything unclean until the end of the week because you would see my passing and the birth of Samson given for a new journey."

As soon as the sound stops, I felt I was picked up by two angels and I was led to move out from the highly decorated hall. We walk and pass a small bridge, but it was different from the one I went on before. There were no guards on the bridge. There was no any special form, arch or shape for the bridge. It was a short and small expansion of flat surface built into the shady mountain with golden chain that shines from the gross darkness and dense clouds. As I walked through those smoky but chilly airspaces, I felt my feet hop off in the air.

In that very moment, I somehow heard a soft voice whispering by my ears: "Do not focus on the death of your dad but rather, focus on the living" said Azrael, one of the angels.

"People were traveling this date. Some could plan out while others can't...I mean death but people need to focus the living as life moves on" said Daniel, another angel.

Without knowing where we were heading, I could only see myself wading through the mighty waters, sea and whirlwind. On those journeys, the angels of the Lord reminded me of the cross that God had in every step of my life. From the moment I entered the Kingdom to the minute I left Heaven, God himself revealed the provision, reign and protection that had never been out of his sight, and his touch doesn't become the problem for any reception or communication channels and networks. Even to the unheard, ill-believed and unknown, God always had his hands open to those who were ill in their faith, in despair, and even the dead. Many times the angels of the Lord showed me that my feet were drifting in the mud of confusion as we dived into the depth of the valley. They also pulled my body away from the turbulence of my suspicious thought and the shaking of my subconscious mind as we flew through the gusting of tornado. Further, they righted my life, as we moved against the current of skepticism and the stream of bitterness. Finally we were caught up in the street, by the corner, and into the building, and there I was released into the dark night. That was the happening from series of deep sleep and sweet dream I had in the Monday night. I didn't recall I made any additional trip or saw any signs in the following night. But deep in my mind, I knew it was the greatest things that I've ever done, and I was anticipating something big happening.

Still, I mentally became a lost soul. I was engaged, drunk and tired. I continued to ponder what I had seen in Heaven and what I had heard from the Lord despite the fact I don't fully understand them at all. I knew that I lived in an earthly flesh, but my mind somehow still hung on to the divine spirit. Whether my journey was a pilgrimage or not, I was so anxious to see what those experiences might lead me. From time to time, I saw myself as someone who was truly blessed to experience the extraordinary from my ordinary life. Regardless of what and how those things turn out to be, I'm convinced that God was actually looking down on me. Perhaps, I was not different from any other individuals who were constantly questing for a purpose. In some secular or humanistic viewpoints, I did not stop searching for something bigger and greater than what I was living in an unknown, hysterical and impregnated life. Indeed, I was looking up to God for some kind of infinite and superb intervention at all times. Throughout my life, I constantly stopped, stumbled, and then was lost and found in some very strange ways that eventually led me to believe "there were new heavens that belonged to God's Messianic Kingdom, and a new earth that was understood as a righteous and justified human society that we were awaiting according to his promise, and in this righteousness was to dwell" (II Peter 3:7 and 13).

By following the Biblical prophecy and true sermon of Jehovah and the angels of Lord, I continued to work on Wednesday as I always do. After leaving work, I went home, ate a simple dinner, took a shower and then headed to the hospital. I pretended nothing seemed to happen, and I even told myself that "it would be all right to me even if nothing happens." I calmed myself without losing control so that other people, including my family, wouldn't find what's going on. I also tried to hide from my feelings that "it would also be all right if things do not live up to the reality." In the time of those long and stressful waits, I literally was not different from a young under-aged pregnant mom who was expecting a painless perfect delivery. I forget Jesus Christ our Lord and Savior never would be late or fail to deliver his promise but could turn things around at any time to work for his purpose.

Time never runs so slow as when you wait. No one knew better than me what was actually kept inside my mind. Subconsciously, I believe this was the time that would justify the means but not the end. It was not the time to doubt God's authority, and it was definitively not the place to question His sovereignty because there was no other gods on this planet could do what He did. There also was no other power in this world that could remove burden and sickness better than His healing hands. Despite my physical exhaustion, I felt my blood boiling, my energy heating up, and my heart pounding so strong that I turned out to be sleepless. I was totally on my feet whenever the medical staff came by the room. Throughout the evening, time remained steadily slow and no extraordinary abnormal findings reported from the routine procedures. Even every now and then, I had some time to chat with nurses and staff to further learn about their work.

I didn't know what time zone I was in. Perhaps I might have dozed off a little bit; however, I remembered clearly that as soon as I get up, I felt the room was a little bit colder than before. I headed to the thermostat to reset the room temperature but later found that it could only be controlled by a central computer and that the engineer was out for the night. For a while, I heard some loud beeping sounds from the room, and I immediately looked toward the heart monitoring machine, but it did not come from there. Then I turned to the ventilation device and soon found its existence. I immediately pressed the button for medical attention because the heartbeat started dropping to a surprisingly low level that I had never seen since dad was admitted. Then an alarm for medical assistance sounded, and nurses came into the room while I was directed to stay outside the room. The paging system sounded off for a code alert to notify the doctor on duty. All of a sudden, the room became awfully crowded and busy. Some nurses were checking on dad's heart and the other was assessing the vital while waits for the doctor's arrival. Some nurses prepared for resuscitation and life support. A male nurse placed his hand on the naso-tracheal tube where air and oxygen were administered through the mechanical ventilation. He opened dad's mouth, made some adjustments and repositioned the tube. Nothing changed or improved during his first move and a few seconds after the second move was initiated, the scary and annoyed beeping sound from the ventilation device surprisingly stop. Then slowly I saw the data returning, and it was a little closer to what they were. Sweat came off their foreheads and smiles filled their faces as they each left the room. The nurse who took care of my dad at the time told me everything was under control. Meanwhile, I heard the paging system cancelling the call to the attending physician.

I stayed alongside with dad until dawn. Within those few seconds to minutes, I witnessed and felt the fragility of life going beyond the wiring process and medical procedure. I had never thought of the death of my loved ones would happen on my watch. Literally, I was truly torn apart and mentally overwhelmed by the matter concerning about the ill and fallen.

For some reason, I was almost immediately lost in the shadow of trees and fog. The odds were I would never find myself in such terrible straights compared to those who ran into their mistresses. If I did, I would not have had my hands wrapped around my head, especially when I had a lot of work that needed to be done. I didn't want to mess up my work even just for a few minutes. When I looked at my dad, his time in the hospital told a fascinating and heartbreaking story. I was about running into some kind of emotional breakdown as well. I had never imagined or thought of how to handle this death-like experience, and it turned out to be a handful when I witnessed grief and agony at the time dad faced imminent death. As I looked at the rain lashing at my window, I felt the storm's warning, and the sense of grieving hit me hard while I looked back at the pitfalls. It really hurt inside because the suffering, which the disease brought, could be as terrible as the actual tearing from the prognosis of cancer, not to mention the aggressive chemotherapy or radiation treatment.

Before daybreak that Thursday morning, I couldn't wait to call home letting my family know what had happened to dad last night. By the time my sister Miley picked up the phone that early morning, I suddenly recalled what God commanded me to not tell anyone about it, and so I mumbled telling her to continue praying for dad because he was still unresponsive to the treatment. But deep in my heart, I was convinced that it was not a coincidence to see the great work from a talented individual and the professionalism from an ardent nurse who saved his life in a split second. Meanwhile, I recall from both prophesy and word that God told me in advance. It reminded me of the parable in which God commands the Israelites to have the blood of a lamb placed on their doors so that the wrath of God and the killing of first-born could be avoided (Exodus 12:29). I truly believe it revealed the will and purpose of God who happened to reach in the very moment by finding the right person to intervene the process. Because His promise remained steadfast, I truly see that Jesus our Lord never would be late to illustrate his love and if necessary, I truly believe He would move the heaven and earth to show us his prophesy, truth and authority.

Throughout the morning, the family medicine practitioner came, as did the pulmonary specialist, to evaluate dad's conditions. They told me that my dad would have a better chance of waking up soon if he continued to show signs of improvement from the objective findings. They didn't know exactly when that might happen. It might possibly be sometime today, tomorrow or even few days from now. The important thing that they were looking for was the rate and amount of urine output to minimize sign of kidney infection along with the respiration capacity to ensure both the lungs and heart continue to function at the optimum level. From a different perspective, I believe it was not a medicine that creates a cure, nor the avocation that restores life but all that contain inside. Instead, it was something in between or something indescribable in term of reasoning or legitimacy.

To accuse or to be accused of something could turn out to be a painful thing. But up to that stage, I humbly said medicine played a significant role in the life of my ailing father and in the process of failing body function or system. Medicine was neither developed to be the answer for a promiscuous disease nor did it intend to be the solution for any myths or questions related to the nature of life. Certainly there was no absolute in any absolutes unless the absolute redefines and emerges from all assumptions. Whether it was a fact, fiction or myth, history revealed that science doesn't always live up to our expectations and there was no pure or perfect science unless the measurement or justification was perfect. Due to that sense of irrationality, a connecting dot was missed. Jesus our Lord indeed was the one who knew what was in and around our life and only he chooses to show up at the right time and in the right place where all of the best doctors on earth provide no answer to the problem. When the world gives no answer, God extends his healing hands to reach out and touch the sick. Given that, I truly believed my family and I should rest our faith on the provider and creator of this universe and allow His will be done on our dad without questions being further asked.

All through that Thursday evening, dad made no significant improvement. Perhaps this is not such a big deal for those who've never experienced, physiologically or pathologically, a major loss from sickness. But it could be a big problem for those who have experienced life and sickness, suffered despair, grief, fear, loss of consciousness, long-term disability and even death. The prior likely would apply for those who seek medicine or alternative treatments as a way to promote health and to improve total well-being. The latter would contribute to those who seek immediate medical attention for their late stage of disease or illness and some other specific health concerns. As for our dad, he definitely belonged to the second category.

Life could never be much more boring than being in the ICU. Despite the latter's monotony, life indeed could somehow fill us with some surprise and wonder. Of course, that isn't always true for those who stay in the hospital for their treatment or for those who live with the sick during their hospitalization. For me, taking care of my parents and family was indeed an honor and privilege, not to mention that it was the right thing for me as a child to do that because he, the father, first loved and took care of me. That was absolutely true to follow with what the Bible teaches me in the First Commandment: "Love and honor your parents so that you may live longer." That contrasts with the attitude of being cold, irresponsible and sensitive. Certainly, no one knew what a caring could lead us to, but at least we realized leaving our parents alone was not going to be the right thing to do, not to mention that the obligation and fulfillment that could rank it as high as any calling for active duty in any profession or culture.

Sometimes no news can be good news, and no changes might not necessarily be a bad thing. Indeed, recovery from a coma was something that my family, friends and the healthcare workers were all expecting and awaiting to see, but it somehow became a big challenge for dad. As for me, waiting for something to happen often was painful, and it consumed a lot of time and energy, not to mention it generated a lot of frustration and distress. In the midst of those intellectual and emotional battles, I suddenly heard a cracking and a moving noise from the other side of bed where the nurse practitioner was hanging a new bag of IV fluid. I think that sound might have come from the touching of an IV post and the connector of an IV tube. With a closer look at where the sound came from, the nurse and I found dad might have moved his forearm and fingers that connected to the bed handle despite that he had not yet been fully awaken. The nurse and I continued to wait in the expectation of seeing dad to open his eyes soon. To our disappointment, dad failed to wake up after more than 10 minutes following the movement, so the nurse left the room and came back with a flashlight to check on his eyes and reflexes. She then told me that dad was still too weak and perhaps by giving him some more time, he might wake up soon.

In the midst of an emotional and spiritual breakdown, I become physically tired and even emotionally worn out, especially when the early morning arrived. Between the anguish and languor, I feel asleep comfortably. During that wonderful sleep and sweet dream, I found myself once again traveling to a dessert, a beach, or by the sea where I don't see any human beings within 500 feet. I don't know why I ended up there walking by myself in a lonely and strange world. I appeared to be looking for something though I had no idea what it was. I could have been in some kind of trouble or was lost so that I didn't know where I was actually heading. There was no background music or noise that blocked me from clearly hearing my inner voice. Certainly no one could stop me from finding my true self. While I walked on those lovely sands, I saw a big crowd of people having a good time on the other side of road. For no reason at all, I walked down this quiet road where there was hardly a soul. Before I realized what was happening ahead of me, I was stunned to see a man who happened to be sitting on a rock in the middle of road. My heart began to pound so hard, as I become frightened and intimidated because I didn't know what could happen to me next. With a closer look at this strange individual, I found that he was totally different from some traditional savaged beggar or homeless in spite of his thin beard, long hair and old clothes.

"Excuse me, Sir! Were you all right?" I asked.

The man looked at me. "Yes, I was fine kid! What about you...are you all right?"

"Yeah...fine." I hesitate a little bit and then mumble, "What were you doing...in the middle of road and do you need some help or something?"

"Help...No! Not for me. Why were you so pale and shaking? Were you in some kind of trouble? Were you sick?"

"Oh, No...I just pass by." I tried to turn back and run.

"Where do you think you were going? Come here!"

"Actually I just forget that I had left some stuff in the back of my car."

"Come here, kid! Were you afraid that I, an old man, might hurt you?" He laughed. "Don't worry...I was in good intention and as a matter of fact, do you know that I had sat here for quite a while waiting for you."

"I was sorry, Sir! I beg your pardon?" I don't believe my ears and begin to question the man by saying "you wait here just for me...I don't know...why?"

"Young man, don't be afraid and look at me closely"

"Forgive me Sir! I'm not so sure that I know you...but if I do, please let me know anything I could help you with."

"What's holding you back so bad that you can't recognize the old man and the principle that he came to represent?"

"Permission to speak the truth, Sir!"

"Free your soul and let's hear it."

"You know...we were living in the world of setbacks that highly emphasize on addictions, drugs, corruptions and violence, not mentioning murder or crime. It was not unusual for anyone to not keep some distance from anything."

"Right...go on kid!"

"We were also living in a culture of obsession that encourages anger, jealousy, dishonesty, deception, lies, manipulation, ill-treat and rebellion. It was very common to find that almost all tried to come up with good measurements or excuse for the kind of temptations they were having."

"If so…why not let go of what does not belong to you."

"I was not sure that was the right thing to do, and besides, who were you anyway?"

The man, without saying a word or breaking his temper, turned to me. "Listens carefully to this and tell me if you recognize it."

Suddenly a voice broke out of the woods across from where we were standing, as lightning flashes across the man's face. "Fear not to the thick clouds, hail stones and coals of fire, I would hide you under the shadow of my wings and draw you out of the water of conflict and confusion this world imposes on you."

"Please forgive me…" I'm emotional and somehow begin to cry and to a point that I don't know why and what was that all about.

"Look at me, kid, you should not doubt about this," the old man continues. "Be faithful and He would be responsive to you."

"Show me your wisdom so that I knew what you were talking about."

"Do not rely on your wisdom and the word from this world. Put your weapon back to where it belongs. For those who use the weapon and word from this world could reap the damage coming from the pre-empted purpose. There was a time you would find fallout or shutdown whether you could be so confident to own it or not, you'll come to realize thing could walk out of you regardless of perpetual commitment or unwillingness to change."

"If it was possible, would you tell me what should I do with my life and my family in this incredible time of challenge?" I ask.

"Be strong! Go and tell nobody about this and be ready to speak the truth when your father recovers tomorrow. Look at the footprints over this sand and remember that they were the promises God had for you."

"Sir! Could you tell me who you are before you go?"

The man smiles, and few seconds later, I seem to see a familiar face from the reflection of light but I'm not sure where I had seen him. Strange enough, I hear some voice whispering by my ear, "When the time comes, you'll be my witness across this place and over that water. You'll see the comforters and know the way."

As soon as the voice stopped, I saw the old man disappeared from the middle of road.

The rest of the night while awake, I tried to determine what I could do differently to hopefully induce my father's recovery and to seek the immortal through the spiritual identity. I realized saying that infinite peace could be sprung from a limited body with the fact that eternal security could be found by the taste of salvation, the smell of spirit, and the feeling of divinity was not rational. What I didn't understand was how God knew what I was thinking, and why did He send some intelligent person to talk me out of it? Why does God do what he does, not to mention the unexpected presence he had in this very moment of my confusion? Certainly I didn't expect to have all that answer in a second. Even if God showed me what they were all about, I still wouldn't believe that I could fully understand them. And by the time I understood what they really were, I wouldn't believe I was able to live up to that kind of expectation.

By the morning, dad was still in deep sleep and during the routine re-evaluation and progress report showed no sign of recovery. His heart was beating, his vitals continued to be recording, and his breathing remained in the correct range, except he was not yet awake. Looking at his pale appearance, I was aware of the fact that was quite difficult for dad to keep himself above the physical condition of his illness. And judging from a healthcare perspective, I was encouraged that dad remained strong in this stage of the unknown and I couldn't imagine how worst can he be if not came out of some desperate situation. Certainly no one could tell what his future holds, but one thing my family and I could be assured for now was because we give him the best we had even if he happens to quit for now at the worst of his moment. I began to realize that it would be quite different by the time dad wakes up. Anyhow, I encouraged the rest of my family to tell dad what had been going on with him regardless that he may not actually have heard and understood it. At least, that was our obligation to be honest with ourselves and to those who we love dearly. Subconsciously that could help us to look straight into his eyes by saying "Job well done, Dad; it is time to get up and leave this place."

When I left the hospital at around noon, dad still showed no sign of being awake. My nephew was instructed to report back to me if anything happened.

While I was at work, my mind continued to ponder on the conversation God had with me. What I didn't understand was why God chose that day to be the one that my dad was going to wake up. I don't believe in the hypothesis of random selection or coincidence. Instead, with my full faith and belief, I was certain nothing could stop God from doing what he thought to be right for his purpose. No one knew what God's plans were until he called them into existence. Certainly that could go beyond my comprehension for what He had in mind, and it could always be greater than I ever might imagine.

For the entire afternoon, I worked with an easy-minded and lighthearted attitude. I was totally convinced by the Holy Spirit because I knew God would stand on his promises. I also realized that He'd do things greater this time than he had done. I continued to claim them as if I had owned the results and I tried to not think of how and why during my work. I'm confident in the leadership and establishment that God leads me through. I turned out to be calm and patient during this period of waiting because I deeply believe our Lord was going to provide us with all the resources necessary for dad's recovery and He was also empowering us with strength and wisdom so that we may be able to live up to his glory.

Before I left work that evening, I received an unexpected call from the family medicine practitioner to give me an update concerning about dad's condition after his assessment earlier in the day. He was also checking on our status to see if any plan or decision was being made from our family since the doctor and family meeting took place few days ago. Shortly after that, I also received another call from my sister Helen, and she told me dad had just woken up. With unspoken joy and almost tears in my eyes, I suddenly came to my senses to acknowledge the truth and promise from the Lord, and as He said, "be strong, my child, and tell nobody about what's happening until the signs were given...Go! I would never leave you nor forsake you."

About an hour and half later, I arrived at the hospital. As soon as I got off the elevator and passed through the waiting room in the ICU on the second floor, I was surprised to see crowds of people gathering in groups and waiting patiently for their turn to visit the sick. The hallway was filled with the background noises of chatting, crying and praying. Suddenly this ICU floor became alive and almost packed despite it was on Friday night, a night when people are supposed to have fun in theaters, stadiums, malls, restaurants, bars and clubs. As soon as I reached dad's room, I saw my sisters, brother-in-law, and nieces who were visiting dad. By the time I got close to dad, I saw his eyes open wide with a dazzling look, his mouth was mumbling with low and unclear words because he was still hooked up with ventilation device, and his body was weak with pale skin and atrophy, especially both of his hands being tied up by the bed rails because the medical staff were afraid he would pull things out when he woke up. At those moments, I felt unspoken joy in the room because our dad had come back to life.

I didn't know how long we spent during that visit consoling dad and explaining to him how important he was to us and telling him that if he thought he needed a long good sleep, that was fine, but he surely needed to remember waking up. Deep in our minds, we knew there would be more treatments. This wake-up was just another break from a long and hard journey. It could be a fresh start for a new life and a new beginning for dad after all those sicknesses he suffered. Then we gave praises and prayers to God for the wonderful gift we'd received. When we opened our eyes, I saw two beautiful angels standing by the wall next to dad smiling and releasing a crystal-like odorless ball of air and bright light into dad's head. Then they waved at me and flew off, leaving a vapor trail behind.

Long struggling with keen disappointment, I previously had a feeling that this hospital admission would require a longer stay for dad. For the first time, I could truly envision dad going on a new expedition to get rid of those that were once dangerous and miserable and that threatened to his life. I was convinced dad was capable of doing it by himself. I was certain dad was going to put on a good fight, for each time I held his hands I could literally feel his spirit.

For the next few days, dad showed some signs of recovery. Every time I saw my dad was still intubated, my head constantly spun and I didn't know how long it should take dad to get off this invasive treatment because I truly didn't want to see any damage to his vocal cords, thus jeopardizing his ability to swallow. After a few consultations with his pulmonary specialist, I began to see the remarkable improvement that dad made because deep down in my heart, I realized my dad was a very tough fighter who wouldn't settle for living with only the equipment's help.

I believed he could certainly make it through. As time went on, I found that to be true, as dad was soon disconnected from the ventilation device because he was able to breathe better without it. And based on the data and results, the pulmonary specialist recommended oxygen therapy to help dad enhancing his respiratory function. Day by day, the respiratory therapist was scheduled to come by every two hours to test his oxygen saturation levels and then placed medication into a plastic apparatus connecting to the oxygen switch. During the 10-minute treatment, the medication was delivered nasally into the lungs and other respiratory system through the use of convection and evaporation. The goal of oxygen therapy was to improve the skeletal muscle metabolism, correct the arterial hypoxemia, reverse the alveolar and/or tissue hypoxia and further enhance the physiological condition associating with chronic obstructive pulmonary diseases (COPD) or any chronic lung disease.

With restless care and progressive treatment from the medical professionals, dad gradually was able to talk and laugh again. He was then released from the intensive care unit. He heads to the regular impatient recovery unit where he was monitored and followed up for changes. From his coolness and composure since he gets sick, dad had surprised us with his character changing from quick temper, aggression and optimism to being withdrawn, depressed and debilitated. Oftentimes, we saw him working himself so hard to keep his emotions from flattening out. Recovering from his coma once again contributed from his strong mind power and reflected the grace of God.

Life was not easy and sometimes could be tough with what was going on. Dad saw himself as someone who was enthralled and trapped in the desert of sickness. He acknowledged the journey through the wilderness could be long and perplexing when he tried to look for ways to spiritually and physically get out of the depressed state. He realized that he had been lost and wandered back and forth during the desert of his comas while he battled with and against unknown threat of sickness, despair and even death. He also knew that he was caught up in something bigger and more dangerous than the drought he experienced during the final chapter of his life. He could hardly imagine that he might live up to the time when he saw the oasis and the fountain of life appeared in front of him so that he could catch his new breath.

Hope was a strange thing. It came when one had reached the lowest point of life. Contrary to hope, wishes came when one dreamed of the impossible and when one tended to drive himself into the unpractical or crazy thinking. Sometimes there was a fine line between a hope and a wish; however, there also are times when we might see no lines, signs or boundaries, and among them were when we were in deep trouble. There might even be a blackout from hope and wish when God was not present, and so no light was lit before the shadow of doubt, darkness of thought, and desert of mind. In fact, dad was both a strong fighter and a principled believer who claimed man could be as tall as his deeds. Dad believed in the notion of exceptionalism, and he rejected the idea that one is unable to think or act properly as one ages, not mentioning the fact of inability to eat, drink and walk properly when one undergoes serious illnesses. He also believed he could and would become one of few elders who maintain unchanged in structural and physiological functions in their late 80 years of age.

There was a time when the perception could bypass all kinds of random thinking, and there also was a time when the mixed feelings could make clearing of our mind difficult. In between those moments, we really didn't know how that could happen and how they played out. There was one thing we could clearly see: the overwhelming comfort found in the Bible verse "our Lord would supply all things according to the riches in glory Christ Jesus had" (Philippians 4:19). One amazing thing for all that had happened was that adversity aroused our deepest emotions and brought us closer to God. For dad, it was the illness that led him to fully understand God's love and healing over his life while the "dead" or "nearly dead" experience drove him into repentance for sin and reaffirmation of faith. Further, it was the dream or dialogue with Christ that eventually compelled dad to be spiritual rather than religious because he was used to carry on with his Buddhist view on fornication, perdition, idolatry and emulation.

One late afternoon in the middle of week, my sister Helen headed out to the hospital to relieve Kim from staying with dad. During that visit, she was told that dad agreed to accept the surgery that was recommended and encouraged by his family medicine practitioner during his regular re-evaluation and consultation. While his family doctor was making referrals and contacting the gastroenterologist for the surgery schedule, dad told both Helen and Kim about what actually happened in his dream on the previous night and explained to them the reasons why he now made up his mind for the surgery that he'd previously rejected.

In a world of sensuality and confusion of wandering in dream and sleep, there seemed to be a lack of intercommunication between intellectual and spiritual perceptions. During sleep, the world moved in the cradle of illusions, of ambiguous and unclear meanings. This kind of perception was also true when the world of sleep was a nightmare; however, not all that happens in a dream were so vague that they couldn't unfold the facts of existence. Oftentimes, they could help the conscious mind to comprehend mentally and materially and then proceed differently in the awakened state.

There were times when our life could be complicated, but they didn't have to be that way. There also were times when things were not meant to be put together, but they were. To some individuals, they could feel quite frustrating to see things out of their control and to get into their way. But to my dad, it was just the opposite because he said the dream turned out to be the right influence on his life at the time. He recalled that two nights prior to the surgery he dreamed of a man dressed in a white gown and sitting in white chariots visited him while he stood at a crossroad in a remote country farm. Suddenly, dad heard a voice: "Young man! Why were you holding back there?"

"I don't know Sir," dad said.

"Are you in some kind of lost or trouble?" Said the stranger. "Where do you think you're heading, young man?"

"Honestly, Sir, I truly had no idea...I can't remember this was the road where I came in." Dad pointed to his right side.

"Do you know where you might be going?"

"I think I do...But now I'm a little bit confused. East, north, west, south and they seem to be the same from this part of the road."

"No roads were alike, young man! It was not the roads that confuse you but rather, you let your emotions getting into the way."

"I'm so sorry, Sir, I'm not following what you're saying?"

"Sure you knew what I mean."

"Hmm..." Dad was silent for a while not knowing what to say.

He then looked at the stranger on the chariots, and by the time their eyes meet, dad was shocked. Dad began to open up his eyes, as big as the sun, and suddenly felt light shines on his face.

"Who were you and how do you know that?" dad asked.

"I was the one whom was sent to deliver you from the lost. Let go of your fear and you can tell me anything...Now, what could I help you with?" Said the man.

"You really mean that...anything?"

"Oh, yes! Why not?"

"I was not sure...But you knew I had been ill for quite a while now and all those doctors seem to not know what's going on with me. They did a lot of tests but had a hard time to tell me what the real problem was with me."

"How do you know that they were not doing their jobs?"

"You were right...I can't. I don't mean they were not good, but how could I keep my faith in their treatment of my renal failure and difficulty swallowing, which I had been fought off for so long?"

"Faith was something that can't be based on commercialism and objectivity. It was something you knew when you happen to run into it."

"You were suggesting that I should not think about them. If so, how could I break that barrier, or should I stand still and not even cross the road?"

"Young man! Don't confuse your stress with distress, your test with mistress, and your pain with suffering. It would never been too late for anyone to accept and reaffirm their relationship with God especially when the day was hard, the road was tough and the spirit was low."

"How should I know that the plan was working for me?"

"You should never doubt about what God puts into your life, nor should you be questioning about His righteousness," the man said. "He would never give you something that you can't handle. Believe in the man who was going to do what was good for you especially when you were aged. Remember that there was a time for sow, there was also a time for reaps; when there was a time for sick, there was also a time for recovery."

"Is that right?"

"Take a look at this road...Is it that one was where you say you came in and now, you don't know where you were supposed to head out, correct?" The man points at dad's face.

"Sir, please tell me what were these all about?"

"You really want to know, young man!"

"Yes Sir! You seem to know a lot around here. Please help me."

"Nothing could be more serious than this. Look at those roads. Some are narrow. Some are wide. Some looks longer than the other. Some have more twists and turns than the other...Every road had its use and purpose whether people pay attention to it or not. Some roads reveal heavy use in wheel and footprint. Some roads look smooth in the absence of marks, but that doesn't mean that it should be replaced by something else, do you understand?"

"I see...but how do they relate with me?"

"Why were you rushing through, and how do you know that they had nothing to do with you, young man?"

"Sir! I was sure you were right, but now I truly want to know where I would be heading."

"No rush, my child, and listen to me carefully...Believe me and by the time I finish talking with you, you'll know the real answer to your problem."

"If that was what you say, I truly want to hear the rest, and Sir, please tell."

"Every one of us was no different from all these roads. As you might know, some people live longer than other. Some people get richer than others in term of experience, passion, and devotion to life. Some live in higher darkness, deeper fear, and greater doubts. Some carry smaller dreams but stronger positive attitudes and take on bigger challenges. Some appear to be healthier than other...All these were a part of road and lesson of life."

Dad scratches his head. "I see it now, but still I was confused by what that had to do with me?"

"Your life had been hard, you were tired and you knew that you need some higher level of care so that you could move on better, faster and easier...do remember that nothing terrible happened to you and absolutely nothing could drown you except your belief, thought and discipline relating to other people's expectation."

"I indeed get scared and many times I think about giving it up."

"You need to give up some of those false beliefs."

"Why Sir?"

"Negative and dangerous thoughts lead to self-destructive behaviors. They were harmful for personal growth and ineffective for a better life."

"Sir, does that mean the surgery was good for me, even though it could be scary sometimes?"

"What you had been is not as important as what you're going to become. There was always a hope and a future for you even you were in the dead bed. It was not sins nor ages that lead you into this predicament but rather, this was the Master's plan that brings you into His grace period. Remember that in your weakness were His strength...and when you came out of these fogs and the crossroads, you'll be glad how you become."

Before dad began to understand what the words were and how they were meant for him, the chariots and the man were gone with the wind. As the dust continued to circle off from the road, dad suddenly came to his senses that it was Christ and the comforter who delivered him from transgression, disobedience, hardheartedness and grumbling. By the time dad finished telling his story, both my sisters were impressed that God did a great work and a miracle to revive not only the stubborn mind dad had, but He also revealed his promise to heal the broken heart and to save the lost soul.

On a warm and sunny Friday afternoon, dad was prepared for his PEG (percutaneous endoscopic gastrostomy) surgery. The pre-operation procedure was done a few hours prior to the time scheduled for the surgery. No feeding and no IV tubes were allowed. Vital assessment and registration were performed by the pre-operation nurse, also known as O.R. nurse. Evaluation and instruction were conducted by anesthesiologist who reminded us of the precaution, permission and administration of anesthesia and its possible side-effect during and after the procedure, including the authorization of blood transfusion if necessary. Shortly after that, the gastroenterologist came into the room to reassess dad's abdomen and to check for any abnormal bowel sounds. He then told me that dad would be transported downstairs shortly for the operation. As soon as the surgeon left the room, my sister Miley, dad, and I joined hands in prayer. We prayed for God's wisdom to be with the surgeon and his team throughout the procedure despite that we saw dad was calm, alert and relaxed.

Less than two hours later, I was greeted by the surgeon in the waiting room downstairs. He told me the surgery went well and my dad was resting in the recovery center. Then I was directed to the post-operation recovery center where I see dad recovering and awaken. Looking at his appearance, dad no longer revealed himself a man of strong will, firm belief and non-tendered faith. Instead, he became accepted, understandable and optimistic. His expression somehow revealed the sense of relief and comfort from a new person who exercises faith in the Lord and trust in the healer despite being physically exhausted. Shortly after being carefully assessed by the O.R. nurses, dad was transported back to his room upstairs where he was connected to an IV for electrolyte balance and to prevent the body from dehydration.

Our family was happy to see that PEG tube was easily put in during surgery. Certainly it was a big adjustment for dad during the early use. With the precautions of the health care professionals and the thoughtfulness of family members, a selected back support was given and attached to dad's abdominal area to prevent him from unintentionally pulling the feeding tube. On the other hand, the surgery revealed a great breakthrough from science technology and also a master skill by the surgeon himself when one looks at the tiny and delicate opening few inches above the umbilicus with plastic tube directly attaches and connects few inches away to the superior border of stomach. With PEG tube in place, we could worry less about dad suffering from malnutrition and electrolyte imbalance. Yet, we also were aware of risk from blockage, contamination and infection if both the tube and surgical area were kept unclean or in a not good hygiene condition.

We learned from the doctor that dad was slowly making progress and his health conditions also begin to be stable throughout the past few days' evaluation. The surgeon told us that the PEG tube was a temporary procedure that could be removed if dad was healthy enough to swallow by himself. But up to that time, the tube and the treatment were the best way and effective procedure possible to help prolong dad's life. If nothing worsened, the surgeon said that dad would be scheduled for release home tomorrow.

Having received mixed signals before from the healthcare system, I knew this system had sometimes failed and disappointed us. Looking at the treatment dad was getting, I thought that we might be unwise to continue diving in for more frustration. I truly understood the heart of all of this. Though I never knew how to get rid of that terrible feeling, I believed in miracle and forgiveness that made healing and caring practical. If we loved dad, I thought that we had to accept all that went into his care and that we should be happy for him because he was now in better shape.

Within a day or two, welcoming dad "home" turned out to be a reality and a blessing for our family, not mentioning the incredible journey and the stressful burden rested on our shoulders in those boring days and sleepless nights finally disappeared. To me, I believe Christmas wish is all about what we want and that allows our dream to come true. In addition, I truly believe Christmas is a special holiday that allows us to trust our heart. To all of our family members, this recovery of dad once again proved to be a wish coming true and the greatest gift that God gave us, especially few days before Christmas – a holy day for the birth of Jesus – bringing new perspective of hope, joy and salvation to the world, including peace and comfort for our entire family. Looking at the cold air passed through our body along with the beauty of spectacular holiday decorated lights on the streets, we could feel the warmth of winter and Christmas was in the air.

Chapter 4: Lessons of Faith

Faith was the substance of things hoped for, the evidence of things not seen. (Hebrews 11:1)

In this age of uncertainty and in a world that is as secular as it is cynical, there has never been a time that we've seen so many people turning away from their religious beliefs. Sometimes, most of us tend to confuse material consciousness relative to the sense of self, while some of us tend to doubt more when we do not understand our sense of true being. Indeed we should realize that every one of us has problems in life and making a decision or choice out of our belief systems or perception can be a challenge, often requiring an adjustment and even a big compromise. A lot of times, we might go too far and too fast that could get us lost or out of control. Eventually we don't know who we are and what we stand for. We seem to be knocked out of whack. We might be in danger as in the middle of railroad track. We don't find any help or there was no one stands up to confront us and say "enough was enough." And in the middle of all those confusions and chaos, if you think that you were not getting help from your neighbors or families, you suddenly see a hand out of nowhere. What if there was really a hand, and would it be something that you could hold on to and something that you could take to change and shake up your beliefs?

As an old Chinese proverb says, "A house could give you a sense of wealth, but it does not give you the sense of belonging." From some perspectives, that is quite true because the concept of a house was far more different than that of a home. By definition, a house had four walls and one roof where it was used for dwelling and shading. It could be filled with honor and pride. It also could be taken away by disaster and debt. A home could be quite different from a house. A home was not just a physical object. A home could be filled with love, warmth and dreams to the homeless or less fortunate, both emotionally and physically. It could also provide protection and healing to those who were sick, hurt and lost. A home should be a place where it could give accessibility to the needed, not to mention the memories and supports in term of finance, religion and morale.

Life was full of surprises. Oftentimes, we see people were busy working on and with their schools, careers and businesses. They work tirelessly to climb from one social ladder to another. They like to show how they are productive and competitive toward others in term of objective goals and physical or spiritual achievements. Some people were chasing their dreams in the raging storms of the social welfare, environmental issue, community health, common wealth, and even world peace because they believe in the equality and freedom through successful political campaign. They further believe that conflicts could be resolved through the deprivation of political, cultural and religious differences, justices or any governing means.

Even more than that, we see people working restlessly to pursue their broken relationships. Some of them took pride in treating others with no deep respect while others just enjoyed a little good time by driving others into insanity or a miserable life. For youngsters, it could be commonly seen as the fight or the matter of boyfriend and girlfriend in term of physical attraction, sexuality, drugs and alcohols that could be caused by jealousy, cheating, abuse and/or addictions. For adults, it could be mostly seen as having an affair in term of lust or vanity, but it could also be seen in social or moral corruptions that could be caught in between intimacy, fame, power and/or wealth. For elders, it could be the lack of connection with an extended family or possibly divorce, the threat of an illness, and the agnostic contempt of a religious cult that could cause them to be extravagantly frustrated, sentimental and hardheaded.

In fact, the problem leading to most of the broken relationships should not only be the problem of an individual in term of commitment issue. It could be a form of attitude that tends to be influenced by a previous experience. It also could be a trend that was indirectly affected by family or some kind of peer pressure. As the unhealthy event piled up over nights, it could cause poor decision making that eventually could turn into some crazy thoughts and weird behaviors. To a point, it should not be restricted in just breakup anymore, but it could drive people up for violence, revenge, kidnap and murder. To some extent, it by far could become a morbidity that began to invade our spirit, culture and belief because it was socially permissible.

From the Holy Scripture, one might find that the holy birth of Jesus Christ into human flesh was to become a ransom for our sins. His life was indeed a total reflection of faith, obedience and deliverance that God the Father puts forth for the completion and perfection of love. In addition to the physical tortures and afflictions He suffered, Jesus revealed himself as a new covenant to bridge between human nature and deity. He also helped to restore the broken relationship between God and mankind with the promises that He was the truth, way, hope and life for those who believe and accept him as their own savior (John 14:6). Certainly Jesus was not designed to see what a dysfunctional family or disrupted bondage should look like. Instead, it was the will of God who intends to make every empty heart or wicked soul as the home for the poor and the final destination for the lost.

Due to the fact that most people had animosity and disobedience toward God, sins, sicknesses, fornications and transgressions were once the causes of death eventually turning out to be a grace and salvation, and as Jesus said, "I came not to condemn but rather to save the world" (John 3:17; Luke 19:10). Unbelief, hatred and denial were indeed subjected to some form of condemnation. They could be grounded on former guilt to become a resistance against remedy. They could be sprung from the love of sin in some form and the enmity of the human heart toward God. They could also be sprung from the principle of lie, doubt and temptation that the devil took pride in tyrannizing Christianity and patronizing the fallen.

Unfortunately, not every life was an open book. What one person would share another might not necessarily disclose. Whatever was held inside, though, might not possibly be available and openable again. The chance for revealing the truth could be quite rare because we frequently lock ourselves up or hold ourselves back from our traditional values. In fact, we were not perfect, and we were far from being perfect. There was nothing perfect in our lives except the one who created the perfect life

Himself. Whatever constitutes our life should be considered a gift from the Almighty God because only by His grace we were able to overcome our inadequacies, shortcomings, setbacks and negatives and to thus enjoy the love, peace and security we had. And there were times when God used some tragedy or disaster to drive us to the end of our selfhood and to thus get our attention so that we could remember the blessing and experience the joy we could hardly find in this earth or in any other religions.

Sometimes the most obvious lessons in life can be the hardest thing to talk about. There were times when we think that we had all the answers, but in reality we end up with none. There were also times when we think that we were in control of what's happening in life, then suddenly we see that we were no longer in charge of the situation. Perhaps you might have all the plans in place for your business, career, church, family, children and/or love life, but they could disappear at the twist of a storm. God indeed does not need to check in to get your permission because He always had the conditions under control. Whether you believe or not in the sovereignty of God, He indeed does exist and has selected a plan for you and me right before we were born (Psalm 100:3; Jeremiah 1:5; Jeremiah 29:11). We might not have a lot of choices to not invite him into our life because he knew us completely from the inside and outside (Psalm 139:1-3). Nor was our excuse left to our discretion and ignorance to not recognize the peace, comfort, joy and prosperity that he provides for our life to an extent that this world can't.

Imagine knowing that our world was full of confusion, commotion, competition and cynicism. We have a constant sense of urgency regarding our needs. We think of the presence of God, as He supplies our need for what we ask from our prayers. What if God did not and was late in His response to our prayer request. Would that mean that God was no longer trustworthy or that He failed to be faithfully followed? Given the fact that we were Christians and followers of Christ, does that mean we had rights to change God's mind and favor? After all, we might be smart enough to figure out and seek through His words, but God would never do something that interrupted His purpose of goodness in our life because He was righteous and good.

Perhaps we were indeed smart enough to handle problems in our lives, but it does not take much time for us to realize when something unexpected breaks our hearts and the hearts of those whom we love and cherish. Remembering the time when my dad was discharged from the hospital and headed home for Christmas shortly after his PEG surgery and throughout the Christmas holiday, my family and I felt that it was a true blessing from the Almighty God who happened to give us a precious gift on the top of the greatest gift He gave to mankind. For years, my family and I were told the story of amazing grace in sermons and hymns, but we certainly could hardly imagine that it turned out to be an unforgettable miracle and truth that God promises to deliver. Despite the fact that the holiday was short and the weather was chilly and breezy in the absence of snow, but deep down in our heart, we felt warmth, joy and comfort when listen to the song silent night and the Christmas carols as our father joins us in the worship.

Generally speaking, a good time never lasts long, but a tough time does. In early January 2009 and shortly after dad had his PEG surgery a few weeks ago, we found that daddy was sick, pale and he also had high fever on one late afternoon. After monitoring his symptoms for few hours without signs of improvement, we were advised to check him in the local hospital where his doctor would be ready to stand by and see him. By the time we go through all the evaluations and lab procedures, we were told that dad needed to be checked in for his kidney infection. That was the fourth time and incident in approximately seven months since the first episode happens in July 2008.

Life was unbelievable and she seemed to know how to play trick on us. It was very frustrated for us to go through the kind of life that was once recognized as both an agony and nightmare with the stress and illness combined. Certainly we wouldn't expect anything less than insanity because the process repeats itself. In the meantime, we were also aware that history could repeat itself. Sometimes the lyrics might develop in different way, but the process could certainly be cohesive or even match up with the previous one.

Sometimes God allows bad things to happen in our life. But there was also a time when something strikes us in the absence of His will. For instance, adversity was one way that God forced us to confront our honesty. Sickness, on the other hand, was neither God-given nor self-constituted, as Mary Baker Eddy, founder of the Christian Science movement, pointed out. The cause of disease or sickness was mostly unknown or mental. From scientific perspectives, heat and cold were products of a mortal mind while temperature was the byproduct or perception from a mental power. In general, the presentation of chills and/or heat expresses itself in a physical form in which fever manifests and surpasses to a point of self-destruction over the physical state. Ignorance and disrespect of the cause or approach of disease could induce sickness leading to the stage of fear. If the mental state becomes confused, the belief system would be disturbed and gradually send the wrong signal or message to the mortal mind when the sense of fear, doubt or despair may lead to a bad result.

Fevers could be caused by the effects of both fear and the errors of the mortal mind. Fevers also could be the sign of a disease. The quickened heart rate, the weak pulse, the pale skin, the febrile temperature, the pinching sensation and the pinpoint pain could all be perceived by the mind and thus reflected onto the body. Science revealed that the material body can't have the ability to feel pain or sickness and to thus suffer from a fever if it was controlled by a mortal mind because that would create a false belief, alarm or disturbance to the harmony of the body system itself. According to Mary Baker Eddy, by definition disease doesn't have intelligence or capability for reasoning because intelligence could only be embedded or perceived by mind. But disease does have the capability for manifestation in term of germ theory. For instance, many people are told or diagnosed with cancer or cancer-related problems. The worst part for any malignancies might not necessarily be the process of the treatments such as radiation and chemotherapy to kill the cancerous cells and in the same time to diminish the function of healthy cells as well. Instead, it is the belief of the mortals to think of the procedure as a failure that eventually reproduces the potent and lethal results they dread. Many patients are informed or experience the so-called vitals as a significant part of their health if they suffer from heart disease, hypertension, diabetes or illness of some kind. From time to time we see people working very hard to keep up with their medications, diets and exercises to ensure neither inflammatory nor torpid action be found in the system. In reality, many patients tend to forget about the fact that one of the thriving forces leading to major death is not about the excess of dormant factors, sedentary lifestyles and unhealthy food choices but rather, it is the false belief that not only affects the invalid's health but also destroys life of the despairing mind.

The human mind indeed could produce the organic disease that results in hysteria, hypochondria, paranoia and hallucination. By definition, organic disease is the term that describes a physical alteration in the structure of an organ or the structural changes to some tissue or organ of the body as opposed to the functional disease which shows no structural alterations in the tissues despite an abnormal change in the function of an organ. Despite that organic disease usually contains the observable, detectable and measurable results or disease process, its predisposing causes could be traced back in term of anatomical and/or physiological functions rather than for mentality and spirituality. The organic disease somehow could also be manifested and built on the top of fear phenomenon that weighs down mankind with the focusing point on errors, sins, lies, sicknesses, guilt and even death. The human mind, in other words, was not different from the mortal mind that helped to justify the functional symptoms by giving us the perceptions or ability to feel, suffer and enjoy in term of material or physical sense. This so-called mind could be formed by the results of experience, education and belief. It could further be changed by divine healing power and the immortal mind.

As for my dad, his admission to the hospital once again could be related both to the functional symptom and organic disease that require follow-up and advanced testing. Just like few of his previous admissions, dad always had a handful of treatments. And as old as he was, this admission took great pride and strong courage to accept what a condition dad had to follow through with what an outcome he might get. Certainly, what happened yesterday might not be the same for today and what occurred today might not necessarily repeat itself tomorrow. With the degree of his alertness and stamina, we could see the relentless tortures and sufferings that he was going through hadn't taken their toll on him. In light of all that had happened, dad was brave enough to live up with his journey of faith, conscience and belief. No one in our family had ever doubted that the outbreak of sickness was related to a matter of heart, lungs and kidneys, but more likely the mind was the matter that leads him to face the end stage of disease.

During the previous few days of treatments, dad showed great signs of recovery from susceptibility to infection and his inability to resist gas reflux. Gradually he was released home. And for the past seven months after the fourth hospitalization, dad became bedridden and his life gradually turned out to be dependent upon nutrition from the tube feeding. Due to his physical weakness, dad surrendered himself to the mechanical and continuous feeding that ran 18-20 hours per day from the Kangaroo pump. Whether he slept or not, both the blinking light and the peeping sound continued to run along with the wholehearted devotion from his caregiver. With careful guidance and instruction from the home health nurse and therapist during the first few months, our family began to step up and take care of dad to the best of our knowledge and abilities.

With dad's health conditions improved and stabilized, I begin to direct his attention to alternative treatment. And with the impression and knowledge that dad had been bedridden for quite a while, I also realized that getting back on his feet and especially getting him to walk again could be very challenging too. But I wouldn't take "impossible" as an answer. Dad definitely needed and deserved time to get everything back on track. In addition to prayers, I decided to use chiropractic as a way to reduce his stiffness between the spinal nerves and joints. I also used the fascia release technique to reduce tension in the paraspinal muscles in addition to turn his body side to side after he sleeps every two to three hours. Every other day, I carefully evaluated his vital screenings and cardiopulmonary functions before I mobilized his joints and rehabilitated his extremities. The goals of the treatment and therapy were to maintain a global health, develop homeostasis within the body, and further reduce the level or degree of physical weakness from the long-term disability.

Perhaps one of the toughest jobs as a provider or practitioner in any healthcare profession was to treat your family members. Just like other medical practitioners, I truly have not thought of that assignment to be easy at all when I would expect my family members to listen and follow through all the recommendations unless they were in some kind of excruciating pain or mental unresponsiveness, as that of a coma, for instance. Certainly that was not the case here. In addition, when I decided to take on the assignment of treating my dad, as that of my patients, because I needed to earn his trust and treat him with good results, otherwise, dad would not accept anything other than traditional and Chinese medicines.

Like many others, I had been seemingly lost and confused in the sea of reasoning, and yet I restlessly continued to read through all kinds of medical textbooks and references to help me understand the science of the healing arts. Looking at the increased suffering and the continual bedrest dad put in day after day, I truthfully could say that not shifting the course of treatment before the time came in which nothing could be done for him was unwise and incomprehensible. By the time I began to see a change in the discord and disease, I knew that I might have had a chance to correct dad's physical and mental conditions. After several weeks of consistent chiropractic and adjunctive therapies, I begin to see acceptance, discipline and relief going beyond the sense of chronic pain, debility and other illnesses. Words become indescribable for the ill because an adjustment had been made within the body itself in addition to the medications and material remedies. The result then turned out to be the greatest reward that I had ever asked for.

When chiropractic treatment was no longer a form of rejections from dad, it turned out to be a new excuse for him to use for back pain relief. Generally speaking, chiropractic care was designed to treat mechanical back pain or any back problems. Since dad had been bedridden for quite a while and since he doesn't want to overload himself with additional pain medications, the best way available for me was to use what I had been trained in chiropractic to facilitate the structure and function in his thoracolumbar spines. With a specific approach and instrumental adjustment, I restored and induced motions into his spine to reduce joint fixation so that dad could use his back with extra strength for support and locomotion as well.

With this new approach, I begin to work on dad's shoulders and thighs in addition to his spine. I focused my treatment and therapy in the re-education and strengthening of his deltoids, biceps, gastrocnemius and gluteus muscles, as a way to maintain the tonicity and agility that help to provide dad with strong stability and balance when he stood. Then I slowly support, assist and train him to walk one step at a time. Because his extremities remain very weak from not putting in use for so long, this rehabilitation process turned out to be quite long and difficult. In the beginning, dad was very impatient and upset when he catches himself in the trios of fasciculation, weakness and limitation to use his hands and legs for simple task. As time went on, dad began to slowly turn himself around. He learned to use his arms and picked up things, and then he started moving his legs and would keep doing so until he become exhausted. He also started to move his upper body such as head, wrist and upper trunk without difficulty. Every now and then, we help him to make use of the strength from the lower part of his body so that he could get up and down from the bed with assistance.

With time being the key factor in this recovery and rehabilitation process, I certainly realized the importance of remaining patient when dealing with the aging condition. I also learn that Rome was not built in one day and so as the restoration of complex physiological and musculoskeletal systems. What makes dad different from other patients were possibly the unyielding faith and a never-give-up attitude that carry him over the physical therapy session. Every day was and could be a test for dad because he had to remind himself that his life was totally related to how he responds to the training. Certainly no one could make him to do anything that he doesn't want to. Dad should know that his problems would not go away anytime soon unless he actively engages in the change. With my modification and family's encouragement, dad worked very hard to overcome his inferiority complex and he began to sit up from the bed by holding the rail after the rehabilitation for three months. To us, this improvement was the total reflection of team effort and collaboration between dad and the family. There was never been a time we doubted that dad would fail in his treatments, and so we continued to press on because we believe in the mind power and the promise of God.

As dad's health conditions become stable and secure, I begin to empower my family to take good care of dad more while I shifted my focus on to my work and the restructuring of my business. Recalling the time when dad was firstly hospitalized in July 2008 to the fourth time he was released from hospital on January 2009, my life seemed to be in chaos because I tried to balance myself between my family and my business during a time of worldwide economic turmoil and the bursting of real estate bubbles in the States. For those who were in their businesses or entrepreneurship spirit, they might know that it could be a double hit especially when I deal with a less than two-year-old business.

Looking back at my business, with the time, money and effort invested, I found myself dipping into a deep hole of disaster as my deficits rose. I gradually realized failure was a terrible blow to my vision and all the little devotion to things that meant so much to my life. As days went on, my mind was busy, and my stress levels rising. At one point or another, I literally forget about what it means to "live" my life. Every day was just a day that I invest my personal savings into the office and my energy to grow the company. I worked diligently and tirelessly to leverage whatever financial outlets I had, and yet I continued to see my investment slipping further into higher debt. In the meantime, I continued to struggle and panic about whether I might possibly be able to pay the bills and expenses on a regular daily basis in the exchange for a hope that I, on a later day, might have found other options to get through this tough time. Despite the raging personal battles and possible bankruptcy looming ahead, my entire life was shaken up when I strove to balance my vision with the harsh reality. I felt like I was wrapped up in a complicated love and hate relationship, as I began to deal with keeping my struggling company alive and my father battling to stay recovered.

With the turmoil from the global economy, small businesses across the States suffered. Certainly that was no exception for my company as well. With the fact that I experienced moderate breathing difficulty from the stress of my business, this recession left me feeling like a walking zombie. Day in and day out, I felt so ticked off with the whole situation. And even there was a time when I become so down, discouraged and impatient that I felt I'd lost touch with where I came from and what I do regardless of where I might be heading. In those moments, I truly thought that the world seemed to have given up on my growing company because of the tremendous stress and frustration of dealing with the lack of good patients and the potential of new clients. From time to time, I felt like jumping off the bridge, and I also become lost in passion as that of the putting off fire from a big dreamer who was badly beaten and deeply wound when wage through my struggling business.

During those turbulent times, I could hardly forget that my life was completely and totally upside down. For many nights, I failed to balance my checkbooks while I tried to figure out what I should put on the dinner table for the next day. Fortunately enough, I didn't rush through by making stupid or unnecessary decisions. Perhaps sometimes I had dreamed of a perfect life that focused on ideology or perfect logic, but at that point I didn't think that – or my ego's demand of a perfect medical practice – was possible. In those very moments, I suddenly recalled a famous quote from Patrick Overtron, "When you came to the edge of all the light you knew and were about to drop off into the darkness of the unknown, faith was knowing one of two things would happen. There would be something solid to stand on or you will be taught to fly." Certainly at that time I didn't expect flying was within my ability, and it tended to be far beyond my comprehension as well.

Surprisingly, life had thrown some good curve at me. I don't forget this special night while took care of dad at home. Though dad was still on a feeding tube and bedridden, he remained very calm and awake during this early morning. We talked and exchanged quite a bit regarding my love life and religious life. One thing I would not forget was how he came up with idea and advice for me to grow my business.

"Dad, are you hurting somewhere?" I ask when I see him toss and turn for the past two hours.

"I was all right, son," dad said.

I look at him. "Are you looking for something?"

"As a matter of fact, my backscratcher was here a moment ago, but now I just can't find it." Dad points at the boxes on the right side of his bed.

"Dad, did you drop it or leave it out somewhere?"

"No…it was here earlier, and I was using it."

"Would you think it over and you might put it up somewhere…under your blankets?"

"I don't think so…if I happen to hide it underneath my blankets, it would hurt my back because I was lying on the top of them, don't I?"

"Right," I continue. "So you might leave it in the living room then."

"No…of course not…look underneath my bed ok?"

"Nothing on the floor, Dad, and I don't see it on the sofa either."

I truly don't remember how long I spent looking for the lost backscratcher. I eventually found that it was hidden inside the thick, folded blankets that dad was used to put at the bottom of bed near the right side of his bed rail. Then I pull it out and give it back to him. I also reminded him to keep his backscratcher because if lost I didn't know if I could find it again.

"Thanks, son, for getting it back to me," he said. "This lost and found backscratcher was not much different from your business."

"How and why you say that, Dad?"

While dad was holding his wooden backscratcher, I was surprised to see that it had remained so shiny and smooth and was unbroken for the past eight plus years. Many times I tried to talk him out by changing a new one, but dad refuses all the time.

"You knew what...son, think of your business as that of my backscratcher. I have been using it for so long that I don't fully remember when I first bought it. I don't want to throw it away not because I can't afford to buy a new one but because it was useful and effective for all these days."

"I see...but how could it possibly relate to my business?"

"You don't know it well then." Dad turned to me by showing me his backscratcher. "Your business – and I mean chiropractic practice – was indeed similar to my backscratcher. I was just like your clients or patients who've used the service before. Hopefully some repetitively use and benefit from your services. Though the service could be old and outdated, it remained in good use. Though some people happen to forget about your business just like the loss of my backscratcher, but when people found it again, they would remember of its value."

"I see it now, Dad, and please go on and let your son hear more."

"Remember when you tried to get me to replace a new backscratcher, but I insisted on keeping it, right? The reason was I had built a relationship with my backscratcher after all these days despite the fact that it might not be a beautiful and perfect one. Your chiropractic practice is the same. Your business might not be good at all times. It could be up and down, as all businesses should be. Sometimes it could be worse because of some economy situation or because some people forget about your office and that was just like the feeling when I lose my backscratcher."

"But how could I assure my business running well again?" I'm confused.

"Business could be down at any time but not the mindset and especially the spirit of entrepreneurship. If you lose confidence in your business, you would not have energy to look for ways to change what you were going to do. You see, even though I lost my backscratcher, I continued to look for it because I believe I was able to find it again. The same theory could be used in building and reconstructing of your business...Some people actually lose confidence in your practice because of certain reasons at a time, but they could come back one day after they find your true value and if you were able to show them how effective and important your service was to their life, then they'll cherish and keep it as long as they can."

"Yes Dad and thank you."

"Son...you indeed are intelligent but you just got a hard bump on the road. There was a long stretch down the road. Besides you have a long way to go. If you truly believe in your gut feeling, go with full gear and do it now before you might end up with regret. I am sure that you would live thru it and live it beautifully."

For weeks and months, I continued to build my practice based on the concept dad shared with me that very night. I started to adopt new strategy by developing and maintaining good relationship with my patients, both new and existing ones. At some point, I was surprised to find how intelligent and experienced my dad was even though he was still quite sick. I had never thought of the fact that dad was very sharp and clear-minded despite that much had changed since he ran his business thirty plus years ago. I continued to press on by following what dad told me.

During many sleepless nights when I was clueless about all that was happening, I suddenly remembered some evangelistic preachers from the national televised networks claim that "the gates of hell shall not prevail you" (Matthew 16:18). I searched through the Bible for divine intervention and guidance to nourish the depth of my emptiness. From several perspectives, hell represents the abode of condemned souls. Hell indeed was a place filling with devils in some religious senses and it was also the place where eternal punishment for the wicked after death was hosted. The gates of hell could be defined as the battering rams of Satan or an evil attack of human spirit with storms of hardships, floods of sins, and thunders of failures. Hell could exist in terms of metaphysical and personal forms. It indeed could come into our life in form of temptations, mishaps, sufferings and even death. It also could lock us into condemnation due to our ego, failure or error in life, but only God's grace could encompass and deliver us from the gates of hell. When we human beings make a mistake or tripped, we frequently took the blame or experienced some kind of unpleasant feeling and we might fall into some kind of suffering and damage physically, spiritually and intellectually. Dealing with mistakes could certainly help us to solve the problem, but it would not get us off from the experience of hell in the process unless we focus onto the Rock, which was a symbol of God as the source for our spiritual refreshment, to fill us with comfort, endurance and protection. In a physical sense, no one could escape from the lesson of hell in terms of pain and suffering from sickness and death. No one could literally live their life without facing some kind of criticism, hatred, jealousy and lie but they were far from persecution and conviction. In the spiritual arena, no one could possibly deny the existence of God even from the theory of Darwinism or by being agnostic. God's love indeed extends beyond those who were confined to hell and even to those who would freely, finally and everlastingly reject him. God agreed to enter willingly into solidarity and loneliness with those who condemn or are locked up in their own world of sin, despair, guilt, failure or addictions. Through faith in Jesus, we could escape from hell and receive an eternal salvation by accepting him as Savior (1 John 5:11-12; John 3:16). Certainly no one could provide a vindication of hell unless they condemned their own, and no one deserved a miserable life if they prayed for the deliverance and mercy of God even from the bars and belly of hell (Jonah 2:7-10) because God was always our assurance to peace and prosperity that neither powers nor principalities could hold us accountable in hell. Literally, there was nothing could separate us from the protection and love of God in Christ Jesus (Roman 8:38-9).

Indeed, the idea that people always spend time to repair relationship issues or to address problems we might have no solution for is scary and sad. We can't continue to spend time worrying about others without knowing the danger we might face. Sometimes we have to realize the nature of things is to only happen in some ridiculously bad way. Perhaps we might feel that walking away from our dreams is impossible, but sometimes we have to let them go, at least temporarily. To some extent, we'd be better off setting our dreams aside and then coming back to them when conditions were better. Indeed, many of us haven't left worldliness behind in one way or another. As for me, I do thank God for those lessons that he allowed me to learn from my business. The truth of the matter was that if I didn't have that hard fall, I possibly would have had no idea what I was going to do with my business, my career, my family and even my faith. Without knowing what my future held, I thought that the problems might never end. But one thing that I could be sure of was that I was fortunate enough to have found strength in the Lord during that very moment of my life, and His choice for me was clear from the beginning, and so I pressed on.

Quite frankly, most of us do understand that we human beings might not have all the answers in life. But sometimes taking chances was all right. There were victories and setbacks in every culture and race, whether it was in the time of turbulence, tranquility, peace, war, prosperity, depression, health or sickness. The point was not to blame but rather to learn from the mistakes or failures by working together for the common good. Whatever our occupation, career, education, race, religion and belief could be, life was always a reflection of choices we make and its result became a difference from what we do. If we paid more attention to what was around us, perhaps we might not miss out the wondrous stories of God's mercy, wisdom and blessing that happens in our life.

Recovering from my financial drought and the survival of my business continued to be twin problems during the six months dad was home with me. My worry was compounded because of the instability of the economy and the lack of confidence in consumer spending. I didn't know how long that recession might last. Every now and then, I truly felt the time was too early to predict what kind of role our government would take in the process. What mattered most to me was not what policy the government employed, though; instead, it was how I was going to respond to the business environment without further breaking any more of my nerves.

We should always feel good about having expectations because they became the primal force for a movement. Generally speaking, we usually could get things done more smoothly and better with the right attitude because it could fire up our enthusiasm and passion, resulting in higher quality results for all we do. However, there were also times when expectation did not match up with the result. By trusting one's efforts and by reinforcing the positive attitude over illness, health and harmony can be achieved. Unfortunately, that was not how it worked in the system of healing. In a metaphysical sense, healing was the direct result of moving from a lower to a higher rate of vibration or even to a higher state of consciousness. It pertained to the physical or spiritual body in terms of harmony. It usually could be a process, but sometimes it could be an instantaneous act over the conscious and subconscious mind. It tended to capture the mind to think and plan, regulate the brain to direct and control, and to further enhance the substance to form and develop into our desire.

Everyone, from all walks of life, needed healing. The elderly needed healing. The sick needed healing. Even children needed healing. Whether people agreed or not, we needed some form of healing, and we indeed needed healing more than we expected because our bodies carry sins and illnesses from this lifetime or inherit from the traumas of the past lives. At some point of our lives, we might need some kind of simple healing or perhaps a special healing. Some people might need more healing than others because of the excessive loads they bear. Some others might need just a healing at a certain time or for a short period of time to keep their body moving forward. Despite the reasons, once our bodies started to heal, then we'll keep on healing, for days, for years and perhaps for eternity. Generally speaking, healing was a form of expression, an art and science that tend to remove the imbalances or distortions from the body spiritually, mentally, emotionally and physically. Healing also could be a process and an evolution that created a change or formed a new system within the body itself so that the body could function better when it could overcome injuries, sicknesses, thoughts, grief and beliefs.

We all know sickness could come in all size, form and shape in the absence of our consent or apprehension. There was never been a clear pattern about how a sickness should come and what it should behave for a specific person or at a certain time. Sometimes, one disease could exist in the form of another and meanwhile one disease also could be destroyed by another. Whether the moral or physical belief in our efforts could be strong enough to destroy the mortal dream of sin, failure, error and fear in relating to the sickness remained a question to be answered by our own selves. For instance, cancer, tumor, heart disease, stroke, inflammation, pain, injury and joint deformity, just to name a few, could all be overcome by healing of some form. Whether the healing could be completed in days or years, it indeed depended on the element of matter and the cause of the problem.

As for dad, my family and I were pleased with the results of his therapy. Our expectation had been and always was to see dad fully recovered and in good health so that he could take care of himself. My family and I continued to work with him until he was no longer bedridden. Until he was able to walk, bathe and eat on his own, we prepared to respond to any wear and tear inside his body. We also were fully aware that the remittance of sickness and remission of disease could be fatal, as the recurrence rate was high. The high fever, severe pain and indigestion indeed reminded us of the discordant manifestations and fearful attacks dad had during his past few episodes. But they were not so scary until a smooth collapse and a comfortable doze off from the chair where dad was praying scared the breath from us.

The incident happened early one evening on a late summer when my elder brother and sister came home from their out-of-town trip. They were there for a reunion and first anniversary celebration for dad's recovery from his semi-stroke or TIA condition. The weather was a little humid that night when our whole family gathered in the family room to chat and learn about God's words. In the midst of all those laughter, chatting and worshiping, dad was asked to pray and give a blessing for our family. In the beginning, the prayer went so well, and then it turned a little emotional. Then the voice of prayer became unheard, and by the time we open our eyes, we were startled to see our dad had apparently dozed off. I checked his vital and found that he was still breathing and had a pulse at the time; he was just slightly unconscious. Then one of my sisters called the elders and pastors of our church.

A few minutes later, the elders and pastors from our church came to our house and continued praying with us. Another sister of mine then put an ice pack onto dad's head because I found he was sweating and with mild fever. The prayers all of a sudden become louder and louder along with hymns and gospel music that eventually echoed over the roof. We literally felt a strong connection of current circling both the family room and kitchen where we all stood. With hands laying onto dad's body, we continued to feel the strong energy or heat among us. The prayers circled the room while I monitored my dad's situation just in case I need to provide any medical emergency response. I was ready to standby for any CPR if necessary before medical assistance arrives. No one really knew how long we had spent in that session of prayer. One disturbing thing was that we started to see some weak response. Dad was still physically breathing, but his respiration sounds were low and his pulse was irregular.

While every one of us were busy with prayers and out of the blue, we hear a loud voice that yells, "Who puts that things on me? It was cold... take that ice off me."

We saw dad slowly open his eyes.

Shortly after that, dad told us what he dreamed. Dad remembered that he was pressed by some tremendous unknown forces and was forcefully dragged and pulled away by some villains who he had never seen and did not recognize. He was thrown from a cliff; and when he hit bottom, he could barely move. His breathing came so hard that he felt as if he'd been encased in marble stone. Dad began to cry, confess and repent for what he'd done, as he was enslaved to idols, witchcraft and spirit-worship. He once believed in the false priesthoods, tribal sacrifices, and ritual offerings to appease the anger of different gods who could bring destruction, punishment, sickness and death to those who resist in the bondage of spirits and demons. Dad also realizes the power of darkness that could come into lives in term of curses or healing in the presence of witches and different gods. Hypothetically speaking, dad was afraid of reading what was once to be the haunt of violence, sin, guilt, wicked and darkness that fill the poor and the reckless, as he came close to the end of his road. He was fortunate enough to be removed from the clamor of punishments, uproar of enemies, destruction from demonic spirit, and vengeance from debtors. In that very moment of continuous prayers, dad had once again overcome his own death because the grace of our Lord set him free.

All of us who luckily had witnessed the testimony of transforming life and had experienced the miraculous healing of prayer remained speechless. We saw what happened in the house when the pastors, deacons, elders and the family prayed together for just one thing. We prayed by taking authority over the forces of spiritual darkness, and we commanded the evil spirt and cast out demons in the name of Jesus. Indeed, it was the feeling and emotion that counted, during and even after all had been done. I didn't believe that anyone would take that experience for granted in term of what it means to believe in the truth and principle as if from God's words themselves. Certainly no one took less credit to what it meant to be in control until God's grace was taken away from the context. From a broader sense, I believe the battle against hunger and thirst for gospel was really not a physical or social battle. Just like the nature of fear and denial, it was a spiritual battle that could be greater and harder than any chemical or political warfare. It could kill or destroy any human being by condemning that to a wasteful and desperate life. Without a doubt, it was not the matter of the heart, but rather the heart was the matter that revolutionizes faith and all else. It could make this journey possible and for many others to continue believing.

Personally, this unexpected incident tended to cause me drifting myself away from my life rather than the other way around. For less than a few seconds, I literally could see what was stretched out in front of me – my belief, my pain, my dream, and above all my life. I tried not to relate that with my business failure and errors. I managed to keep my coolness, anger and fear to the lowest so that I could live with more flexibility and to keep up with my joy despite the unrelenting pain. Meanwhile, I could hardly imagine that at a certain time I might come close to a point where I could be free to dream and plan and to be able to act on those dreams and plans again. I also knew I couldn't, all by myself, take care of my dad and business at the same time not because I was incapable, unprepared, unavailable, impossible, undependable and incompetent. The truth of the matter was that I had no intention of being disappointed and learned of where to proceed from this point and beyond.

Sometimes things that tend to be nice and beautiful came with an expensive price tag. For instance, the ornaments we normally use to decorate on the Christmas tree could help to warm up our hearts during the season. They were not just a glass cylinder or a metal mold. They become the art, craft or collective designs that shape up the fantastic coating to represent the thoughts of the special ones in our lives. The tattoos on the arms, back, neck, face and elsewhere on a body tend to reflect that person's personality and character. They had to go through the use of machine with needles connecting to tubes and dyes over the skin. They could also be done in selective ink or some printable designs. Those who had successfully reduced their weight generally got all the attention and admiration from other people they know while the obese ones might undergo some tough time to adjust themselves over criticism, isolation and temptation. They might have to restrain themselves from indulgence, overeating or anorexia coming from peer pressure. They might also have to force themselves to keep burning more fats in excessive and enduring exercises than they could earn from all high calories food intake. Obviously, life could never be easy for anything good to come, and all good things should not come without paying a price – and that price usually justifies our need and want.

At some point during our time on earth, we human beings had to realize where we came from and fight hard to get to where we wanted to be, to keep what we had, and then to hold on to it. There were times when things happened in life that we can't physically get done while, some days, we could become relatively close to what we want. Certainly it could be hard for anyone to not figure out a way in term of want and need. It was also unwise for anyone to disregard what was not there in the first place. Sometimes the saddest thing was to find what was not existed but we kept searching until that turned out to be the problematic ones for us to continue. Perhaps, you might have someone who you could turn to when you need them to fix your problem. But it doesn't mean that your helpers need to become your babysitter and they had to be there when and where you need them. What if your safety net didn't exist and your problem solver was no longer available – did it mean that you had to let go of your life and carry a doing-nothing attitude or world-complaining mentality to expect royal treatment from some mysterious movement?

Perhaps my family might have no idea about what was actually going on with dad or his condition. But it didn't make us less guilty or innocent than what had happened to dad. There were times that we wish we could roll back the dial on what had been happened. There also were times that we were impossible to turn back the clock or turn away from the happening. And obviously facing the reality and accepting the fact could help to avoid a nervous breakdown while skepticism wouldn't make the problem go away. To be fairly said, my family and I had no idea of what had happened to dad on that last and surprising knock-out. But deep down in our hearts, my family and I had witnessed the miraculous healing and taking authority in prayer. This incidence indeed proves the change of mental state or moral power over our physical state. It was clearly illustrated by Christian Science, as Mary Eddy pointed out, once the levels of our spirituality change, then the restoration of health or physical healing follows. I truly believe that this form of healing could only be seen by and through divine love because the acknowledgment of truth helped to set us free from anguish, dread, fear, pride and despair. It was the humility and honesty that gave us a chance to learn about God's control over the mortal sense. It was also the genuine emotions and faith that filled us with strength and chance to overcome sickness and death as well.

For a few days after that incident, dad showed some signs of recovery. We saw and felt the sense of guilt being uplifted and taken away from his heart. Dad started to read Bible despite he had hard time to read between lines and to thus fully understand God's words. With repentance, dad captured the beliefs that Jesus Christ's death on the Cross was to preserve the eternal harmony and originality of life. Dad realized that the Messiah's works and Divine interventions into mankind were to destroy sicknesses, forgive sins, and cast out demons. But it was the Father's desire that Jesus came into this world to destroy any painful state of fear, lies and death in term of corporeal sense and mortal mind. It was Jesus the Lord who broke off error with truth, replaced mortality with immortality, eliminated hatred with forgiveness, and condemned curse with love. Since he carried this kind of attitude and mentality, my dad eventually felt happy when he started to live in divine healing.

One cool day in the early week of September 2009, my sister Kim and I took dad to a follow-up appointment with his medical doctor. An evaluation and tests showed that dad had made good recovery. The family medicine practitioner didn't find any problem with his heart and lungs. Daddy told his medical doctor that he lost consciousness during recent prayer at home and was wondering whether that had anything to do with his health. The doctor, on the contrary, commented that dad was making good progress from his medical history and age-related conditions. He then recommended us to consult with his gastroenterologist. Two days later, my sister Miley and I took dad to see his gastroenterologist. An examination and evaluation revealed the bowel functions and the activity of the PEG tube were normal. The doctor then reminded us to keep the tube clean and follow up as necessary. Medications were given by both the family medicine practitioner and gastroenterologist to reduce pain and to further prevent the progression of sickness.

When Christianity came into our home and since divine healing became a powerful testimonial among our church, our family changed from godless and emotional into spiritual and syncretic. For decades, my family and I had sought health through physicians, drugs, herbs, natural remedies and even different gods. With no great success, we gradually realized that science and health came from the Bible, silent prayer to God, and reborn faith. Every day we found joy, strength and comfort through the study of

Holy Scriptures. We wouldn't forget the transformation and regeneration of life by fully obeying Divine truth and by faithfully executing Divine law. Sometimes our perception with the Lord might be different from the reality. Because of that difference, it required exceptional courage to obey God and to follow his command, especially during the time of cynicism, setbacks and frustration that become greater than sicknesses. I was also ashamed, and possibly guilty, that had taken us so long to finally realize we had been running away from the grace of God. Yet, His love remained steadfast and He, without reservation, continued to welcome us, as if we were the prodigal son.

Throughout various doctrines or theories and even modern mythologies, I could hardly find good solid proof that helped me to understand the presence of life and intelligence in term of matter, not to mention the miracle that overcomes sin and death. And even from my previous encounter of faith, I rationally believed that life presented in matter while sickness or sins could yield to the reality of spiritual life. I also believed that pain and pleasure, sin and sickness, life and death were the total reflection of spiritual manifestation or at least from a biblical perspective. They form in the material sense or substance in nature. To our family, this entire process and experience of dad's repetitive episodes of comas underline not the story of dying but instead was all about living the spirit of not giving up what life had offered. Hypothetically speaking, there was no identity crisis in terms of revelation. And yet there was no true conviction or sentence of death before the judgment was finalized even though we had already faced enormous challenges and dreadful sufferings that no one might happen to understand and possibly comprehend.

Every day was a new learning experience for me. Whether it was in my professional duty as a healthcare provider or in my managerial position as a business executive, I was humbled to serve the multitude of people whom I associated with. Even if it was in my family role as a child and in my spiritual life as a young Christian, I put my heart into the avocation or assignment that I was responsible for. I tried not to accept anything less than "impossible" or "unattainable" without giving myself a fair chance to work through the situation. I also realized the existence of limitation in things, physically and materially. One thing, which was indefinite and unlimited with the likelihood of matter, was not about the lack of compatibility but rather, the cohesiveness of spiritual life because it was what God lays the foundation of his truth.

For a long time, I looked back at my life to see what had been drifted so deeply inside of me that I was unable to see clearly of its existence. With the lack of consumer spending coupled by domestic fragility and global turmoil, businesses, small or large, gradually experienced bigger deficit and the economy also began to go into recession. As long as I could remember, the year of 2009 was the most difficult time for me to try balance between my business and my faith. Days in and days out, I set sail to hopefully come close to or into the Promised Land because I believed in working with enthusiasm to find the true way. I tried very hard to forget about what an impact from the economy played out on my business. I put all my focus on to my business and lay all my heart out to do what was best for those who come to seek help for their health conditions in term of enhancing their daily lifestyle and reducing their pains or discomfort. Occasionally I think that this life was better off if I could at least deliver the quality care they need even I might be underpaid slightly due to the structure from the current healthcare system. Unfortunately there were times when things got out of hand and plans were off track a little bit. As soon as I looked at the mud of mess that I created and the hole of trouble that I got my head into, I thought of divine existence and I wondered how I deserved to own that kind of adversaries. I gradually learned, without doubt, that if I happened to be apart from him, my life could be way out of control.

Day by day, I worked very hard to see how far I had mistakenly led both my business and family until one day when I finally understood it all from the spiritual perspective. Simultaneously, I believed "fear" was the biggest factor that caused me to wait for an unknown in the expectation of having them. I tried to put good faith into works that gave a possibility of success no matter how slim the chance could be. I always thought diligence and perseverance to be my virtue that could be highly prized. In the meantime, I felt the universe was telling me to move forward by leaving my physical life behind, and as apostle Paul once said, "I press on toward the goal for the prize of the upward call of God in Christ Jesus" (Philippians 3:14). I also believed the universe had brought me back for a reason despite that I didn't know what and how that might play out before I rediscovered God's purpose in my very life. Whether I was on my feet or off my hands on some business project, I could literally perceive that I was into something bigger than what my life had put together. Indeed, all these things were total disaster with the consideration that I would not be able to fix my past no matter how hard I tried.

Commitment was a journey, not a destination. What I saw was the locking of myself into something that I needed to figure out. What I didn't see was the sad entertainment of unlocking my inner self to see what was getting in the way. Whether or not I was actually crossing the line, reflection on my past somewhat tended to be a drawback because I didn't take life for granted and for anything less than perfect despite that it never had been perfect. On the other hand, I truly didn't know what the real color was for the mockingbird in comparison to that of my heart. That was no reason for me to continue upsetting myself and to those around me. It was also absurd for me to accept defeat of my life and to think of failure as the gift of the Holy Spirit. On the contrary, I recognized some mighty struggles with error and the pinching pain from false beliefs. I was not discouraged and intimidated by hardships and setbacks without giving the Holy Spirit a fair trial. For every bump on the road, small or large, I realized that bump would only make me stronger with little resistance compared to what Jesus went through in term of ridicules, persecution, contemplation, mocking, spitting, finger pointing, stoning, beating and bleeding. Notwithstanding the costs to myself, I was yet convinced that no one needed to confess their spiritual blindness and physical disability without putting the Holy Spirit to work unless they were struck by not doing that. Of all of the changes and events in my life, I found security and refuge with the acknowledgment of power of life rests in God alone (Psalm 27:1-3; Psalm 91:1-6; Job 24:23). And because of the unquestioned integrity and positive proof that God speaks through the Words and my vision, I couldn't lay my burdens down until my worry disappeared and my pain started to heal. Then slowly my heart began to loosen up and all traps of burden, the shadow of fear, and the loop of pain resulting from failure or error vaporized in the light of truth.

Generally speaking, failures can't be finalized as yesterday dies in last night's memory. Whether failure was small or large, it indeed was hard to forget and tough to let go. Failure can come in different forms, styles, shapes and sizes when our expectations don't match reality. Failure can come to all kinds of personalities, to people with different levels of confidence, and to people who've made various levels of preparation. Anyone fairly might say failure could become insignificant if people realized and were willing to get to the root of problem without doing a cut and chase or a twist and turn. And to some extent, repeated failure could be avoided if people accepted and treated their failure as a learning experience.

By far, failure tended to come into life more quickly when egotism consults and manages team spirit. The damage could be greater when the individual effort outmatches the contribution from others. To some people, it might be all right to have other people staying out of their business. To some others, it might not be so all right and brilliant when the idea of individualism results in being isolated and shut off from their loved ones so that they could move through their problems. Resistance could be expected, and resentment could become highly destructive because both disenfranchisement and disassociation in return could decrease the chance of success. Throughout history, one can find that the worst enemy of mankind tends to be selfhood that drives us to the end of the road. In the spiritual world, egotism or self-centeredness were sins seeded by the Devil to drag human nature away from God. It was not unusual to find egotism parallel with failure or error that could literally lead us nowhere because sins fall short of the glory of God, and the wage of sins is death (Romans 3:23; 6:23). In the corporate world, individualism and egotism could indeed make us stand out sometimes. Individualism does not literally mean smartness or superiority but rather a bad attitude that could lead us to being all by ourselves. Egotism tends to welcome no new ideas or input from people who work with us or those who wish to help us for the common good. Other people won't take too long time to figure out our intentions and that could decrease the chance of cooperation leading to benefit and success.

There was darkness before dawn – and there was also twilight after dawn. Apparently, life had her ups and downs every step of the way. Sometimes we might think that we have been healed, found success, and feel fulfilled or accomplished. Sometimes we might feel as if we have blurred vision, are fatigued, and have lost hope or suffer some kind of unexplained discordance. And before a cure and a solution could be found, we most likely find physical pain and emotional weariness tied to our search for material accomplishment. The sense of infinity when anyone denies the omnipotence of God also was natural. We can understand the existence of desperation when we happened to believe that God was limited due to the co-existence of evil and the sharing of power in material sense. What could be worse was the attitude of not expressing doubt or speaking out the truth so that other people could share in the wholeness of joy or sorrow. In return, a priori reasoning could be found on the top of the true knowledge and experience thereafter.

For years, I had been told and taught that I couldn't and wouldn't out-give God no matter how hard I tried. I found it to be true when I put all my thoughts into the drought of my finance, in the dead end of my business, and in the lock-up of my career. I literally could see both the titanic movement of humanism and my willingness to serve life sinking deep along with the loss of purpose and the perplexity of an unfinished mission. I understood that as soon as there was a division or disconnection between religion, thoughts, beliefs and/or faith, God's preference and his Kingdom's culture would not show up in life even though I cried out aloud to Him. I also realized that I might not have all the answers for why I pursued my life in the way I had, but sometimes I thought that would be all right if I was taking a chance. Life was phenomenal when I continued to stick with my own pace despite the criticism of being hard-headed because I was the dream chaser and career maniac. Of all the captivity, productivity and achievement I made toward my commitment for a better life, I was certain that the endowment and endeavor from the Almighty was the one who made them possible and affordable for me to have a plan, a will, a dream and a vision that I could proudly testify his love.

For months following the incident that God performs his miraculous healing in our house, I continued praying God for a renewal of my faith. Every day I pray and wait for the covenant to work. I let go my tears from sorrow. I learn to suppress my emotions during my grief. Gradually I found my balance among the ongoing challenge and the disturbing relationship. I feel that the longer I let all these problems holding on to the towel of unsettlement, the more expensive I would discredit my perseverance on any inflicted overcoming. I continued to stay strong and to hold on to my faith even I really didn't know the result, but I was going to find it out. I take no excuse for the errors I made in covering my weakness and also the failure I charged against my hardship. Among those stony trails and in the rusting grasses that I passed, I somehow heard him speaking to me elsewhere. Time and time again, I believe that my life could hardly function and I could remain miserable if I was not going to surrender my mortal error and physical sin over the deep water of bitterness.

While my faith was shipwrecked, I felt a deadly curse and was not oblivious to other people's moods regarding the ailing person's depression. I tried very hard to weigh my judgment and emotion in and out to match up with my conscience so that I wouldn't feel regret when I looked back at the issue. I constantly believed that there should be a limit to my endurance of the error to justify what constituted the mortal mind and moral decay. Day by day, I began to see the road was going to be long, hard, and with no turning back. I also realized my fight was going to be tough and rough when my health, hope, intelligence and productivity were put on trial for the security of my beloved. Though I was not physically ill – only psychologically – I found myself steadily growing worse with a diagnosis of losing myself to an unknown suffering. It was similar to that of post-traumatic syndrome except that I carried no explicit symptoms.

For some reason, I had heard nothing of the healing power and curative practice of Christian Science or Christianity. I managed to not judge things from their appearance without finding out more about them. I also happened to realize that "hurrying" didn't seem to be the wisest way to conduct business, especially in this highly competitive world of marketing. Usually, the sense of good patience yielded high dividends to those who followed wise counsel and made smart choices. This was true not only for corporate finances but in relationships as well. Whether in business, family, professional, spiritual or personal decisions, we tended to be better off when we had sufficient information from which we could draw conclusions and to make appropriate decisions. Every now and then, I worked very hard to understand the mythologies and logic behind until my reasoning became caught up with spiritual regeneration. During this time, I looked for and looked out to the Lord for the inspiration that helped me to grow and to figure out what had been so wrong in my life.

Still, I remember how vaguely pleasant I had been with varying experiences of life. In my loosened memories, I truly don't think that I was too late to find the droughts and storms in life before God showed up to tell me how the breaking of my emotions could lead to the journey of His love. Up until those days, I wouldn't forget about the visit over the rolling rivers and the walk over wasteland that served as a significant turning point in my life. Because of those wonderful experiences that literally transform my professional life and my business mind into some things that I had never dreamed of. If it was not because of his awesome plans built into my personal life, I probably won't happen to see miracles from the lives I touch and the inspired stories I share in people's journey of faith.

One Sunday afternoon in late September 2009, I was taking a nap shortly after the church service because I felt a terrible band-like headache that I hadn't experienced for quite a long time. After a quick and simple lunch, I headed to bed thinking my headache was possibly related to the lack of good sleep a few nights ago when I tried to prepare a new budget for the upcoming fiscal year. I had a hard time falling asleep during the first half hour, so I ran downstairs to drink a big glass of milk and then went back to sleep upstairs. A few minutes later, I fell comfortably asleep. In that hot, sweating and drunkard-like sleep, I began to vividly see that I was traveling instead of sleeping. I found myself coming forth to the due time that the Lord clarified me from some confusing expressions people had thrown at me, the parables from the Biblical figures, and the remnant of blessing off the House of Israel so that sins were all cast off and then traded for peace.

The journey began with the visit of two friends who happened to be concerned about my sufferings. These two friends dressed in simple pullovers and jeans. There was nothing special in their appearance, voice or character. They claimed that they were friends of Mr. Johnson, whom I had little knowledge of. The purpose of their visit was to see if there was anything I might need for help since they had just come back to town. I told them concerning those accidents and incidents that my family had experienced. Gradually, their insistence and sincerity convinced me that I might have been misled or deadly locked in some types of confusing rhetoric until one of them points out the perplexity they saw in my eyes. Then they kindly and generously offered me a chance to meet his friend who believed he could help heal my pain and solve my problem as well. Since my life from the boarding schools to the healing business as a healthcare professional, I had not been really taking any good therapy or counseling especially from someone who claims to be the greatest healer of the time. With no disagreement and rejection, I was willing to travel with them to see their mysterious friend and healer.

By the time we started our journey together, I slowly realized my contemplative life and my entire body were flowing above the air. I felt the agony of not having oxygen, of being in a vacuum. In the meantime, I felt like my personality, conventional wisdom and aptitude were being hijacked. Sometimes I felt all right, divorced of apprehension, discernment and dissolution in life. I thought that all that mattered in life was spiritual composition. I realized the naked truth also could be revealed by the reasoning from the intellect. Of what awaited me to investigate and to satisfy was how I could set my standards aside from the material life to form an intimate relationship with God.

As we continued flying over the streets, trees and buildings, we began to encounter some kind of unknown high pressure. I don't know what I've gotten into or where I am. All I hear was some kind of roaring and ramping from my ears, and I could hardly see anything in front of my eyes anymore. Every time I tried to see what it was and it turned out to be a blurred view covering my entire eyes, and to a certain point I think that I was blind. Perhaps I'm tired, worn out, and frightened because I become lost in the clouds of my eagerness, desire and expectation. Gradually, I become so exhausted that I thought I might have fallen so far behind that I was incapable of catching up with my friends. In those seconds of mixed signals and thoughts, I felt a strong hand picking me up and then slowly I was flying with him. I didn't know how long we had been flying in that way and side by side. The feeling was terrific and phenomenal, one that I had never experienced before. I then realized the sense of new birth of which men may be revealed by the angels, the true ideas or presence of God, and the spiritual sense of being or belonging. The supposition was that I might have been so bad and wicked that there would be nothing and literally none could save me from my mistakes, mishaps and sins. There isn't a sense of growth and reorganization out of the vague hypotheses that human evolution and degradation of beliefs descend from the animal instincts and survivability. Still, I had learned that there was something more than just mysterious building inside of me despite I had constantly suffered from fear, anger, agitation, and distress since I was thrown in and out of thin air and thick clouds. Many times in this journey, I lose control without knowing what was ahead of me and so as what leaves me behind. And before I figure out where I am, I had been released onto the ground, a plain field and in front of a beautiful mountain.

There was always an elephant in the house, though many would deny its existence. We tended to only believe in what we physically see, rejecting or denying what we don't perceive notwithstanding the form, shape and appearance. Whenever there was a disconnection in our intellectual and spiritual beings, the presence of God was more likely there to address the identity crisis, and there also would be intervention of a divine nature to help us escape the decay, rottenness and corruption of this world. Surely I was not much different from any other people in this world. Apart from the physical mind and material laws, my experience to this new environment unveils my ignorance and distortion to the reality of spiritual realm. I catch myself in the middle of crushing my rationales and beating up on my beliefs. By the time I erupted from my hungry thought and self-conceit, I began to feel the spiritual uplifting in the presence of an infinite theologian who happened to speak with me face to face for the first time in my life, as I got in touch with some kind of fire-dazing eyes and silver-lining face.

"Master! By your grace, we had brought you a new person…He needs your touch," say the angels.

"Well you do the right thing," the man says. "Hurry and brought him over here. Let's see what we get."

"Hello, young man, come here…do you know where were you at?"

I turn to the man. "No Sir."

"Do you know what brings you here then?"

"No Sir! But they tell me that you knew a way…they say that you could show me what was wrong with me."

"What about you and do you believe that?"

"To be honest with you Sir, I was confused when I first start. I had been thinking and worried along the trip. When my eyes were dim during those rumbling and darkness, I somehow felt safe. It was quite weird I guess."

"So what's really bothering you?"

"I was not sure, but I somehow recognize that I had been drifting away from what it means to be for matter and for mind when I had hard time to set aside that in my life."

"The Scripture teaches us that by faith we understand the universe was formed at God's command, so that what was seen was not made out of what was visible (Hebrews 11:3). Mind and matter were total opposites that work together for one, and that is in Divine's law and principle. What we can't see in the physical form can actually be manifested in the intellectual or spiritual form. What we can't perceive in terms of mind does not mean the non-existence of matter or the absence of thing at the dispensation of His Truth."

"What you ask from your prayer can be seen from those stored inside the house of the Lord, and they will turn out to be the matter and thing that you certainly have no idea about because they have not been given to you yet. But it does not mean that *impossible* is the answer. The world and the mortal mind think of sin, sickness and death in terms of matter such that the wicked thoughts came in the middle of the night to destroy and steal what belongs to the darkness. If you believe the Word or Scripture originated from God, then you should know that healing power was a supernatural gift God gives us to enrich our spiritual understanding to the divine science and His promises would be stood firm among his creations such as what you just saw the beautiful rainbow, as the sign and promise for a better world to live."

"Yes, Sir, so how do we know that God listens to our prayer, and He gives us what we pray for?"

"You shouldn't have thought of that, and only if you had faith and believe in it, then you would understand these verses quoted: ask and it will be given to you; seek and you will find; knock and the door will be opened to you. No earthly parents give their children stones when their children ask for fish, right?"

Perhaps I might have been overwhelmed or preoccupied with things, as I became perplexed and wondered why there were times we might see what we get might not actually match up with what we ask or look for.

All of a sudden, this strange fellow continued. "If you see and look back at what you pray for, then you would find 99.9% God happens to give you more than what you ask for. Even if he did not give you exactly what you ask, then it does not mean God was unjust, unconcerned and powerless. Instead, you should realize that God was working on it and the process might sometimes take a little longer than it should because God wants to deliver thing in the right time and for the right reason. Sometimes, He just happened to work on something and someone for whom they could be delivered. Despite of what your prayer might be, small or large, you shouldn't have doubted but instead, trust your God because He would not fail you the way this world does and His love for you was eternal."

"Sir, could you tell me how and why we do find failure in our life and does it have to do with our prayer?"

"Listen to me very carefully, young man! There was never been a failure that God put in your life. How you look at and measure for failure depends on how well you knew him and his Words and how you were going to make use of his Truth. Look closely at this beautiful mountain, the rock, and the water. They were put together with a true purpose and genuine meaning so that we all could learn from them. There was no coincidence for things to happen here or there. Every success in your life was the fruit of your labor and the seed of mercy being given to you."

"Do not confuse failure in terms of workmanship because the works of man don't necessarily reproduce the fruits of success unless they fall in the Master's plans. The world looks at success in terms of material and physical values as that of wealth, power, fame and achievement. They tend to be clustered into sin, desire and lust in other senses. They were totally opposite to the divine laws in term of spiritual affluence."

"With faith, you could conquer almost anything in this world. If you surrender your mentality to the deity by finding a way to get over the top of this tall mountain, you will find beautiful scenery and spectacular views from your dream. But this world tends to impose upon you a different view, one from the perspective of the challenge or obstacle you face. On the other hand, the finite or limited mind could manifest all kinds of mistakes originating from the material beliefs that could eventually lead to failure or a miserable life. With the divine mind set into your spirit, you could build your moral steadfastness as that of the hard rock, calm the overflow of your desires against any moral decay, correct or broaden the horizon of wisdom so you do not dip into the deep pool of error, and also destroy illusion of physical weariness over any desperate situations so that disappointment and perversity would not water down your life with excessive and potent temptation than it should be."

"What could we do to get rid of our spiritual or mental slavery so that we could share in the prosperity and freedom this life had to offer?" I asked him again.

"As a Christian, you knew that you'd end up feeling tremendous pressure from the outside world. Certainly having a good solid spiritual understanding was crucial for the journey of your faith, but you had to keep your material beliefs from interfering with spiritual facts so that you won't be confused it with religions, denominations, sects or cults. It had to be a personal choice. Because of divine love for the world was indefinite, you were free to choose what you believe in spite of the sinful nature and rebellious mentality we had."

The man paused for a second, as he looked at me, knowing that I was confused. He then took a close look at what was around the boat. I don't know what he was looking for.

"Our mission as Christians is to inspire and influence other people to live, think and act in accordance with the direction of a transformed life. Look at this motor engine here, and perhaps you might find that it had little connection with the movement. In fact, due to its equipment with cruise control and the navigation device, it helped to propel the boat forward, backward and against turbulence. We Christians are like this motor. We should function as the motor engine to lead and guide the lost or those who are in despair for a better direction so that they can find their purpose. There was always a place and time for us to serve. We should neither be afraid to confront moral decay nor be intimidated to take stands on ideas and beliefs that don't represent Christian values."

"We need to realize the biggest division in the church and religion today was not about the lack of the anointing and the absence of the Holy Spirit that tends to slow the healing process or delay any expected miracles. Instead, it was the inconclusive sense or mixed signals from radical and cynical views, the sense of neither a hot nor cold attitude from some revolutionary agenda or dogmatism, and the finger pointing from the ill of faith and backseat individual or groups. Sometimes the lack of unity and the fallout from church leadership hindered the process of re-attesting the faith. Sometimes we might see egotism, corruption and discordance of trust within church and their leaders were the compelling and dangerous cause for decline in morality."

I turned to Him. "Given the fact that we Christians were saved by the blood of the Lamb and God's grace, then how could we be sanctified from our wicked nature and mortal thoughts so that we might be able to be flourished and practiced in the Christian healing or Christianization of our daily life?"

From some perspectives, this man was not good looking, but he indeed had some extraordinary knowledge.

I put all my focus in this time as he pointed out, "God was the representation of divine Principle of Science and the Law of Universe. The Prophets and Scriptures highlight the teaching and demonstration that all physical matters and material mind manifest in sin, sickness, and death. They were parts of the false claims and beliefs based on sensuality from this world. They were destructive to morals and health because they contradicted the truth and the principle of love that God has. The life of Jesus proves the dignity, obedience and faithfulness to God's supremacy and spirituality that eventually form the antidote for suffering, subordination, immorality, selfishness, wickedness, materiality and mortality.

"Listen up and look closely at this world; evil could be always revealed by goodness, materiality could be disclosed by spirituality, error could be replaced by truth, mortal could be substituted by immortality, and sickness could also be taken away by healing. There was nothing God was impossible and incapable to get rid of in term of material senses or law unless people completely turn away from His omnipotence and ignore the signs of His omnipresence."

"So you were saying that we should be doing...something special?" I asked.

The man must have realized that I knew nothing about what he was saying, then he pointed to the sea and said, "Take a close look at the way the water was moving. You will see that the water always flows in one direction and that was heading forward unless it was blocked or hits something like a rock. Nobody told and showed how the water should flow at a given time or at a certain place. It was the way it should be doing. All things could be and would be done for you. What happens to the water as you see, the same theory could apply to us all.

"One big difference was that God gives you – that is, mankind in general – the wisdom to distinguish the bad from evil. You've had the freedom to choose from the intelligence being provided. God, in fact, had not intended to demand you to do anything, and if he does, he certainly could and will, notwithstanding the kind of emotions and good deeds you have. As long as you were still holding on to your faith and your beliefs of the Truth or Principle by asking God and the Holy Spirit to cleanse, forgive or guide your life, then you will find strength and wisdom, even if you were in the deep water of failure or hardships. You will feel the comfort and peace even if you were in the storm of sickness and death."

For few minutes or quite a while, I had been muted and doubted about my faith. I still had no understanding of what I'd heard.

He said, "Look out, and see those jellyfish drifting along the current over there. You might see that they could be found both in this side of dirty water and so as over the other side of the clear water. I knew you might question or wonder what had they in common and how should they relate to you, right?

"Listen to me carefully. Human beings do worship dreams. In one way or another, our lives were a total reflection of the kind of dream we live and believe in. Some lives indeed tend to be better than the other not because of the environments, and I mean the environments as water here for instance, we were in, but it had to do with the kind of acknowledgment in what we could make use of those environments to cultivate life as well as dream. Look at those colorful jellyfish from the clear water; not so many people realize and see what the fish were or turn out to be that beautiful, not until they come off from the dark water."

"In fact, our lives could be no different from that of the jellyfish. How we live our life, how we choose to hold on to our faith, and how we make our dreams, do matter not just in the process, but they also are quite different in the perspective of values and beliefs that we live by. No two processes are alike, and no change could be any different other than the yoke of faith. Christians need to live out their faiths by example, parents need to live out their words by actions, professors need to live out their teachings by illustrations or analogy, the wise people need to live out their lives by remarks, the strong men need to live out their strengths by their character, and the leaders need to live out their promises by testimonials or living proof convictions. Regardless of what people might think at the time, no environment or surrounding was too small and too difficult for anyone to get around. Some people might have no moods for games, dreams or even life itself, but they gladly enjoy to have the world burned in their minds. Eventually the journey to battle for dreams lies in the rationality of fair play, the logistics of God-fearing attitudes, and the totality of using available resources to preserve life."

"There is indeed sin in soul and corruption in mind. The most important thing you can do to defeat it is to mutate the sense for material achievement or to lock up the door of your wisdom by focusing on God so that you can be reborn again before life fills you up with the false sense of matter, substance and intelligence. There was a time when you begin to understand the blessing and leadership from the anointing Spirit, then you would be hungry for His presence into your very life. There also was a time when you realize forgiveness was greater than sin, guilt, and failure combined, then you would be once again tirelessly and seriously begging for His intervention to take over your miserable life."

"Sir pardon me for interruption," I said. "Given the fact that Spirit should precede or exist prior to thought, what should we do to keep our beliefs in a place where we could start a fire to centralize an unseen specter?"

"You should not doubt or second guess what God promises to do for you despite that you might have no clues in what they could be. Even though you happen to know or might find what they tend to be, it doesn't mean that the matter and thing were going to add up the way they should be. When matter or things don't match up with your expectation, you shouldn't think or ponder with denial, rejection and reluctance toward His provision. You shouldn't carry hostility in any fashion or direction against God, Spirit and Truth. Instead, you should take everything in appreciation, by prayer, and with thanksgiving, even when your life happens to be at its worst, but with God's constant polishing and furnishing, all things would no longer become the degrading ones because His workmanship was perfect."

For a while, I heard nothing except the wind blowing on to the water. I also seemed to hear some soft smooth sound coming off the clear sparkling wavy flow.

Then I heard him saying, "People could provide you with their beliefs or wisdom based on matter, and that could trap you between errors in thinking so that you are confused. By the time you are fooled by the presentation of a thing or matter – the bondage you create due to the love of this worldly possession – you've already fallen in love with it and dive deep into materialism. If you really want to know what God's plan for you is, then you should put all your heart and soul into His words, ask for his forgiveness in term of daily cleansing, and turn to His cross claiming for the promise and victory he had for you."

For a long time, we didn't talk, and I was not sure what I should be asking him because this special healer expressed an extraordinary wisdom. All of a sudden, the burden in my mind was taken off. I had never felt any relief from anyone and any authority back then in terms of tribulation, distress, nakedness, nagging and guilt. And at my no expense and knowledge, this mysterious speaker and healer begin to lift off the boat where we had been sat for so long. He was just like a stranger who had known me from inside out, grasps me at the refreshing of warm spring, and speaks through my ears in some strange manner but familiar sound. Before I realized what was brought me, I felt that we'd started flying. This flying experience was different from others because I was taken into the hands of some supernatural force. I found no one and nothing standing between us. Apart from what could be seen or what had been told, I gradually came to realize that I was going to fall into a higher and a holier consciousness.

Perhaps I had been closer to his holiness than I should, but I had been chosen to live the fullness of my material life. I was indeed given the glory and an honor to stay aside with my spiritual protector and salvator – angels. This was the time that allowed me to fully understand what brought me down in this environment, not because of my entitlement or settlement from the spiritualization of thought but rather, the humility and apprehension coming from the personal relationship with God. Certainly I had no idea of what brought me closer to better understand the supremacy of Truth and the supernatural gift of spiritual healing. I happened to realize the material sense or mind tends to not correct the healing or any saving grace even though it was a little late for me getting to where it was despite I had disregarded the voice spoken to me since my journey with this spectacular stranger began.

As we continued flying over the mountain, sea and land from continent to continent, this amazing but fascinating journey opened my mind to change the views I had of the world. I truly didn't know what could happen next, but I realized that it was my legal responsibility to share them with self-centered and narrow-minded individuals, and it was also my desire to make a difference in the lost world where gospel should be brought to enlighten the darkness. Without fear of what it is, I opened my heart to invite the judgment of God. While I was in the process of condemning my sin and error, I felt a strong electricity or current sweeping across my body to alleviate my tightened chest and my strangled heart. I came to realize the nature of a sinful, sick and dying mortal can't be connected with a deity and live in the likeness of God at the same time. So I tried to speed up the growth of my faith by asking "Master, where were we heading?"

"Son, were you lost or in some kind of trouble?" Said the man.

"I don't know. Quite frankly with you, Sir, I see all the places we've passed are beautiful indeed. I truly am clueless and horrified of where we were heading."

"Why should you? Instead, you should know and rejoice in the Lord always because the peace shall be with you."

I truly don't remember how long I had been silent. My curiosity and anxiety focused on discovering where we were going to land and what we were going to do afterward. Somewhere deep down in my mind, I had never doubted or raised any questions about why we were flying. While I was still pondering those questions, I saw I was a little late for that because, out of nowhere, I was landing. Obviously I feel that I am correct to be worry about my situation because people of a certain age could produce certain action of thought. I tried not to underestimate what I could or couldn't do in the context of thoughts and especially to those thoughts that I had not been completely connected. I also happened to understand that this man was above those who claimed to be angels. Despite the fact that he was not God, he had a way of showing all the good things about God. No matter where I was heading or how hard I was working on, he was there in some unspoken way, and his ability of staying on the top of things was incomprehensible.

As my mind pondered, I happened to know that location or place proved physical existence in the presence of reality. Generally speaking, selecting the right place was important for all kinds of businesses, but it didn't mean the process of selecting a location could be so significant. I did not know the decency, expectation and respect of a location had something to do with the perceptual sense of wealth and reality. Instead, it was about the plan, vision and knowing of what we do to be worth what it should be. Though most people do not see the presence of physical sense as necessary, but when material concepts and spatial sense disappear, the spiritual exist in the eternal order of divine science. Obviously, reality could be spiritual and sensual because human mind was limited. The sense of reality in existence was not about the availability at the time but rather, divine purpose continuing until the Master's plans were carried out completely.

Continuing to fly over the open horizon, I realized that literally nothing I did could change my situation. I happened to understand that God was not unfeeling to not listen to my prayers, but I knew He had a decision in mind. Besides, there was no reason to be emotional with God because he was the intelligence of all the intelligences of this world combined. He had all the rights to call things into existence, and He definitely had all the reasons to change matter into the ways that they should become. Indeed, He had a way of showing it, and sometimes it happens to be in the way that we could be hard to understand. Sometimes I think that we might have all the excuses, justifications, and reasons for the petition to the court of this world, but in the court of divine law, I believe that my basis of reasoning became useless in the spiritual science because it was up to God's discretion that things or matter would be given the fair trial in accordance with their premises.

According to Zig Ziglar, "it was not what happens to you that determines how far you would go in life, it was how you handle what happens to you." Indeed, that was true because we human beings were given the freedom, rights and wisdom to change the environment in a way that helped to best fit our circumstances. Comparing that gift with other animals, we were definitely blessed to control and govern God's properties. Though we could be powerful and intelligent enough to figure out what could be going inside the material sense and mortal mind, that still didn't give us the privilege to reject or deny the spiritual presence and divinity because God's way was still the highway, and it remained the best way ever. Throughout the entire process of flying, although I was given the supervision and protection within the journey of divine life, I was personally abused by the hypnotism-like faith that almost pushes me away from the safety net of my spiritual heritage. Many times, I literally could feel that I was tossed up and down by the evil content of guilt, sin and wickedness. I was robbed of my belief and faith in terms of mortal mind and error that tend to push me off my selfhood. I had never felt this upside down coming from the turbulence of nature itself. I worked very hard to set aside my fear to get some balance from the immortal facts until I hold onto the spiritual beings. Before I found the experience or consciousness of dying to life, I was taken to land on a mountain-like place.

As I landed on the sloppy hill, my heart was slightly loosened up and my body also started to cool off. At first glance of what surrounded the hill, I caught my breath. I was at the summit of the mountain, and below me spread the finest wilderness. Perhaps I might have put my rage, shame and disgrace when I first looked into the land of hardship and fruitlessness. I might be carried away by the blaming mentality and rudeness of absolute truthfulness. This piece of land seemed to be depleted from the rich and plentiful resources because I hardly see crops, vegetables and plantations since my landing. Certainly I couldn't complain of what had physically happened all the way here. I was not upset about my situation, but I'd allowed my emotions to get in the way. Somehow I saw that this was not something I did in my daily life, and it shouldn't be something I took pride of the faith that I practice in my daily encounter and it certainly shouldn't be my standard to not live in harmony with Jehovah's guidance. Between those unanswered complications of anguish and incompetence, my anxiety and eagerness to learn about the Truth did not deepen until I was called to start my new adventure.

"Son, had you found what you were missing?" he said.

"Sir, I was not really sure as of now and I don't think that it was what I was looking for…Maybe I do but I seem to not see it happens yet."

"Hating what you're doing and loving what you're wrestling with could always be something we need to balance, not because we could humbly walk away from our fears, but because we could boldly walk into the life of our sins."

"Master, please slow down because I am not sure how I can stay with you. Please teach and show me where I have been wrong."

"Keep your chin up and remember the promises God had for you even though you might feel dread and fear and be clueless at what was in front of you. You should know that there were no disappointments if you make them as your target. Be not frightened with dreams and terrified by the visions that you had no ideas about. Never turn down any opportunity and especially the one that provides you with new inspiration and wisdom against the financial meltdown and intellectual infrastructure this world attempts to set block into your life. You should not think of the obligation to do anything other than not being distant from the presence of God. Be alert and mindful at the situation and diligent in the course of your work."

"How could I know that I was not misleading…I was doing right in terms of my institutional and vocational assignments when other factors point to my disadvantage?"

"Don't be confused by your gifts and talents when this world prevents you from getting your assignments done. You should keep in mind that your integrity and wisdom are at risk if you allow them to get into the way. Take a close look at this hill, and you might see or feel nothingness because of the plain and dry wasteland it appears to be. You might question how and what it had to do with you and your life. I certainly hope that you could relate it with the lack of result or failure when your faith became rootless. Any attack from the outside world could threaten the growth of your faith and move your heart along with the gusting wind."

The man paused for a while and then he pointed to his left. "Don't worry about what you can't see at the moment and focus not on what you could see now because our Lord won't give you anything that you can't handle. He definitely won't tell you if He believes all matters or things working against you. What you see here was neither the real presentation of a thing itself nor how it should become.

"Oftentimes people see things or measure matters in term of physical and intellectual standards; however, God tends to make them a little different. We should stop perceiving things or matters not from the way they look but rather think of them as the process or materials that were waiting to put together for developing a fine and perfect product. If your intention was correct for the work you were doing, then you should not worry about why, what and how the result becomes. Otherwise, you should not do it without a better explanation. On the other hand, if you look closely to your far right ahead and to the lower left behind your back, then you might find the views are changing not because somebody intentionally does that to play tricks on you; instead, it was your eyes and mind that fool you about what you've just see few minutes ago."

"Master, I am not quite sure…but I see what you pointed at…both the bad and good sides from the view. How could that happen? What should I do to change them?" I was shaking my head and my eyes kept rolling back and forth to follow his fingers, but I seemed to not see what he meant besides the direction.

"You know…it was a hard thing to say or describe what you had not seen, and it was also a strange thing to see what you had not said. The drought in your life was similar to what you see from the unfruitful plants and wastelands we passed earlier. It was natural and easy to see all these grasses and plants uprooted from wind or fire, and the damage could be imaginably huge for the owner on those farms. It was not so much about the kind of seed that produces the type of fruit it should. What you don't see is the successful bearing of fruit and the revelation of a good plantation on the other side of the hill because the right seed had been planted onto the right soil. Remember, the spiritual life was a process, word was the seed, and soil was the condition or environment to nurture."

"What happens in your life could surely reflect the line of work and the kind of environment that you were engaged in. Normally, we might find that no results were alike even when applying the same application. One difference between the harvest from the crop still in the field was evil's misleading of you and a rejection of God's provision. What drives you away from your success tends not to be the same as what leads you to failure. You should not be confused with the application of plan, techniques, strategies and skills that defined the outcomes. Instead, it is the development of passion, faith and consistency that redefines the purpose. The drought on the farm could be overcome by sufficient water, good sunlight, and enriched soil. The drought in your life also could be turned around if you give your true heart and soul to God. The drought in your life also would be broken off when you surrender your life to God fully, completely, wholeheartedly and intimately."

The journey had been a hard and stressful for me. I had never doubted my blessing to perceive omnipresence. I realized that a mere utterance – known as a Rhema – through the Divine Spirit could brighten the sick and bless the poor. Perhaps that was because the conceptual senses were perplexed by the metaphorical representation of mind or soul outside the body. "Sir, please allow me to abide in your thoughts and show me how to fight off my absurdity," I said, "and to take authority and command over my error or relapse?"

"There was no real error except the one being lost in the perfect Principle. You should know that all creations including ideas or matters were the perfect reflection of God's workmanship. The reason that Jesus Christ spent His entire life illustrating obedience and love was because God was perfect, loving and righteous, and therefore, Christianity became the common culture, popular science, and an extraordinary mission. In fact, Christ was and should become the center of religion and of all things to all people. Certainly the path of following Christ is never been easy and smooth. You will have tremendous pressures and suffer setbacks at the hands of those who don't like you and your approach to the divine principle, not mentioning the fact that people don't like you to be like Jesus. You should know secular humanism and materialism tend to provide a worldly view and scientific method to solve the problems of mankind without God and the presence of His intelligence."

"As a Christian, you shouldn't be ashamed of yourself to testify God's love, become his testimony, and hold your position defending the Truth. You should realize that your life was a reflection of God's grace and mercy despite you might experience errors or failures more than expected. If you were faithful in your beliefs, then God would be faithful and responsive to you. Error or mistake that you make in life should not be the excuse of holding you back. If you let it dominate your life, then you gradually would invite the condemnation and curse from devils and eventually it would ruin your life and also the life to those who came to help you with. Instead of carrying the loads of guilt and shame from the mistake you're committed, you should run toward your God for the solution."

"How can we know that our prayer and request were answered? What must we do to ensure that God was with us especially during the time we felt or experience dying in that moment?"

"If you believe in the Son of God and his death on the Cross was to be the ransom for your sin, you should know that it gives you the pardon for death sentence so that you have eternal life with Him. You also should know that whatsoever you ask in the name of Jesus Christ you will be given according to His will. Do not doubt that God hears your prayer or He gives you anything you ask for. If you do, then you should first ask for his forgiveness before you claim your possession. Knowing that God loves you no matter how, what and why you do, but as long as you bend down your knees to invite Him to clean up the mess in the locker of your heart and in the darkest corner of your life, then you'll find there was a sin that doesn't lead to death and a mistake that doesn't earn the rights to hell as well."

"Sometimes you might see or experience a delay in God's response to your prayer and request, but it doesn't mean that He was no longer in control of the problems you have. If there was a time when you found no action coming from the Lord, you should not turn away from your beliefs by transferring your trust to different gods this world presents to you in exchange for recklessness and betrayal of the divine principle. Instead, you should be confident in the promise and provision that our Lord has for you because he happens to work on the perimeter of things or matter so that you can have the miracle. Sometimes you happen to not see the miracle as quickly as expected because He was working on somebody who happens to be the rescuer and solver of your problems."

"You might have died by not jumping off the bridge of your error, mistake, sin and guilt. But if you happen to allow God's intervention and redirection into your life, then there was nothing for you to lose other than the fruitful life you're missing out because God always had a plan and a blessing waiting to be delivered. Look at those beautiful views in your far right side and remember that they, just like anything else, are waving their hands at you and are waiting in line ahead of you. Be courageous to run toward your calling and be responsible to take on your work and environment according to the calling you have. Don't run away from failures and setbacks. Don't carry on life with a delusion or any demoralized senses without thinking over in what it was and how it should be."

For the first time in my life, I began to clearly understand the goal, mission and calling of my life. I had never experienced such a strong feeling, especially after the dialogue and conversation with someone whom happened to be far more intelligent than my college professors, more skillful than my mentors, more loving than my parents, much closer than my best friends, and more knowledgeable than all the philosophers and world-class speakers combined. I had never seen my financial problems coming off in red-light and the structure of my caring business turning into a completely different perspective of light. I even had hardly imagined all the loose ends of my emotions, captivities, expectations, sensitivities, understandings and denials to Christian principle turned into a tight and genuine relationship that inspired me to be highly committed and strongly weighed into a set of new standard that was larger and greater than all that was inside of me. I was completely and overwhelmingly convinced to make both immediate changes and a necessary impact to my life. This awakening and revival did not frighten me as other missions I had been on. This exciting encounter with a deity and the valuable teachings from the mystery man indeed revolutionized my life to get in touch with the Holy Spirit, to acquaint myself with the Stewardship, and to further connect intimately with the Lordship, as I had never done before, either intellectually or spiritually.

As I recovered from my spectacular journey and left the divine life for the physical world, I sought counsel from older Christian leaders and continued to gather information from church elders, including those who were in different denominations. For weeks, I stepped out of my comfort zone to search for my true soul, and I also listened eagerly to anyone who could give me advice on entrepreneurship, business competency and religious faith. Though I had learned quite a few hard lessons from my painful trial and error, I came to not concede myself against the destructive advice and disappointing help. I refused to compromise my reluctance and decision against God's wisdom and his vision for me because I truly believed that was a reason why God revealed his spirit to me. In my go-getting spirit, I always felt that there were no rules meant to be broken, no works meant to be unfinished, and no dreams meant to be not discovered unless I put a stop to it.

Sometimes we think that our plans could be perfect and delicate enough to obtain a desired result. All unknowns, by nature, were mysterious, complicated and beyond prediction, however. With the implementation of faith, we could fine-tune ourselves and put all we have into something larger than our own lives. From the nature of faith, if we put our mind into something larger than ourselves, then the notion of overcoming the illusion of fear or uncertainty, the mental meltdown from error or failure, the threat from sickness, sin and death, could no longer be a fancy roadblock to Christianity or Christian faith. In reality, this was never a problem of how faith should be structured in every degree or scale of thought process but instead was how faith should be put into the context of both the physical senses and moral standards so that clarity and certainty could shine a light on the sense of reality and also allow it to be visualized from the science of being.

Life had thrown lots of curves, moves and transitions at me, and constantly I found that my way was somehow filled with the unexpected. There was a time when I actually could see disappointment and heartbreak ahead of me. There was also a time I hardly knew what I should do with things or matters hiding in the shadow. Day by day, I worked very hard to stay on my course by opening up myself to whatever came my way so that I could find my balance. Many times I found one common reason that most people, just like me, were likely to fail in life was not because they let go of their dreams but because they tended to trade what they wanted the most for what they wanted at the present time. I think that we all deserve exactly what we want and even the best, no matter what, and literally none of us should settle anything for less.

With changes and corrections being made, I strongly believe what sets forth in life should not necessarily be the right thing to do. I had been told of what was not meant to prioritize with would not likely come into the circle even if I tried hard for it. I also happened to see that most of the time if I don't make good plans and control the plans, it was more likely that I either miss the boat or miss out the opportunity to get things done at least in the right way. With years of trial and error, I learned that there never has been a perfect or failed plan in place other than the one that was broken loose at all ends and also the one that was not given a fair and complete workup. Sometimes the process could be complicated or mingled with uncertainty, but it should not become too personal or cynical to a point that we had to set it aside by doing nothing so that we could make all people happy. Instead, we should know that no one can go back and start again unless they're committed to make an end of the past by starting fresh in today.

Clear mind initiatives were important to coordinate with daily routines and lifestyle choices. Human willpower was indeed a part of material senses and couldn't stand against the divine science. What makes this mortal mind to become materially important was that the mind could weigh theories from human speculations and help minimize errors. And what makes this physical thought from the mortal mind was that the commodity of material senses covers both the good and bad cognizance to a point that it reproduces comprehension, perception and observation. If there was any mystery to unveil the mind from ignorance, it was the Divine Principle or the Science of Being that guides the thought or mind to redefine any captured senses at the functioning and manifesting levels of matter.

Ego could be elusive and sometimes it tricked the mind with skepticism. Every now and then, we understood that we could be in trouble with our day-by-day routines because we are clueless and get frustrated with things, leading to some kind of insanity. If we had a fear of failure, fear of triumph, fear of sickness and fear of accusation, then we might live under the shadow of condemnation, accusation and denial. For instance, some of us might know that we could live and win over a tumor, cancer, stroke, sickness and disease to a point we might think that we were unable to overcome our hopelessness or despair, then we also should know faith protects us from the fallacy of material senses and the temptation to resist the truth. Recalling the parable that Peter sees Jesus walking on the water highlights the revelation of faith. Indeed, faith was neither designed as the healer of distress nor the terminator of doubt. Faith was the expression of trust in God's works and the affirmation of beliefs in what God could do and would do to repair, restore and heal the broken heart. Faith was not the pledge of individual success in the work and belief of selfhood but instead, it was the combination of personal experience and God's modification that eventually allowed matters to work through the corporeal sense and an unerring mind.

Each of our lives is a working process and a reflection of reality in our own ways despite that we can fear or worry about how things might play out in our thought process. To capture every thought of our fears, we need to resolve personal differences on the basis of harmony or materialistic perspectives. There is a time when fear is necessary to put a brake onto our aggression, but we need to know that fear can't help reduce our pain or agony, not until the suffering turns out to cave in some destructive thought. At that point, we could suffer a mental breakdown. There also is a time when, because of our limited intelligence, we overreact to problems and underestimate the progress of matter. Oftentimes, we are born into this world where we were meant to be linked together because of divine and brotherly love. But somehow we part from each other because of our cynicism, over-criticism and insensitivity over the issue of matter.

I saw my financial hardship as a byproduct of the financial meltdown. I put all my heart, wisdom and labor into obtaining clients, but consumers were not responding due to the lack of consumer spending, the insecurity from the financial market, the lack of confidence from investors, and the high number of both home foreclosures and the unemployment rate. From the Broadway of cosmopolitan city to the Main Street of a small town, I literally could feel and touch the pain, despair and tear in those desperate eyes. Stores were closing, companies were declaring bankruptcy and laying off workers, and laid-off workers were lining up for their unemployment benefits at their local welfare offices. Almost everywhere I went between spring 2010 to fall 2013, I saw disappointment, upset or even anger in the eyes of many, and I also gradually got a feeling that people were giving up their hope to look for jobs, not mentioning the landing of a dream job and/or the passion for job creation because the expectation or incentives had faded away. The recession became worse since the past two decades despite there were reports shown some sign of steady growth. For most part, due to the excessive budget deficit in both the state and federal reports, the maintaining of an existing job or business even became extraordinarily difficult and challenging while the culture of corruption remained high, not to mention the fact that downsizing, benefits and holiday pays were off the chart for a lot of businesses.

With all the turmoil and uncertainty coming out of the corporate world and financial institutions, life became harder for me and everyone else to live the way that we used to. Discouragement, hopelessness and broken-heartedness turn out to be the best and perfect description in the days and nights when the value of dollar didn't come close to match up with the amount of sweat. I felt frustrated to see how the bad choices we made could change our lives forever. I also felt very sad to know a bad decision could affect those who support us and those who continue to support me.

Life was not about making excuses for why something was not working in our favor. It was not about playing the blame game so that we could look better by demeaning others. Throughout history, not a single success or achievement of any kinds without losing some bloods, breaking some hearts, and dropping some tears. We can't lie about the nature of an assignment, the condition of a risk-taking opportunity, and the reality of an economy. We can't take away the energy and vitality only to reconnect with the negativity, to break down cynicism or criticism, and to respect the commonality. The world tended to be better off when we accepted our mistakes and worked together to willingly, humbly and wholeheartedly overcome our differences. Our problems tended to be little when we paid attention to what was happening in and around us without fearing the impossibility but instead taking precautions on the hard hits, tough sales, and dangerous plans.

The world collapses without the mind, and humans could fall without their intelligence. Neither skepticism nor philosophy can help us to surpass the material senses. Neither knowledge nor experience could save us from the mindfulness of matter and the supposition of reality if we don't put the best hypothesis and methodology into practice. What locks us into the world of complexities was the definition of self-existence and self-expression into infinite goods or belief. Almost all material knowledge and finite thoughts were limited and could interfere with the reality of existence. Even faith of the wise could lead to the physical timidity because the mortal mind was somehow non-spiritual and could be very destructive. The vision of the mortal mind could be restricted in the geometric altitudes or parameters, and the production of the mortal mind could only be measured in the social and physical sciences.

How sufficient could a positive attitude become and how insightful a mind could be when the plan revealed the thought process! No one and nothing could discredit our judgment and understanding to the matter or thing except when we put a stop to get to the bottom of how a thing should be. We should not carry the idea of ignorance or fear to confront the naked truth. We should know the sense of irresponsibility or careless attitude that removes us from the object of pursuit and the lessons of a learning philosophy. Oftentimes, we were led to believe that the illusion of physical weariness and the toil of mentality rest on the commitment level without paying too much attention on the shape, size and degree of the issue or matter. When mentality gives a strong push to the body, we could take control of the situation. We might even fall every now and then, but the important thing was to have the courage to stand up again and to reorganize ourselves with the energy needed for a next round of combat. In general, we should not be bombarded by the distance of the fall but rather what and how we do to stand up matter most in comparison to why we believe in. One best remedy for any kind of fatigue or give-up in any form was to learn the power of mind, the belief of soul, and the lesson of failure. Without the mind or determination to learn from the past, we would have no feeling or strength to look into the eyes of the impossibility.

If decision-making was left to the mortal senses, the spirit of the devil could surely drive us away from our Lord. If the success of individuality was based on the material senses, the mind could trick us from material accomplishment and push us aside from resistance and disengagement. From the Bible, we probably see the now common attitude toward the money pursuit that said, "Where your treasure is, there lays your heart." It was absolutely difficult to give up our material beliefs in term of mind or matter, to turn away from what seemed to be impossible, and to even deny the possession of matter in the absence of spirituality. In fact, seeking the best to reward our life was always the right thing to do, and it was always that kind of dream that fired our passion to honor the right path we choose. However, Christianity encourages us to first focus on God in order for the abundance to be released into our life. Perhaps the most rewarding moment besides the sense of greed was to know that we were moving on the right track and that we were actually making progress to preserve the greatest. Indeed, the universal sign of having a good life is not the focus of physical stuff or material things. God wants us to continue sticking to him until the end so that we can get things done if we think that was the only way out whether our fight was for love, freedom, health or wealth. Rejoicing and trusting in the Lord were also the decency and respect that keep us from going one way or another so that we not only can enjoy in the savory flavor that this earthly life had to offer, but we also can lay up our treasures and resources in Heaven.

Though I realized that my road to financial recovery would be difficult, I gradually pulled myself together by tightening up my spending on programs that didn't bring in prospects for sales. I turned down any offer that meant a big investment in new innovative equipment or medical devices for my practice. I learned to restrain myself against any temptation for new technology to attract high traffic and new patients. Instead, I begin to aggressively network with other healthcare workers or professional individuals and reach out to the community or small businesses by educating them in chiropractic and wellness. I provided them with information over the web, email, telephone and office tour so that people could have a better knowledge of what I did in the office and came to understand the dynamic of chiropractic in terms of my practice and philosophy. As my mentor and coach once told me, "If we want to build big for a business or if we wish to be successful in any industry, we need to have great team work, the best business associates, and good resources in term of manpower in addition to the controlled plan or willingness to work through difficult tasks." Certainly, I realized building a successful business was not easy and took years of hard work, dedication, fear-not-spirit, and dare-to-fail attitude. It needed a good system to cut off time from trial and error. I also happen to realize that to be successful in any types of businesses, I need to know how to closely follow rules and regulations relating to the profession that the business was conducted. I came to my senses that the more networking and association we have, the quicker we could move up the social ladder and the greater we could become. With the not-faded-away attitude, I begin to hang out with those who had tough minds, think far ahead, and share same values to keep my spirit up so that I could build strong alliance by opening up door of opportunity for wealth. Despite the fact that chiropractic remained under-valued in the healthcare structure, I still kept myself busy by welcoming the chance to learn and grow together with someone who hasn't got in touch with or especially with those who had not been informed of chiropractic so that I could share with them the true story behind the profession.

Not all roads were smooth and not all works were perfect. I knew the time had been tough and things had not been easy, even if I was still a Christian, but that was not going to change anything a whole lot in terms of hardship and tribulation. I still believed in the stumbling blocks and those dark steps that reminded me of what I had been going against. In those shadows, I constantly reminded myself to not spend money that I didn't have, especially in a time when I couldn't make up for it. I convinced myself to let go of my ideology of a perfect practice, to not retain the "keep up with the Jones" attitude, and to not criticize anyone other than myself. And in those ditches, I came to realize things and matters did not fall into the extent, scale and degree as I expect them to be. In that state of brokenness, I saw the reflection of my true self, who happened to grow so much from my own difficulties. One thing that helped to keep me away from a terrible fall was to hold on to the Lord. In those journeys, I learned to love waking up each morning by acknowledging that I was going to make a difference in someone's life. I also encouraged myself to rest at every night, knowing that I was in the right profession because of the impact I make by helping somebody achieve good health and better lifestyle. I constantly believed that life was meant to be lived out loud, and so I was going to live it up and enjoy soaking in every minute with all the things in it and would worry less about what was happening so that I could be attracted to the abundance of life and the beauty of this world that God offers.

In conclusion, reality is always a projection of happenings or a reflection of our thoughts, but our thoughts don't and can't really mean a lot if we don't have desires or the urgency to make things happen. With faith in religious beliefs, with eyes focused onto the infinite magic, and with diligence toward achieving dreams, I do believe the universe will lead us to the path of abundance, so long as we do not give up our hopes and dreams by making excuses.

Chapter 5: Science and Divinity

"I found it quite improbable that such order came out of chaos. There had to be some organizing principle. God to me was a mystery but was the explanation for the miracle of existence, why there was something instead of nothing." - Alan Sandage

Life was both a big physical science and was a complicated social science with all the experiments that were ongoing and not yet completed. Boredom was natural, sickness was inevitable, and truth could be questionable when people realized the world was filled with lots of uncertainty and doubt. There was a time when we might experience the constant toils, agonies, deprivations and exposures that could be indescribable. There was also a time when we can feel condemnation, sin, guilt and curses even though we tend to believe that they were not a part of what we should have. Still, there was a time when we move into a relationship that we had not yet been committed to and become clueless about how we should take it to the next level. Literally, we tend to go rogue without knowing what they could be taken us to overcome our transgression, depression, addiction, affliction and distress.

For years, I had never lost sight of my curiosity to unravel the myth and mystery about this so-called "life." As far as I know, I had not lost sight onto the vast intelligence from this science and I love exploring the infinite beauty from this life. I see people in my life as the reflection of abundance and the beauty of diversity. From time to time, I think the thing or matters happen in our life as the medium between our fantasy and recognition, and I also think they tend to be the consequences between our choice and decision. As long as I could remember, I had not lost any minutes to not look for alternatives that help to explain why it took me so long to understand the difference of what life was and how life should be.

How many times in your life that had you been told the mind could only do one thing at a time? Was it true that was all what the mind could do? What if the mind actually could do more than one thing at a time? Did it throw you off or bother you at all if the mind could handle more than you could know? Imagine a time when you visited your friends' houses but all you actually see was the physical extension of the building itself. Their houses had no lights on. Does it leave you wondering about whether you came to the right place or if you might have gone to the wrong place or at the wrong time?

There were times in life that we were allowed to bounce back and forth in what we do during our daily lives. Every culture and every race can be different because of its structure and heritage. Even in those moments when some of us were allowed to live a life that others don't, some of us still can feel the pressure coming from behind. Perhaps, some people expect us to live in a way that they could understand and accept; however, in some regime or religious beliefs, people were told to live by certain standard, and if they happen to be out of line, then they would be more likely rejected, condemned and persecuted.

Logically speaking, I remembered the universal sign of accepting and welcoming other people in the old days meant an open door policy and a well-lit sign that allowed guests to know that they were at home. Depending on the type of relationship people had, meals might possibly be prepared and provided at the owner's discretion if they respected the company they keep and if they could afford to do that. Generally, people would not turn off lights in their houses unless they were not at the house even though some guests were meant to be unwelcome. Given the fact that homeowners might happen to forget the exact time when their guests were to arrive, but they wouldn't be careless or rude enough to not even leave a notice for guests to know that they would be appreciated and to wait.

Our world functions well when all people pay close attention to the formality and principle of the Golden Rule. When the knowledge of a good reception helped to reflect friendliness, courtesy and respect could contribute to the well-being of a healthy relationship. To some people, the meaning of reception could be not much different from having or throwing a party for the standard purposes of attention, fun and company. To others, the meaning of reception could be the same as setting up for professional networking with style and elegance. To many people, the meaning of reception could be regarded in terms of intimacy, affection, love and friendship. In general, the act of reception expresses how a person cares for another, not mentioning the thoughtfulness.

There is no better place to have a reception than at a house. Generally, a reception at the home or a house party provides a sense of warmth, love or special meaning that allows people to appreciate more about relationship than the celebration itself. Going beyond the reception, the formation of the house can be similar to that of the mind. But the mind tends to have a more sophisticated and delicate structure with complex function and complicated organization than the brain. From a scientific perspective, the brain and mind were interchangeable. From the biochemical and physical standpoints, the brain was the hard cell that belongs to a part of the human body while the mind covers the inner part of psychic content. From a physical view, the mind, as a part of the eternal soul, helps to connect humans or spirit to the energy of Creator. It connects and controls all senses that were highly processed from the brain and above, especially the sense of cognition and the sense of being. According to Drs. Guyton and Hall, the authors of textbook of medical physiology, there were billions of neurons to be found in the brain and there were also billions of neurons in each transmission of an impulse. Each impulse could be generated by the interconnection of electrons and neutrons to carry out chemical signal and movement in per second interval. The fluctuation of each chemical to secure the transmission was crucial for stability of how a signal could be correctly formed to appropriately initiate into action. Once a signal came out of the central nervous system, an image was generated and conceived by the brain. An impulse was then triggered and processed into information to allow biochemical or physiological response in term of cellular level, biofeedback, visceral reaction and physical sense. Generally speaking, the process of nerve impulse and signal transmission could happen in any place or at multiple levels. That process depended on the availability and strength of the impulse itself. In a sense, the mind either could perceive one or multiple things and matters at a time depending on the synapse or synaptic process while the brain helped to process signals that produce images, emotions, communication skills, like or dislike, smells or sounds, and just to mention a few.

According to Ernest S. Holmes, the mind is the principle of self-conscious life or living. The mind can become an entity that allows humans to express and reflect their feelings into the physical world. The mind is a branch of mental science that allows an individual to explore the deeper meaning of life and to figure out the subtle sense, mystical presence, and divine truth with the choice and freedom from the ever-expanding intelligence. The mind creates inner world from the cultures that allow us to highly adapt to some risky behaviors or complex decision making. It also coordinates and controls all of our daily activities so that we can think, speak, behave, and act out life accordingly.

Imagine that a person doesn't believe in reception as a way of treating others with courtesy and respect because he or she might see it as something else. Regardless of what it could be or means differently, it indeed became a perception that captures in the mind except the action could be modified differently because of the social values, religious beliefs, and educational limitations. Some people found unusual ways to relate reception as a way to expand their feelings. Some people found reception as both the time and place to celebrate other people's achievements or joy while they also could reduce sufferings with those who happen to be living amid sadness or tragedy. Regardless of what and how reception was really formed, it certainly could be understandable because not all people were brought up or taught the same, and there was no absolute right or wrong unless it became socially and culturally accepted.

Truth or error and right or wrong could come at the expense of the mind. For years, I had learned that culture could make a significant impact on people's lives with little to almost no influence from education regardless of the level that one obtained. People in the East tend to believe seeking a traditional treatment is the best approach for their health. Their first choice would not be a medical doctor or medicine unless it was some kind of emergency or life-threatening condition. To Easterners, the concept of conventional treatment or therapy includes but is not limited by the combination of herbs, vitamins, acupuncture, reflexology, Chinese medicine, Yin Yang therapy, Tai Chi, Chi Kong, chiropractic and naturopathy in terms of alternative medicine or integrated medicine from the West. Quite understandably, culture not only plays a significant role in Easterners' lifestyle but also the kind of experience they have with the method of and results from the treatment. Despite that human belief could misinterpret the intelligence from mind power regarding healing, the mind indeed holds a key role in perception, decision making and speculation of matter or thing. The level of confidence tends to be high for those who were acquainted with and found no error in any form of the conventional treatment, because the mind and its mental state tend to govern the physical truth and thus control the consciousness of being.

Most people grow up in some ways that they might not know what they really want in the first place. Sometimes people might wonder why they always tend to want or go after what they didn't have. Though people don't know what they want, but they surely want to be respected. For instances, some people want to get out of their small town because they think their lives were too boring and they couldn't wait to see and live in a big city such as New York City. Some people couldn't think of the kind of manner that had been left out over time, but that manner helps to define who they really are. In the early days, people in the East believe sickness happens in the parameter of matter or things. They knew the nature of the beast. They realize things would not exist in the absence of matter when sickness manifests in the body. The big issue in managing sickness of any kinds should not be the focus of reducing pain with relative elimination of toxicity in the system itself. The big concern in treating sickness of any kind should not be limited in the legalized resources of some specific marketplace or industry. The measurement and protocol should develop in the long-term productivity of eliminating the sickness instead of focusing on what was available to solve the problem at the time.

Westerners tended to embrace the big idea of medication coming off the rhetoric of research development and scientific breakthrough. Perhaps many Westerners love the painful state of mind and the deteriorating health that could be improved by the break of a tablet or the drop of a solution. They seem to enjoy living a little more in the very moment when short-term relief could bring them back into their busy lifestyle. Day by day, they further indulge themselves in the fallacy of pharmaceutical intoxication or chemical purity that catches their breaths in a world that could be dying from substance abuse, drug interaction, depression, eating disorders, mental disorders, and other complications.

For decades, America was recognized as one of the leading countries in advanced science and sophisticated technology. America still leads the world in the revolutionary idea of epidemiology and public health policy. Yet, in terms of keeping a good quality of health, America ranges thirteenth in the world. According to the research and statistical study, American ranks forty four in healthcare efficiency among other industrialized countries. Privately, and in the community as a whole, the vast majority of Americans seem to not quite understand the true concept of health and the way of achieving a better, healthier life, not mentioning the fact that the American healthcare system is somehow broken. Most of them were influenced by advertisements from big pharmaceutical companies or lobbying groups. Many believed in the concept that a pill could literally and almost instantly take away all of their pain or health-related conditions. Still, many were addicted by prescriptions to treat their disease. Few really cared or wondered about the reason why so many drugs on the market were recalled.

In fact, Western civilization had long been bombarded by the so-called medical model, and it indeed has become tough for the Westerners to change their mindset. For example, many of us, whether it was Westerners or Easterners, were overshadowed by the fallacy of the drug. At some point in our lives, we probably indulged in a drug therapy for our health-related problems. Every day, the concept of drugs as the antidote was seen on billboards in the country, in the city, on buildings, at the top of bridges, and along the highways. Radio broadcasts and television shows claimed that medicine was the only way to solve health-related conditions. Magazines, newspapers and direct mail were delivered to homes and offices showing the success of clinical trials and the effectiveness of a drug in the treatment of certain diseases. Wherever people go, they could see and hear the promotions of drug. Whenever people turn on the television or radio, they often found an attractive pharmaceutical discount. Every year, pharmaceutical companies spend billions of dollar in sale representatives and advertising to push their drugs into the hands of medical doctors, hospitals and clinics. Oftentimes, we see medical doctors giving patients more or higher doses of medications. With those perceptions in place, the vast majority of Americans and general public seemed to be fed on pills, leaving not enough room for the average person to find what could be really beneficial for their health. What if all doctors told their patients the truth about the cause of their health problems and provided them with all options available for treatment? Would our world be better off?

Recalling the time when drugs were not quite popular and overwhelming in the early eighteen century, people in all walks of life sought through what they found and worked through what they thought to make them feeling better and healthier. Up to this date, the value remains relatively the same except the attitude and expectation have shifted significantly. The problem is not about the change in the levels of education or wealth, it instead is the perception being driven by availability, convenience and cost. The mind has been challenged and the culture has been redefined in term of choice and desire. Perhaps every individual is entitled to speak out the use of pills, vaccination, surgery or supplements in term of cause and effect, but the overall goal should be focused on the long-term cost in relationship to the nature and condition of health.

Perhaps an undeniable truth is that all individuals were free to choose what could be best for them. We should remember that life was good with all options on the table despite that we might or might not believe in the provision and existence of God. There were times when some options could be better than the other. There were also times when having an option was definitely better than none. To many few people, having a clear option and finding some new way for a better health could be worth for a try. Instead of focusing on the conventional method, these people represent the new blood of our society and the new breed from a generation that wrap their life around the naturals with little or no help from artificial ingredients and chemical interventions. These individuals believe that one of the best healing methods or procedure to disease of any kinds lies in the herbal and dietary supplements, the minimal uptake of drugs and surgeries, the healing art of non-medicinal science, and the do-it-no-harm principle from the naturopathic treatment. Indeed, the mechanical approach, which is adopted in the allopathic medicine, focused on the use of pills and it did not fully solve the health problem, especially dealing with the chronic disease. We should seriously think about setting aside our differences, thoughts, and criticisms. In the meantime, all healthcare professionals should come together to explore new alternative, to exploit new initiative, and to form new strategy for the health problems that people face together as a whole.

In retrospect to the birth and development of the antibiotic drug, ancient histories and the Western medicine reveal the prophylactic and therapeutic arts of healing go far beyond what we now know as via science. Looking back at the discovery of the world's popular and first true antibiotic, Penicillin was an accidental discovery from a "mold juice" that Alexander Fleming found in one early morning in the late 1920s. In his early remark, Fleming noticed from his petri dish that one cell culture was contaminated with a fungus and those colonies or properties of staphylococci surrounding the fungus were destroyed. That mold was known for Penicillium Genus, and it was a fungus growing in the form of some multicellular filament known as hypgae. This Penicillium Genus had the ability to produce a substance that could kill a number of disease-causing germ or bacteria. Even to this day, aspirin is widely used and sells approximately 50 tons per day worldwide. Its mechanism of action in the treatment of body aches, pain and fever were fully documented in term of basic physiological response to the pain, but its mechanics were still largely unknown. Across every continent of the globe, people historically learned to deal with their health problems by using plants or seeds from the earth and by using foods or patches of mixtures apply into the areas of body where the pain or infection is. From a psychological standpoint, the ancient people learn to overcome their sickness by raising awareness in conscience, the sense of mind, and the fear from death. From a theological perspective, Christians in the early days discovered that a useful means or effective way of healing over sickness was to pray, fast and repent instead of seeking solution from any other sources. All these deeds proved the nature of a true physical healing to disease or sickness of any kinds exceeding "the one size fits all" theory and there were alternatives that could be unexpected or not explanatory in term of science when search for solutions for disease, sickness or any health-related conditions.

A drug or vaccine is a mixture of chemical compounds and was also a combination of multiple physical substances gathering to form an antigen from the scientific or technological process that could reproduce a resistance against antibodies at the cellular level. From the standpoint of Western medicine, drugs and surgeries were used in both daily medical practice and clinical trials to figure out the nature and cause of a disease. They represent a direct, straight-forward and risky intervention in term of treating a disease. From the standpoint of alternative or complimentary medicine, the concept of looking into daily lifestyles, chemical factors, spinal biomechanics, environmental issues, genetic makeup, hormonal balance, and/or toxic levels provide essential clues to help treat disease properly and effectively. From the standpoint of homeopathic medicine, drug fails to treat disease because the drug can only help to remove and suppress the symptoms. As a result, multiple and high dose of drugs were needed to remove a symptom at a time while another symptom could arise because of the interaction with another drug. The problem was the culture of our health care had been strongly emphasized on solo practice and that problem, in effect, was always the limitation of matter and humbly speaking, collaboration among other healthcare professions or from people with different healthcare backgrounds should be promoted to deliver better care, and continual research should be the best approach to unlock mystery that was not yet found from the principle of basic science.

Perhaps, the successful treatment of a disease or sickness could be related by how well a doctor looks at the problem and what kind of approach he or she took on to the problem. Traditionally, medical doctors focus on the diagnostic finding and clinical assessment in term of pulse, blood pressure, lab work, temperature, respiration and palpitation to find the pathological pattern and chemical factor related to an illness. Medical doctors see disease in term of symptoms or pathology that could induce sickness or other health-related conditions. Scientists, on the other hand, believe in fact and evidence by studying sample, data, and/or statistics to come up with some measurable standards. Scientists focus on the valuable pieces of evidence, fact and background to support their theories. They view disease as a pattern or process that could be treated in term of procedural science and technology advancement. Chiropractor, naturopath, acupuncturist and all other healthcare professionals on the contrary focus on factors or underlying causes that lead to the disease. They recognize all causes could be vested in some self-constituted thing or matters that could be bigger than what actually expresses at the time. What constitutes in the difference of all these professional practice and philosophy tend to be the obligation to legal framework set forth in the provision of healthcare. Indeed, I believe that I was not against medicine, drug and surgery. I truly believe that we need them at their best to help enhance our life. I also happen to realize that they should not be the antidote or the only solution to our health issue alone. I knew that we need more treatment options and better therapies available so that we could live healthier each day. And instead of maintaining separation in power within the legal system, cooperation and empowerment should be the new ground for implementation and strategy to move forward the agenda and to advance healing art or skills into the integrated medicine for the 21st century and beyond.

What was so frightening and troublesome in the healthcare community was not the fuzziness or unclear definition of what healthcare really is but the concept of mind that tends to shift the healthcare paradigm. This is accompanied by a desire to redefine healthcare to be more than it is. To some extent, most people had been frustrated enough to find the strong political and philosophical fight within the medical professional and so as with other professionals while cases of unknown illnesses and thousands of sick people were terrified by the lack of result. Learning that the real focus of some health professionals might not be in the healing business but rather in the political game that allows some to figure out how and who was going to control whom is heartbreaking. The rationale of our healthcare model is questionable by the facts that the sick could be horrified by their "sick" beliefs, the sinners could be frightened by their "sinful" natures, and the healers could be less passionate in their "healing" power, art and skills. If all healthcare professions opened their hearts and hands to accept differences and to abolish prejudices against one another, then good days would be ahead for all people. Beneficial treatment or therapies could be brought into a community where the talents from those healing hands would rise up to help and save patients and their loved ones from despair. Life would be good when all healthcare professionals once again dedicate their best talents to the health of a population instead of focusing on the wellness of a particular profession or an individual practice. If a whole village or a big family was needed to raise a good kid, it should be no difference in the entire healthcare industry to bring forth a team of different professionals to achieve better health or wellness society.

By the same token, there was no sensitivity in the concept of healthcare other than perception from the mind. People seemed not so easy to change their position or shift their mind on something that they had little agreement on and especially in the view of healthcare and its coverage, though change happens every day in the world of business, politics, sports, career, education, fashion and religion, not to mention one's emotions when dealing with crisis. On a separate thought, people know that they do become sick, not truly because the way they think sometimes. Some people might not believe that they were sick, but eventually they do get sick. Some people were sick, but they think they are in good health, and eventually they die. Though sickness might not be completely induced by false alarm or wrong belief, but it could get worse by illusion, fear, spiritual darkness or sin that leads to the dying belief or death. In fact, we all knew pressure could come in the form of denial to truth and threat could also come from toughness of rejecting the wrongdoings. Sometimes due to the fear of making an error and due to the fact that human beliefs could misinterpret the nature of principle, the mind became a big excuse for anyone to learn the truth, and it could bring up false alarm for those who suffer delusions and consequences in term of health and holiness. Every human deserves the legitimate freedom to live in any kind of culture and to hold on to their beliefs. They certainly had all the rights and reasons to shape up thought and live the way they dream of. Regardless of what side of the coin that their reality flips to, no one needed to worry about the quality of healthcare if they happened to understand the true nature of health.

Within the context of health itself, all people should realize that there are three basic systems in the human body to achieve the homeostasis. They are the mechanical, neurological, and chemical-glandular systems. Though each of them could function independently, they somehow were interdependent. Apart from those systems, health consisted of several parts, including the physical, mental, environmental, social, emotional and spiritual. First and foremost, to be physically healthy, people needed to show that they had no signs of difficulty, pain and restriction in their normal routines and activities of daily living (ADL). Secondly, to be mentally healthy, people should have demonstrated that they are capable of revealing a clear understanding between right and wrong or their sound judgment between truth and error. Third, to be environmentally healthy, people needed to cut back or be free from toxins, air pollution, chemical waste, noises, and disrupted lifestyles. Fourth, to be socially healthy, people had to be free from any prejudice or restraints in terms of finance, race, and status so that they could share a better life. Fifth, to be emotionally healthy, people needed to get rid of their bad relationships, baggage and depression. Last but not least, to be spiritually healthy, people needed to demonstrate their religious beliefs stood strongly and correctly against the institutions, laws or policies of the world that could induce cynicism and cast a shadow of a doubt on their faith. Among them, I believe the spiritual factor was the one that brought better, effectual healing for the recovery of sickness or disease.

Scientific, medical researches have found that the brain was different from the mind, and the mind tended to reveal what was inside the matter. Despite religious differences, the vast majority of people realize that we live by emotions, we respond to events with our gut feelings, we conceive or perceive matter via our mind, and we were still living in our daily experience because our souls remain intact in some form. Regardless of literacy, race and ideology, most people recognize that we need facts and truths, not statistics, to help us make good and appropriate decisions during the time of desperation, pain or illness. Along that line, we happen to live with our conscience at the very moment that we were not falling into a drunken state. And as ever, we see that the mortal mind, when the truth was missing or misinterpreted, could literally drive us to abandon our beliefs, and it could send us down the path of desperation and into the sentiment of self-destruction. But how closely had we paid attention to what the mind, in terms of spiritual existence, could do to make an impact on our health?

According to Christian Science, as Mary Eddy once said, the mind could help to promote health and reduce illness. With the acknowledgment that fear of disease and the love of sin are the hindrance to longevity, the belief in our principles and conscience work closely to keep every dream alive. We should not fail to see that the senses could play a trick on what we actually see. By the time the eyes were going to connect their findings with the brain, the brain became fuzzy about what it felt about the situation and that tends to drive the mind into frustration. As long as the mind was still up somewhere, there would be more time for the body to process what had been messing up in the system and to dive deep into the stream of health.

Unless the mind figures out what was actually happening in the first place, the problem won't be the same no matter how hard the intervention could be placed into the process.

Life is too short for anyone to worry about being sick. The problem tends not to be what lies behind or before us but rather what lies between and inside us despite that the matter could be trivial. In fact, nothing was too small for the mind to perceive or comprehend in terms of what needed to be done and why it must be done in a certain way. Perhaps, due to the fact that most of us live by our emotions or conscience, getting comfortable with the good things that life had to offer was easy. But if we live by stacks of standards and values that could work against us, then life could become quite rough for us and for others around us. Obviously, health was not something that we should take for granted, as it would play a significant role as we aged.

How people individually and as a community view their health could be defined differently. With a clear mindset, illnesses and symptoms could be reduced. In science, we use what we tend to understand, and we apply our practice philosophy to the future events based on what was happening now or what could be gathered at the time. Therefore, science was not absolutely pure and far from perfect because it couldn't completely and actually repeat its result based on the sample gathered. In Christian Science, the mind was processed and understood by the presence of real spiritual sources. Whenever a sinful nature overpowers the mind, higher resistance or rejection could be found despite the presence of spirituality. For instance, many of us could relate to the fact that evil spirit or demons could possess and endanger our life when we favored some vicious arts or music, when we rationalized our beliefs in vandalism or idolatry for some superpower, when we tied ourselves in the curse of witchcraft to avenge our loss, when we defamed or demeaned other people's achievements out of jealousy, when we put other people into hostile and terrible environments because they were a threat and intimidation to our ideology, when we indulged our addiction to the pleasure of drugs or sex to cover up excuses or irresponsibility for our behaviors, when we tended to transfer our hypocrisy, lust, hate, cynicism and insanity from the morbidity this world induces. Eventually, our lives could turn into a big mess and tragedy because we allowed them to occupy our mind and to violate our principles.

To overcome the mortal illusions and the fallacy of human nature, we should commit ourselves to the intelligence of the universe. The Scriptures revealed that the Holy Spirit was the presentation of divine principle, and the divine principle covers the basis of His Truth. While the Truth covered the manifestation of love, the love expresses from the captivity of mind, and then the mind bears fruits from the grace of God. Of course, not all journeys or processes in our lives could be the same. What differs between us can't really be the circumstances or conditions we were in but the perception that helped to change our entire situation and to make us different from one another. There was a time when we might see or feel the pain and trouble that other people were going through. There also was a time when we might miss the train of problems coming our way. There were some circumstances that may cause us to fall down or stumble. There also were some circumstances that could literally cripple our feelings and disable our mentality because we missed the boat. One important point was that we should know the obstacles can't be the factor of paralyzing our life without giving us reasons and chances to exploit other means.

Despite the fact that we could be beaten up by the hopelessness this world delivers and could be also depressed or angry due to the alluring lies of the devils, we still should pay attention to the intervention of God. Whenever God presents into our life, the supernatural happens in no measurement of time, no calculation of result, and no breaking of promise. If we were the ones who could imagine of divine miracle and Christian healing, we should not think our problems ever are larger than God's presence. If we believe in God's power, then we shouldn't question or doubt His leadership instead of our cynicism and disobedience. For example, in the Book of Joshua, the Hebrews realized that warfare belongs to God alone. To fight against the Canaanites and to thus take back their city, Joshua and the Israeli people were instructed by God to march seven times and seven days around Jericho. The Israelites along with the priests and the Ark of the Covenant marched around the walls by shouting out loudly and blowing their trumpets. By the seventh day, the wall of Jericho fell. As a result of their obedience to the teachings and laws set forth by the Covenant, Joshua and his people won the battle before starting it. From some perspectives, if you believe in your nature, then you'll follow your flesh, emotion and problem that this world imposes on you. If you present your faith before your God, then the physical mind can't trick you anymore. The reason for that was prophesy from the Lord's blessing went through the mouth of those who claimed by their obedience to be acting on prophetic words. God and his supernatural power act on the mind, the mind then pictured the possibility and allowed the door of wisdom to open up opportunity so that problems could be minimized to a point that they no longer become impossible to overcome.

By nature, God was love and he always answers to our sickness, desperation, failure and/or financial difficulty. Our life, as a matter of fact, should be more exciting and interesting than movie or show. When the doctors of this world give us no answer to the diagnosis and treatment of our disease or illnesses, God – the doctor of all doctors – then stretches out His mighty hands to heal the unhealed and treat the sick. When you were at the end road and before you were going to jump off the bridge, God reaches out to pull you away from the danger and then fires up your mind for a new journey. When you see your works not adding up to the expectation and before things were falling apart, God's faithful arms rescue you from falling so that you could be kept in the shower of His blessing. When you were in the worst or in the drought of your finances, you could either move your life forward by doing something or you could continue complaining about your unsuccessful search for new alternatives. But when God showed up in the midst of tribulations, the wall of financial problems falls off. Indeed, that was not about the ill belief we could be held off from our mistrust or denial to God's grace, but instead the firm belief and attested faith that keep us moving forward and pressing on even though we might face enormous pressure.

When men demonstrate an understanding of Christianity and the healing of sickness, they begin to recognize that obedience to the law of God proves to be the best healthcare. Christian Science, as Mary Eddy points out, believes that disease should not be expressed in the form of symptoms but instead should be measured in the functions of the body. To say the condition of muscle spasm, swelling, laceration, headache, bruise, pain and weakness became the sickness or disease is a misconception because the disabled or dysfunctional organ could, at some point, still function with little to no help to a point where the body could recover. Indeed, the state of fluctuating blood pressure, unstable respiration rate, weak pulse, depleted pigmentation of skin, discoloration of the retina, and open wound could reproduce the condition of disease. People should realize that those were the known symptoms in term of physical form, and they don't necessarily represent the body that operates at the problematic malfunction level. Despite the fact that its function could be affected and its health could be disrupted, the body could still remain functioning at the optimum level if the mental state of mind stays strong enough to disregard the existence of symptomatic illness.

We can see that scientific testimonies and studies in the medical practice can be questionable. From the psychiatric viewpoint, the mental state affects and controls any fear-related health conditions. Psychiatrists tend to see that health had a strong connection between the perception of the brain or mind and the expression of behaviors. Psychiatrists, psychologists and neurologists tend to believe that if humans happen to consciously perceive the objective state of thing or matter in form of sin, fear, danger and doubt, this mental state of the mortal mind could induce sickness and eventually lead to some kind of suicidal thoughts because they lose the sense of respect or awareness and they also tend to forget their own commitment into an existence that was greater than the perception itself. That was also the reason why we see the prevalence of denial, abuse, compulsive personality disorder, anxiety, depression, bipolar, mental disorders and post-traumatic stress disorder that tend to relate to the receptor-producing signals from the brain and the inhibitor-reinforcing signals within and outside the central nervous system. Because of this cause and effect, the mental state of mind becomes a tough assignment in the use of drugs or injections to control symptoms rather than to treat the disease's origin.

Focusing on the mental state or the cause of disease was an important step to unlock the mind-related problems in term of health and wellness. By engaging in the mental state, scientists help to look into the nature of the mind itself, the culture of the mind learning process, the stage of mind perception, the structure and function of brain, and the integrated study of medicine and mind. By dealing with the cause of disease, healthcare professionals learn to read between lines from what patients describe about their health conditions and what the practitioners actually found from their evaluations. For most of the time, these scientists could confidently find alternative therapy or new breakthrough treatment from their research and study to show the reason why drugs give no answer to the disease. Certainly there were lots of anxiety and pressure in the interprofessional study onto a topic because the goal of restoring patients physically through research and practice was more important than the experience of the pain suffering itself.

Conservative Christian believers tend to carry hope and faith when they were in some kind of danger and tribulation. Even the conventional patients show confidence and hope when they found the strong correlation between the spirituality and healing power. By looking at the roots of all sickness and disease, Christian Science revealed the greatness lying in divine mind. True Christians could always relate to the mental and moral issues when their life was a reflection of mortal thought and mind with little to no intervention from the Lord. In fact, sin, sickness, error, danger, suffering and even death was a part of life. No one go through life without knowing that they were a part of problems. Whenever problems occur, they literally can feel the connection to the circumstance that requires them to put forth their hands and works in it. The genuine Christian realizes that all the hardships or tribulations were the total reflection of grace because God wants to draw us closer to him. With that in mind, the genuine Christians see that their problems were a small part or equation in comparison to the sufferings Christ pays for our sins. They knew the only solution to their problems was to humbly and desperately run toward God for strength and wisdom so that they could have all their burdens of guilt, shame, ego, hate, wickedness, sickness, and/or conviction being released and nailed on the Cross where Christ's blood once had been shed and paid for all.

To the contrary, false Christians or atheists see their problem or tribulations as a part of conflicts coming from this world and the continuity of their nature. By definition, our nature was the extension of our flesh in terms of desire, character, moods, behavior and thought. What our motives and acts reflect is the reality of need and want in some unique ways. There was a time when our motives were presented in some explicit forms. There was also a time when our acts were driven by some hidden secrets. Eventually they happen to be a part of mind and belief in ignorance of the law of God. Most of the time, these people believed in their ability to defend their life and were capable of controlling their circumstances. In their subconscious mind, they tended to view obedience and faithfulness to God as a weakness and as absurd. They see fear when confronting problems or tribulations as incompetency and paranoia that lead to suffering. As a result, they could be perplexed by the dilemma and decisions. They could be shadowed by the hidden truth, latent belief, and mortal fear. They could invalidate the mentality of the sick, the heart of the ill faith, and the act of the unjust, but they can't undermine the mind of the Lord and the work of His righteousness. By removing the leading error and the governing fear with the mind, humans were able to overcome the cause of all functional difficulties or impossibilities in term of condition disease. By rooting up the sense of grief and fear in life, we could be healthy and rejoice in the love that God provides us. And as Dr. Yohannan points out that "our spirits, which are eternal and infinitely more precious than the whole physical world, are contained in perishable, physical bodies." Because of our beliefs in the fundamental truth of God's words and the spiritual awakening, the elimination of mortal mind and the breakdown of mental concept apparently prove to correct the false belief in regarding to the harmonious being, constant suffering, and even instantaneous death both scientifically and spiritually.

For better or worse, we humans tend to try living up to other people's expectation. At some point of time, most people grow up not knowing or being confused about what they need or want. Despite high expectations, few people really put their hearts into something they had set their mind on in the first place. Instead, many promises and dreams turned out to be some kind of a joke. Some people even required or demanded the quality service from others while they literally put forth less effort. Among the worst aspects of our modern day culture is that idolization has become a strong factor. The common acceptance of being someone else, such as the idea of "wannabe," makes people feeling "cool" or "special" even though no one is actually sitting next to them in judgment. Acknowledging the courage and admiration to be someone, especially those who wish to be a celebrity, public figure, wealthy business person, or successful professional, could be uneasy and messy. First, to do this some of us need to give up our true self. Secondly, we have to learn and act in accordance with others, such as we need to talk in certain way, sit the right way, dress a specific way, and party at the right time. Third, we might have to live with no or low self-esteem. In other words, no one literally likes to be called "loser" from their painful experiences, isolations and setbacks. And almost none of us dare to act out consistently because we lack the qualification or talents. Chances are if we had to ask ourselves honestly and truthful that should those persona or pretenses were reasonably right? Whatever the expectations or justification we hold in terms of religion, career, culture, education, and/or health, the energy could be explosive, and the thought could be comprehensive. Whether we base our analysis or analogy by age, sex, region, ethnicity, socioeconomic status, the key issue was our attitude to look beyond the matter. Chances were that the more clearly we could identify who we really were and define what we are going to be, the greater possibility that we could make out of the sense of insecurity being whom we were going to be without copying exactly from others because God makes us individually and distinctively from His image. On the other hand, if we tried to be all things to all people, we might end up being nobody, and we'll become everybody else with little to no mark for ourselves.

Life does not really mean a whole lot when we try to be someone else. When we can't recognize who we really were, we should be frightened to learn a few truths by looking at what we do. Perhaps we might come to our senses without getting confused by what brings us closer to our dreams. Whether we were religious or not, our beliefs and values should go hand-in-hand with the way we live our lives. Just in case some were still questioning their ability to make a change in how they could address their attitudes, they should know that they were still held accountable for what was inside and outside of their minds. Generally speaking, all of us were fully and completely responsible for our own expression and choice of freedom in a fair and equal playing field, no matter what kind of circumstance we were in and no matter how desperate or detrimental our excuse could be.

There were times when many things in life occurred, ensuring the management of personal issues no longer were the obstacles or stumbling block for success. Believe it or not, there was nothing ridiculous and impossible to change what was inside our mind and to thus clean up what tends to be the dirty thought in the tricky locker room of our heart.

Sometimes it was quite right for us – every one of us – to seek some space and alone time to figure out what the next move would be even though the chances of recovering ourselves or restoring our confidence could be one in a million, but the process was still worth a try.

In retrospect, the multiple episodes of my father overcoming a coma and diabetic shock during his hospitalizations reflected both a medical breakthrough and a spiritual healing. On the intellectual side, the key issues of finding the cause and getting the right diagnosis focused on the effectiveness of new technology and the availability of a treatment or therapy that helped to reduce suffering and to improve the quality of life. During each of those incredible hospitalizations, we learned that health should either be built or lost. We tend to think that if the idea of having a good productive life was to make better use of each of the healthy organs with the help of a procedure or medical treatment, then the value was the expected result of consistency with less regards to the base and philosophy of a practice. Even the smallest things could have the largest impact. And based on the scientific approaches and Biblical principles, the results of my dad's health exemplified the integrity, the moral values, the ethical standards, and the extraordinary miracle that go way beyond the expected.

During a coma, the body tends to lose the ability to develop the appropriate physiological response. Depending on the circumstances or conditions of the coma, some bodies take longer to respond and for the mind or brain to pick up the signal and thus become aware of its connectivity in term of time, space and positioning sense. For instance, a brain injury caused by a high jump diving could be different from a head concussion from a sports injury; a head injury from a sports injury could be different from that of incurred during a car accident; a trauma from the motor vehicle collision could be different from a fall from tree or building. Technically speaking, the initial treatment or procedure for managing the loss of consciousness or coma was not much different regardless of the injury, but the nature and mechanism of the injury itself can affect the success and recovery rate, requiring more aggressive treatments be attempted.

In general, when the body was in a coma or an unconscious state from any unknown illnesses, the brain tended to lose its ability to perceive, connect and produce. From the physical or spiritual sense, a coma tends to interrupt nerve transmission and conduction from the brain and circulation to the rest of the body. In medicine, a coma describes a profound state of unconsciousness that allows an individual to be unresponsive to pain, light or sound, induces to no voluntary actions, and does not have sleep-wake cycles as well. A coma could indeed result from a variety of conditions, including but not limited to the intoxication, metabolic abnormalities, central nervous system diseases, pathology in the blood vessel, and/or acute neurological injury or impairment.

The severity and the mode of onset were varied from one coma to another. Depending on the underlying cause, some comas do not require major medical intervention while others necessitate admission to an intensive care unit. When the cause of coma is unclear, various investigations or further evaluations were recommended to establish the diagnosis and to help identify any reversible causes possible. When the coma was stable, typical medical procedures were performed to assess the underlying cause; usually a computed tomography (CT) and/or magnetic resonance imaging (MRI) of the brain and blood vessels would be done to locate the hemorrhage, pathology or any source for the damage around the brain, blood vessels, or areas of complaints. There also may be a time when a coma was induced by pharmaceutical agents to preserve a brain from further breakdown. Technically speaking, most comas could last a few hours to a few weeks, but some might last as long as few years. Some patients could recover from the coma while others could progress to a vegetative state with a slight degree of awareness. Still some others could even die from coma or from its complications.

The outcome for a coma or any vegetative state depends on the cause, location, severity and extent of the neurological damage. The deeper the coma, the more severe the condition became and the slimmer chance of recovery was for the suffered. In general, the comatose patients could awake with some kinds of confusion, not knowing how they get there in the first place. In some conditions, the comatose patients could suffer from some degree of difficulty in movement or speech. In some severe cases, the comatose patients could present with many other complications and even disabilities for extended periods of time. Recovery from coma was not impossible and usually it occurs gradually because the nature of coma came from extract or combination of physical, chemical, intellectual, psychological, and even spiritual therapies.

A coma indeed was dangerous and frightening and could even become life-threatening, as in my dad's case. In the beginning, the coma that my dad has was related to diabetes. In medicine, a diabetic coma was a medical emergency with some degree of diagnostic dilemma when a doctor gets in touch with a comatose patient with limited information or medical history known except diabetes. The most obvious symptom for diabetic coma was the unconsciousness that could be due to hypoglycemia or hyperglycemia, dehydration, shock and exhaustion or the combination of all. Depending on the stages and causes of coma itself, the complications were vitally huge and significantly different.

There was a relative connection and perhaps a relationship between the diabetic coma and diabetic shock. By definition, diabetic shock was a medical condition that happens to be caused by a severe case or type of low blood sugar known as hypoglycemia. A diabetic person could go into diabetic shock from a high dose of diabetes medications, predominantly insulin, strenuous exercises, and lack of food. Unconsciousness was the most common symptom for the two. When the diabetic individuals go into shock, they would present with blurry vision, confusion and dizziness. As time progresses, they would illicit convulsion, palpitations and dysphasia. Their face could become really pale, and their skin could turn out to be clammy with excessive weakness. If they leave untreated, these individuals with diabetic shock could end up in a diabetic coma. And without immediate and appropriate medical attention, this could result in vegetative state or death.

From a different perspective, most diabetic people could lose their ability to recognize the symptoms of early hypoglycemia. Research shows that unconsciousness due to hypoglycemia normally occurs within 30 minutes to an hour as the earliest sign and then proceeds with other illnesses or symptoms. The progression of an illness or symptoms depends on the cause, stage, age and condition that could vary from one person to another. Statistics show that approximately 5-10 percent of diabetic people would suffer from at least one episode of diabetic coma in their lifetime due to hypoglycemia or its severe attack and about another 4 percent of all diabetes-related deaths were caused by diabetic shock. In the early stages of diabetic shock, the diabetic may feel exceptionally hungry, dizzy, weak and lightheaded. Before their blood sugar significantly drops, sucking or consuming some sweetened things such as candy, orange or fruit juice, and sugar equivalents could usually help to slightly reverse the situation. At the more advanced stages, the diabetic's brain or any neurological senses may be affected. And at the most extreme stages, the diabetic would completely lose consciousness and result in the diabetic coma.

As for my dad, his conditions underlined the occurrence and recurrent events from both the diabetic shock and/or coma to a point that intimidates and frightens many people into realizing how fragile our health could be. There was a time when my dad happened to suffer from advanced diabetic ketoacidosis that caused him to be in a coma more than four days. There also was a time when he could be in the nonketotic hyperosmolar coma lasted more than a week and it gave him an impaired ability to eat and drink. There even was a time when he might be dead from those aforementioned illnesses and the complications from severe infection or stroke-like symptoms. Our family was fortunate enough to find dad was surrounded by many of those who were not only highly educated, skillfully trained, and fully dedicated professionals, but also genuinely loved, spiritually motivated, and fully committed individuals. These people were truly God-sent with the talents and experiences to help and support dad in those critical moments.

For some time, we speculated that the recovery from sickness of any kind and the manifestation of healing both lie in the perceptual senses. The myth of knowing what constitutes life in the perception of mind or matter drives many of us to look beyond the anatomy of the brain. Science proves that the human mind or the brain had the ability to respond to the basic needs of life. It coordinated and initiated our ability to eat, drink, sleep, move and think. It also captured and regulated our senses in terms of desire, emotion, pain, pleasure, foods, clothing, shelter, power, beauty, wealth and lust. With the knowledge that our body was no longer adapted to the physical or material senses, did it mean that we were of no help from this world? For instance, many of us see or realize that there is a time when our friends or family members were ill to a point that the treatments were ineffective. There always comes a time when medical science provides us with no answers to our health problems or tells us that our beloved or we ourselves had only few months to live. During those desperate situations, what should we believe in?

Presently, as in the past, the mythical theory of material life and spiritual perception came at a time when we humans were at the end of the road of our marriages, families, children, businesses, health issues, financial problems, educations, careers or relationships of any kind. We definitely were entitled to be upset by the entire situation, and we were certainly right to complain about. But there was no reason for us to be upset with our life for what had happened because the animosity or negative attitudes could deepen the problems and wouldn't make them to disappear overnight. If we believed in changing our course or belief, we might have a better chance of getting our lives back and by resolving our problems as well.

Looking at the structure and function of desperation, it was no more than a destructive thought. It was the reflection of a thought process that builds on the foundation of mistrust, misconception, hopelessness, wrongful thinking or pursuit, obsessive behavior, negative attitudes, and denial. Sometimes it was different from a suicidal thought. In our mind, when the result is not what we anticipated, all things could mean nothing. Whether our expectation could be in some kind of simple or complicated form, it tends to be misguided or misled by the subconscious mind. Depending on the base of our reasoning, the conceptual senses could be monitored and changed to a point that even the worst thing could work for our own good. For instance, when we think that we had no hope in our situations, if we just slow down our own thoughts for a moment and listen to things around us, we might be surprised sometimes to be found there was options available only if we give them a try. Perhaps some of us might be severely sick or suffer from the end stage of a particular disease such as cancer, kidney failure, amyotrophic lateral sclerosis (ALS), heart disease, leukemia and/or major complications from any brain trauma or injuries. Indeed, we could be frightened or destitute of hope because we might be the ones who were in the critical health condition or had been told by doctors we had only a few months to live despite undergoing all the aggressive treatments and procedures. Still, we could be wise enough to let go our despair by looking for few new alternatives before we put a stop on anything. The same phenomenon could also be applied to the world of business when merging tactics and cutting cost can't save the company from going bankruptcy. The challenge was not about the lack of the cutting-edge technology but the ineffectiveness of strategy and the failure of global initiatives that eventually took away the life and spirit of entrepreneurship. Therefore, the totality of a failed mentality was to let competency and assurance be carried away by ignorance, arrogance, denial and embarrassment to a point that we might not embrace new ideas and ways for a better change to happen.

Even though some of us or some of our beloved were sick and had been told they had only few months to live, life shouldn't be that way, and no one deserved to be desperate. In general, the nature of a thing or any happenings didn't usually look the way they seemed, and sometimes we might have to buy some time until we start to see them clearing out. In the meantime, we need to start growing up and be honest to our true self. Life was about choices, and we need to courageously take up some choices that might even provide no solutions to the problem we have; however, it didn't mean the choice that we made was going to worsen the condition. Imagine if nothing was going to get our circumstance better, then it might be best for us to not try anything. But if there was some option available, we'd better take the chance because if we don't try, how should we know the impossible could turn into something possible for us; otherwise, we would not get a chance to find out what would or would not work?

Taking into the account the end stage of a particular disease or of being in a deadly coma, life could certainly wear us down. It seemed to be no different than living in the shadow of mental death, as if it was physically not lived. From some perspectives, when our body was in a state of coma or some kind of critical illness or disease, our mind in fact might somehow leave our body to a point that the latter becomes less adaptive to treatment. To some extent, we could assume our spirit might have temporarily left the corporeal body. Christian Science has shown that the human mind could rise above the physical and material senses where sickness and danger were concerned. Especially in the terrible moment of life, the human mind tends to perceive or search for spiritual being and divine consciousness rather than anything else. One reason to explain the assumption was not the prevalence of emotion that gives strong control over the physical body, but it was the spirit that God puts into our body when He first makes us from his image or likelihood. As a result, the recognition of divine healing or intervention tends to be the most effective way when science provides no real answer in comparison to the spiritual law of truth or the principled fact.

There could be no reaction to the physical science and its truth when the spirit leaves the body by falling into some kind of unknown mental world or space. By definition, a disease had no intelligence, as Mary Eddy pointed out, and disease couldn't give us a sense of reality versus delusion. What could be so imperative to the structure of the body was the psychology of fear and the breakdown of belief. It was the assumption of the mortal dream in terms of sin, sickness and death that tend to produce the adverse effect or result to the disease. Due to our perception of the negative, we could project ourselves to feel the supposed disease or any less effective pattern of healing went through the physical conditions. The intensity of anxiety could be imaginably high when the treatment still focused heavily on the type, extent and symptom instead of going against remission of sickness. In fact, mortal belief was a means of destroying the principled truth and the logical fact. But the belief that God is the only spirit ever present was more critical to the mind than the body for retrieving information and destroying all tumors, cancers, comas, pains and infections. Sometimes such belief could lead to a terrible approach if the treatment or therapy doesn't reach out to cover the unchanging result.

We should be clear that the conquest of any kind of sickness lies in the conviction of truth. There never has been any threat or dread than rejection and denial combined. To be fairly said, the mind had a strong ability to address what was lost and misunderstood by error or chances because the circumstance was not going to be over unless the mind started to ring an alarm. For instance, if you were ill, you probably know what medications you should take, what you should not eat, or how you should not act out against advice would be helpless. Though remorse could be great, it could cause you to fall into a false belief or a sense of guilt. If you were the healing practitioner, you should be aware of the fact that you can't restore the confidence and trust of patients by telling them that they could die anytime as soon as the treatment fails. If you were a psychologist or psychiatrist, you might relate the condition of fear, hypochondria and paranoia your patients had when they tell you that they felt disturbed, upset and dying from the ineffectiveness of treatments to their disease. If you were a social worker or city official, you see the safety and security of your residents being threatened by the increasing amount of crime and your neighborhoods torn down by unknown fear. You literally see the social health of your community being ripped apart and destroyed by pain and suffering. Much of the time, some of us might not see that kind of things or matters coming to our way, and so we could be hardheaded to accept the compound idea of nonsense. But for those who see what is happening and realize all matters were the images of mortal thought reproducing in the physical and ungodly ways knew that the heart could destroy any great fear. By the time the mind doesn't perceive disease, danger, pain and suffering as the byproduct of sin or sickness, then dreams and fear no longer become nightmares but instead the birth of newness in life starts to pave a new way.

In contrast, the acknowledgment and acceptance of the truth could overcome depression that stems from either sickness or personal error. Christian Science showed divine truth provides harmony to our soul and healthy remedies to our body. The mind indeed delivered the natural stimulus for the body to heal from pain, grief and suffering. It could provide a healing ingredient coming from the belief of immortal being or spiritual existence. When people let go of these beliefs in immortal being or spiritual existence, they tended to be more vulnerable to defeat, suicidal thoughts, and even death. As physicians or health scientists tend to treat disease and its pattern based on the physical ailment or material evidence, they reduce the possibility of a favorable result because limitation of matter could top off the reason or hypothesis of why a procedure or processes could be less effective. When God, the metaphysician, focuses His healing on the spiritual being instead of mental unawareness or misconception, many people could physically feel hope over fear, truth over error, and finally love over hate. And only to that extent, the mind could alleviate and recover from the lack of harmony and discordant, deranged body. With clear understanding, the mind could break off from the mortal belief and allow us to realize that not all beliefs were created equal and they should go through spiritual purification to have better result.

A universal nightmare of so-called drugs to treat all sicknesses exists. Toxicology studies report that more Americans recently died of high doses or overdoses of prescribed medications such as the anti-depressants, anti-anxiety, and narcotics compared to the sport and recreational drugs combined. It was also a good question to ask ourselves if drugs really could destroy the inflammatory process and heal the disordered function in our body. If the solution to the dislocated shoulder joint or a fractured sacrum due to a diseased pattern or injury could be managed by the administration of drugs or surgery without the interference to the mind, then the results of perception could be different because disease proves to be obtained from and contained in matter. However, if the fallacy of drugs-as-the-antidote phenomenon provides a disturbance to the brain that eventually causes the mind to be connected with or related to the disease or injury that proves to be less effective, then the assessment should focus on the intelligence of mind with the modification of matter to an extent that best fits the body. As a matter of fact, we had no rights to say that life depends on matter alone, and the ignorance of science could lead to a consequence that we might not want to have. Therefore we have no reason to reject the argument of truth that Christian or Divine Science could develop and reproduce instantaneous healing for any disease and danger without side-effect or susceptibility as that from the physical science or medicine.

Ever since Christian Science began to raise the standard of health and morals, the concept of fear should not be the impetus for death. If humans believe in death, they should know that the existence of spiritual eternity was proven since Christ overcomes hell and death to serve as the promised Deliverer in the spiritual realm. If humans perceived sin, guilt and fear as the cause of disease, they should realize the scriptures and teachings of Christ serve as the most effective treatment and the best counseling of all the tribulations we face. If repentance was the reflection of our mind's perception, we would have exceptional strength or willpower to overcome what we had hard times to believe in the changes for our finances, relationships, curses, failures, illnesses and addictions. The presence of supernatural healing occurred when God and His spirituality hear your plea for partnership in life. There was no remedy more powerful than the spiritual healing of the immortal, and there was no drug purer than the living water of a Christian faith. If all the doctors and healers focus their skills along with the practice of their spiritual belief or Christian faith, then the restoration of harmony in life and health could be turned into the absolute supremacy in term of law and science that this world could no longer claim for the shadow of dream, the ignorance of fear, and the misguide to death. If religious faith could precede the adoption of logical thinking, then the development of prescribed drugs or surgical procedures, the application of caustic and/or therapeutic agents, the attribution of alternative therapies or natural remedies, and the vitality of a healthy and harmonious life would form as a laser beam to break through the reality of imbecility and the fatality of disease thereafter.

Chapter 6: Is God real?

"If we discover a complete theory, it should in time be understandable by everyone, not just by a few scientists. Then we shall all, philosophers, scientists and just ordinary people, be able to take part in the discussion of the question of why it was that we and the universe exist. If we found the answer to that, it would be the ultimate triumph of human reason – for then we should know the mind of God." Stephen Hawking

In these days of defeat and depression, the vast majority of people suffer an identity crisis and mixed signals of principle and belief when they've had a dramatic encounter with some considerable, unknown and powerful force. This world could be messy when people attempt to use their right hand to cover up what they did without letting their left hand know. People could be frustrating enough when they hear voices speaking through their ears, but somehow they decide to let those voices slide through the other ear without knowing how those voices might play out in reality. That could be stressful enough for people pretend to not hear from their inner voices. That could even be heartbreaking when people tended to care less about the innovation, new ideas, and creativity. Some of them choose to be moved by the wasteful life of addiction, lust, corruption, narcissism or skepticism. No wonder that life could be depressing when many of us still live in the shadow of our own problems, personal agendas, and toxic beliefs. Not a thing was back to where we could believe in ourselves again.

The battle against fear and loss tends to go hand in hand in both the physical and social realms. Perhaps, some of us might wonder why we should think that way or why we should have to go that way. The fact of the matter was that in one way or another we had to engage in the fight whether we choose to accept life as it was or we need to change our course by directly facing the problem. To look into the proverbial and even controversial issues we have, I was not totally convinced by the assumption that many of us were satisfied with what we had and that even some of us don't like to settle for anything less without mentioning the time and effort we participate in the process. By nature, few of us realize that it must be hard for us to not sit on the top of our world when we do all our best possible to get there. With all the upsetting circumstances and factors happen, it could really drive us crazy but not until we found that some of our loved ones or friends were in a big mess with the abuse of drugs, sex, addictions, certain diseases, crime, financial crisis or reckless behaviors.

Our hearts could be destroyed by our affluence, could die by the lack of personal accountability and confidence, and could also be compromised when we did not know anything about what they were dealing with. There were standard protocol and acceptable way that allow us to better engage in helping others to overcome their setbacks. There was also a compromise in between that encourages us to develop good strategy and plan for any proposal that gives us an advantage to excel others. Further, there was even a "no turning back" sign in the dynamic intellectual warfare that requires us to choose the right road for our destination; otherwise, we were obligated to accept defeat in term of attacks and setbacks unless we improve the landscape of intellectual warfare and culture of the spiritual battle. Whether we fought through our problem by ourselves or with the help from other people, we should know that no rules were meant to be broken so we could turn something to our own advantages. Until then, the curse or the attitude for counter production would cut us loose so that we could top off our losing mentality to directly engage in the battle.

Perhaps one way we could overcome our problems was to follow our gut feelings. Sometimes the best thing that happened to us as human beings was to know how to make use of our common sense that allows us to reasonably express and comfortably share with nearly all others so that we can collectively perceive what a physical thing really means. When I first set my feet into this country, the "land of opportunity" and "freedom," my life as a new immigrant in this strange culture turned out to be an unpleasant experience. To some extent, it was not an easy thing to say that I was really free to do what I wanted to do. This experience was not quite so simple for me to act in a way that matters most to me than to those who happened to be closely related to me. Each of my days saw me facing either obstacles or limitations in life itself. My day became my night, and my night became my day. There were times when I really felt that my life was completely upside down and I literally couldn't remember what it meant to live in exchange for a freedom that I had no real understanding of. There were also times I could hardly know who I was and wondered if what I did really mattered anymore.

When I moved to the United States, I truly did not know what awaited me on the road ahead or what being on the road meant until reaching that point in which I found myself paying a toll. The major problem I faced was of how to get around. What happened to me as a young man in my late teens and as a new immigrant to a strange and new country was not much different from any other immigrant. About two-thirds of my day and week were spent in the long stressful labor at a restaurant or a gas station, and I had to wait for transportation or pickup out of the restaurant owners' kindness or assistance from friends. At the time, I didn't really know there was public transportation that provided direct access to my workplace.

Looking back at the time for more than two decades ago, I had to admit that life was not as beautiful and wonderful as it seemed to be when I had to trade in and to also restart my life from the bottom up as being a new immigrant to America even though my parents talk me out of it. For months and years, I begin to realize the life, which I have, was not different from driving a car with new but somehow broken engine or toxic transmission. Wear and tear could be an instant reaction to the not so good condition or unhealthy life. Even there was a time when I'm sleeping in the early hours of the day, but I happen to feel and touch the cruel reality of dream as that of the nightmare by the horror moment of the night. I become overwhelmed at the size and scale of the circumstance that limit me as a person and my ability as a young man. With the fact that I work as a clean-up crew, a dish washer, a bus boy, a waiter, a merchandise stacker and a cashier who took job that most average typical Americans were reluctant to have at the time, not mentioning the low income, unequal benefit, and unequal opportunity being known in comparison to today's culture. Whenever I see big bag of trash, the funky smell of leftovers, the heavy buggy of cup, plate, flatware sets and merchandises from working in the restaurant, the heavy stock and pile of merchandise, and the frequent cleanup from working in the gas station, I begin to cut lose my emotions to not relate my life with those elderly, semi-retired and low-skilled individuals. Day in and day out, I begin to see narrow-mindedness of mankind and the closing widow of opportunity that literally shut me out of an open space without my intention and my ability to contest it.

By not perceiving setback as an obstacle in life, I didn't see my passion to seek higher education and my commitment to make a better life as a threat or obstruction to the people whom I know. I certainly had no need to say that my willingness to continue doing my best posed a threat to the job security that other fellow Americans or any citizens would be interested in. But I also didn't single myself out whenever I found an opportunity to help improve my skills or education. In the meantime, I didn't mind going the extra mile for personal growth. I also tried to step back from my comfort zone to get a better life. As a young man and new immigrant, I welcomed the opportunity to help me better understand the value of a new culture and to further reduce my ignorance from a stressful lifestyle. As a quick learner, I accepted challenges that provided legitimate answers to why a non-quitter like me shouldn't deserve a decent chance or a second opportunity to change myself and my own conditions.

Recalling the time when my supervisors, colleagues and friends advised me of the optimal choices and promising results if I continued to move forward from my current position, they viewed diligence as a good investment tool in business that helped to get to material accomplishment or prosperity. They also view contentment as a failed policy that would not lead me anywhere other than disappointment. They gave high appraisal for my work ethic, energy and responsibility when I set my feet to work from the morning to the evening. But they seem to not quite understand or fail to admit difference between good success versus great achievement, not mentioning the expression and pursuit of dream especially why and what it means to a young fellow like me. I remember that every time I brought up my idea and plan to continue my education by cutting back my work, I was somehow recognized to be unwise. One reason for that assumption was they believe that my good investment was to seize opportunity making good money while the business world and the investment market were still promising. Another reason for that assumption was they encourage the practical thinking of hard work to bring in a stable income and prosperous life, but they had a hard time to accept or agree with the revolutionary idea of pursuing an advanced education as a mean of closing the gap of illiteracy and as a choice for building good career. Despite of the difference of viewpoint we had, they eventually honor and respect my choice.

Since I stood up for my own beliefs, I realized an excess of responsibility because I made the choice that was less recommended from my circle of friends. With the strong support of my family, I was convinced that I should not make any compromises for my beliefs or give up on my beliefs to make an exchange for the favor from other people. From the Scriptures, I found myself to be unwise to follow the wrong footstep of Esau. Because of hunger, Esau had agreed to give up his birthright in trade for a bowl of stew from Jacob (Genesis 25:29-34). The birthright of Esau had at the Biblical time was not much different from what we had for our principle, belief, or values in this post-modern day. Overcoming temptation could be indeed very hard. I believe that we could always be in anyone's interests to know clearly what was personally wanted. The sense of overcoming temptation was indeed crucial for anyone's minds to be fully aware of how and why they want without setting an exception or excuse for compromise or tradeoff despite the tradeoff could be as small as a bowl of stew. But what if the tradeoff could be something larger or more dangerous, does it mean that was all right, worthy and appropriate for us to do it than the life and all that we stood for? We respectfully agreed to disagree with each other and should be serious about focusing on the real issue and make tough decisions by weighing out the varying opinions and philosophical differences. Since I decided to stand up for my own decision, every other afternoon I had to take off a little bit early from work so that I could go school at night. Whether it was a sunny day, rainy afternoon, or chilly evening, I continued walking to school even it was an hour away from where I lived. I didn't find walking as a limitation to my eagerness for an education. I enjoyed those long and unpleasant walks so that I could learn things clearly from my own footsteps. I don't blame my friends for their sensitiveness for not supporting my stubborn decision, but on the contrary, I'm appreciated by their negative feedback that eventually triggers my interest and fires up my courage to overcome the cheesy criticism. After hard learning and diligent work for almost a year, I not only forgot about their jokes and instead grew more confident in myself of earning another chance to pursue a college education.

There were always some distractions in life. In some circumstances, distractions could be helpful to give our mind a break from anxiety. No distractions could be as bad as something that blocked you from knowing the truth. From time to time, I found that life turned out to be something that I didn't think it was. The complexity rested not in the conflict of my personality, but sometimes I tended to perceive my personality getting in the way of conflict unless I happened to change my situation. In lieu of what my friends warned me of my unprecedented college life, I recalled that I saw my college journey at the time not as a distraction or interruption of my plans, even though that upset those who knew me personally and intimately because they never thought that I should go to college.

When I first set my feet into the junior college, I had tremendous difficulty adapting myself to class and dorm life. The lifestyle of a small community or countryside town turned out to be quite different from that of the city, not to mention the expectations and traditions. In fact, I thought that I could be easier and more economical to start my college education by living in the countryside than a cosmopolitan setting. But in reality, it was slightly different and more difficult than I imagined. What really shocked me at the beginning wasn't the challenging academic courses that were not within my comprehension but instead the sense of isolation from classmates and friends that almost turned my passion off to become a valuable person who my family could be proud of and a highly educated individual who could better serve the community where I lived.

If life was meant to not only be lived in the moment but lived to its best, I guess that I had put my moments to good use. No one could truly teach me how to live my life the way it should be; I just happened to learn and figure it out myself in a slightly non-traditional and bizarre way. During the first few months of my freshman year, I was totally overwhelmed by finger-pointing, figures of speech, outrageous comments, and a liberal bias from some college professors, classmates and even good friends. I understood the existence of a double standard in how I was being treated and realized that I still should respond with courtesy and respect.

Even though I might not fully understand how the double standard played out in my education, I tried to fit into that culture so that I could get some balance in my life. As long as that double standard didn't undermine my ability to fit in, I would not be bothered to hold anyone accountable for something that didn't match my values.

To some extent, I believe that we were entitled to voice our opinions and be able to represent our own agenda. That was one of the most attractive virtues in almost every culture ever known because it revealed the character or essence of free speech. With that understanding in mind, I felt no reason to beat myself up because I might need some adjustment over time. What really frightened me during those years was the prejudice in terms of ethnicity, race and conservatism within the system. In relating to my past, I had never forgotten the first time when I was denied admission to high school during my early days as a new immigrant to the United States. I remembered in those tearful and heart-broken moments after I ran from the Department of Health Services, family and children services, Immigration and Naturalization Services to verify my document and legal status, but I still was not accepted to become a high school senior because I was slightly over 19 years old. I had nothing to dispute the system at the time and I also couldn't blame anything or anyone other than myself.

There is no rose without a thorn. There is no road without a twist or turn. What was so great about the denial from my early high school admission indeed give me an inspiration and fires up my passion to appreciate what I didn't have at the time. Because of my strong desire to learn, I grew deep from my work and tried not to take an easy approach that could draw me close to or simulate my terrible past. Certainly I would not put all of my encounters to compare that with my bad high school expectation. I truly believed my life would be devastated if I didn't hold a high school diploma. As time went on, I persisted in my own walk by accepting the fact that I just had to work a little bit harder than the average American did. I remembered from numerous occasions when I studied late at night, my father was always there to cheer me up. As far as I knew, my dad had not complained about me staying up late in study even if he still sees me by my desk around 2 or 3 a.m. while he got up for a bathroom break. Dad had not given up on me or said anything to discourage me whenever he sees me working on my study. Dad doesn't yell at me because he realizes that I'm fighting for my life in some good ways. Because of my persistence and perseverance, I put up with criticism and left behind all disappointment. I began to stand up for my beliefs with literally little to no defense for myself. I knew better than anyone that if I didn't or was reluctant to leave my past behind, I could be endangering myself with what sets in front of me.

Perhaps one of the best adjustments at that time was to keep my desire and anger down. In retrospect, I continued to believe that perseverance was a big threat to the world of freedom and the life of choices. From some perspectives, people who were naturally born and had lived a long time in the United States might not really care or have any trouble to get a degree, certificate or diploma. Some might not even give any thought about them or how they were going to make use of it. But for me, the concept of having a degree, certificate and diploma means quite different because I believe in greater opportunity and better life pacing a way from those achievements. I had never realized that my persistence in walking to adult learning center at night eventually would give me a chance to light up my dream. I had never thought of my courage to keep up with my hardships and my fight against setbacks turn out to be a big drive to fulfill my dream for college.

Fighting and continuing to fight through difficulties seemed to be a part of my life. I still recall the many hard times I encountered during my job hunt in and around the community where I attended my junior college. From a part-time job to a weekend position and even to some seasonal employment, I hadn't had any luck because Southerners seemed to be neither interested nor comfortable with anyone other than their own skin color. Certainly I do not blame them for that because I, by nature, might do the same if our situations were reversed. What I did love about those small town Southerners was their traditions that they managed to preserve. They loved to promote the charm of their Southern hospitality, both in church and social gatherings. One reason I could not find a job in that small town was because I didn't fully understand the local culture, the nature in the corporate world and its hierarchy when I dealt with the aspect of professionalism and business relationships, and therefore I failed. Time and time again, I saw greater hardship and I faced greater resistance in term of employment and business opportunity, not mentioning success.

To help pay for my living expenses, I had to drive more than 90 minutes away from my dormitory to the Atlanta area where I could get a job.

From time to time, I tried to keep my spirit up and work hard to live my American dream that I was once anticipated to have regardless of the situations I was in. I tried not to focus on the lack of free will or laziness as the excuse for hardships I encountered, and certainly I didn't intend to say I was smart enough to answer and figure out the problems that I faced. Instead, I believed in the kind of American spirit that promoted optimism about success. I also learned that the sense of creativity provides strength to control shadiness and disappointment. For some reason, I noticed that this attitude might be a little overboard because I believed in the power of dealing with problems but not in the power of conflict of personality. In those dazzling moments of living, as if walking in a daze, I learned to deal with my heartbreaking suffering by engaging in the process. During that time, I hadn't figured out how to overcome those challenges and looked at the amazement to figure out how I could rediscover myself again. Before I realized how disappointed I could be in those lonely walks, in which I happened to see my naked emotions from the vantage point of wisdom. I also found myself not being different from any college kids. There was a time when I began to get drunk and party to a point that I couldn't excuse myself to forget about my predicament, embarrassment and difficulty that I faced in my school. There also was a time when I was addicted to the workaholic lifestyle so that I could escape from a struggling and disrupted lifestyle. Some people might think that I was being a young man and college kid who could be easily tempted by the "all things were fresh and new" phenomenon. By the same token, I truly believe that I'm selfishly living for my own fresh, and I was indeed lost to a point that I had never thought of. In those thrilling periods and until then, I'm fortunate enough to rediscover myself in the shower of an unknown blessing and amazing grace that begin to lead my way. I learn to stay on my post and pull myself together even though the difficulties or tragic of life had found and tricked me, but I truly believe the Scriptures tell me that joy came in the morning (Psalm 30:5) if I could endure for the night.

When adversity hit me in the face, I tried to figure out why and where the blow came from. I recalled one of those incredibly humbling experiences happening in the middle of some late night when the cool wind breezed across the window of my dormitory in Gordon College. During the beautiful autumn of my school year, I was required to complete the standardized assessment test or Regents test before I was allowed to either transfer to other universities or to move into the study of my major. Every day of my life turned out to be a battle of not knowing what the future held despite that I knew my future was in the hands of the Almighty. During that time, I made a fool of myself because I thought nothing could stop me. As reality set in, I found my life was a nightmare in which I couldn't slow down to catch up with my studies and balance my part-time jobs. There was a time when I was extremely exhausted and dozed off during my studies.

One late night came a shocking event forever changed my life. In retrospect, I found this extraordinary incidence gave me the very chance to test my beliefs in something I didn't quite understand in the first place. Earlier in that special night, I went to bed before 11 p.m. and I had a good sleep that I hadn't enjoyed for quite a long time. Perhaps one reason for that was because I had been too busy catching up my homework assignments and studying for tests so far that I didn't pay attention to the good things around me. Another reason was because I overheard some noises below the window of my dorm room and so I woke up in the middle of late night in a staggering, drunkard manner. From the top of my bunk bed, I ran into my desk by stepping on the back of my chair and eventually found myself landing on the floor. While I was lying on the concrete floor, I saw myself bathing under a bright and silver moonlight that shined through my window. At that time, I realized I had fell and hurt myself so bad that I could hardly move. Though I was unable to move, I saw my roommate who was still deeply asleep in the opposite corner of the room. Then, before I could decide if I was just having a bad dream, I clearly heard a voice speaking to me.

"Son! Why were you accusing me?" Said the voice.

"Hello…excuse me…Who were you? Who was talking? Was somebody playing trick and being disrespectful?"

"My son! Why don't you say anything?" The strange voice continued.

"Please show yourself. You're scaring me. Are you a ghost? If you aren't…then who were you?"

"Listen to me! I was the Lord your God who you do not recognize and of whom you do not know by testimonial."

"If you really were my Lord and why haven't I seen your face for all these years?"

"It was neither whom you haven't seen nor what you haven't heard. If you knew me, you should know my way?"

"How do I know that you indeed were my Lord and you were with me all through my days?"

"Stop being fooled by the devil, his lies, and his tricks. You've been there, and you knew what it means to be there. There was never been anything really bad happened to you yet…and if it does, there was nothing to be ashamed of…For your Lord always had a plan for you."

"Why should I believe in you? I'm not so sure who you really are, but you surely know a lot about me. When you call my name, I was scared, but I knew something in me must be wrong."

"Listen to me very careful, my son, I was the Lord your God. I knew what you've been going through. There was a time when you might have me confused with some other gods. There was also a time when you even complained of having me in your life being toasted upside down. Do not put yourself in a position that you MUST do this and that. If you're going to be overwhelmed by that kind of work, then you'll be trapped in the framework of guilt, sin and condemnation that the devil twists from the legality of law in which Christ and Lord the Father give you."

"How should I know that the Law given was on my side and even if it is, how could I find things being done in the absence of victimized mentality? You know that I could be cranked up with circumstances in my own conscience and my life had bounced between my bitterness."

"You were indeed on the side of Law since you welcome change from your faith. It doesn't matter how many times you fail to deal with your problems, and even at their worst, you shouldn't let bitterness run your life because it could turn you into a selfish or unforgiving spirit. Instead, you need to directly and openly confess your negative thoughts to the Lord, get ready for God's remission, get help from Christian fellowship, and further accept his deliverance from both the purification and rectification processes."

"How could I know that I was forgiven?"

"You'll know what it was whenever you experience it again. You won't be feeling the same each time you go through it. You'll know that you were forgiven and set free because you would no longer live under the curse of slavery, condemnation, sin and defeat. You'll find new strength and encouragement somewhere all along the way."

"If life was meant to be lived well, and we were responsible for what we do as a human being, then how could I know that things were working in my favor when they weren't from the previous encounters?" I was completely confused and desperate for the solution.

"Life indeed is not built on bitterness and resentment. Sometimes Christians are disillusioned with their faith – and even you've had bad experiences or terrible relationships – but you shouldn't allow those adversaries to deny you having a new and better life. Even if you might not get the answer you wanted, that doesn't mean you don't have a good one."

The voice paused for a minute. In the meantime, I felt a strong energy coming from the bright shiny moonlight covering me, and it circled me with its radiation. I felt like I was being baptized or immersed in the spiritual presence, cleansing, or some sort of electrical therapy. I don't know how long it had been, but by the time when I came to my senses, I found myself being recharged. My body isn't in any kind of pain, and I didn't even find any soreness or broken bones.

Then, unlike before, the voice became so loud and clear that I felt as if I were being knocked off from some kind of electric shock, and then I heard him saying, "From this time and beyond, you will find healing and touch coming from your hands and to those who you happen to come in touch with because of your emptiness and eagerness to discover what was under this light. Your hands shall serve you well, and your mind shall honor God."

For years after that episode, I tried to figure out what those words really meant relative to my dreams and visions. I constantly meditated on God's words despite that I fought so hard with my inner conflict in a way similar to what Dr. Yohannan experienced in his early calling from God. For countless days and weeks, I waited patiently for my Lord to show up in my life again; as Dr. Yohannan once said, "I decided to wait upon God for His plan, both in desperation and fear." I recalled my failure to pass my Regents test a few weeks before that special voice spoke to me. I remembered the time when I was down and out to the point that I almost gave up my school, work and literally my life to avoid stress, hardship and hopelessness. Day by day, I saw the world around me as a picture of gray. I kept digging a hole of desperation, with me at the bottom of it. I felt like I needed psychiatry and therapy. There was a time when I felt like of falling so deep into the ditch of darkness, mess and defeat, I no longer could hear anything from the Lord and anyone, never mind my intention to run away from Him. But one good part was that I didn't and dared not see myself as too desperate to give up my own life. Strangely enough, after I had been baptized by the Holy Spirit that night, I cried and repented for the sin I'm committed against God by realizing His presence and blessing in my life. Since the anointing from the Holy Spirit, I found myself in a different boat, and the quarter after that I pulled myself off by passing my Regents Test and was then admitted to more prestigious and private school, Mercer University. I then realized what His words really meant. I continued to work my way up until graduating from Mercer University and became the first person in my family to earn a college degree. I realized what His promise was, for the Scriptures say, "He would lead me to the still water" (Psalm 23-2). Indeed I was in debt and afraid, and this world tended to confuse me. I had never imagined my calmness and peace during those turbulent and upbeat moments of my college years because I found no security at all. If God happened to spare His mercy on me, then I could boldly say that I might have been a spoiled brat, drug addicted or an idler. I could have ended up somewhere in the street or even worse than that.

At some point in our lives, especially when going through tough times, knowing we were worthy and why we were worthy was good and significant. But sometimes I happened to see we could be better off knowing nothing about what was working against our reasoning. To some extent, I always thought that I should have a new life and good job after college. But a good life does not necessarily mean the pursuit of happiness in terms of physical and material possessions. From time to time, I felt my life was far from being good or close to what I was expecting because I hadn't found what I wanted in those possessions. On the contrary, I felt emptiness and a feeling of missing out. I knew that there was something out there, and I had a hard time identifying what it was. Though I happened to enjoy my new job, I seemed to not find any fulfillment in it. Deep in my heart, I tried very hard to save something that I loved without knowing how to get there. There was a time when I was not so sure of what I was looking for, but by the time I held a few material achievements in my arms, I fell short to confront my fear and was shy to compare with what few of my classmates had. In other words, I somehow truly didn't know what I wanted or needed at that time because I was perplexed, shaken up and speechless.

Perhaps I indeed had nothing to save for myself until God gave me the best inspiration ever. There was a time when I tried to tear down my inspiration of how to make my life even better, even though I knew there was no easy way of doing so. I still attempted to tear it down piece by piece so that I could fully see what was inside it. But once I started my compelling thought, I'd loved to fully play it out despite the fact that I might be stressed or disheartened sometimes. As always, I didn't want to be in a business in which I shared no part in its development whether it was good or bad.

I truly found my search for graduate school ridiculously amusing. I had to admit that might be a bad karma to say I cared more about a career change than for anything else because I believed that I deserved the best for working so hard all my life up to that point. I sought professional counsel in the academic setting and ran detailed searches to land a career. I tried all alternatives that I could possibly think of. From the schools of business, dentistry, pharmacy, medicine to even law, I found myself to be not too excited or motivated because I didn't see myself as a good candidate. As I didn't have the intention, I felt no regrets over fitting myself into that areas. Honestly, I tended to carry a guilty feeling if I found myself to be incapable of getting into graduate school because deep inside my heart, I really want to follow my grandfather's footstep to become a doctor and healer, even though he practiced Chinese medicine in Southern China province, Cambodia, Laos, Vietnam and Southeast Asia. But surprisingly enough, I become so crazy in believing in the passion, mission and calling of a profession that I was once clueless and frenetic about the opportunity I received. Though my family had been against me and few of my good friends even ridiculed me in that choice, I was pleased to press on in my belief that eventually changed my life and made me into the type of person whom I am today. Before I really knew who I would be and what I would be doing, I finally learned that decision was indeed the greatest and most significant plan that God had ever placed and planted deeply in my heart. For all those years, I regretted to say that if I knew my gift, and if I figured out my profession in relating to what God told me while I fell in my dorm room at Gordon College, I would be better than whom I was. Looking back at the entire process, I truly admit I couldn't overcome that difficult and contested graduate school even though I honestly believed faith and diligence would pay off eventually, but the only reason I actually did it was because God first set His eyes on me, and He actually planned it all out for me before I knew it.

While I sought answers in my quest for life, the answer laid in my basic understanding of obedience and faith. There was nothing wrong with my conscience, principles and workmanship. I didn't think that there was anything I could lose other than time. Due to the shift in priority from a desire for something to be passionate about to the frustration of searching for a career, I finally realized my craving for the dream turned out to be similar to a feeding program, which could save a man dying from the starvation and deprivation of "all-you-can-do" manna throughout the long journey of exploration. While my situation at that time didn't necessarily change my heart and mind, I was not different from an atheist, agnostic, skeptic and Pharisee who not only didn't believe in the truth of salvation, but tended to land on a "nowhere island" to engage in a mission of accomplishing nothing while "doing business as usual." Eventually the discovery of this foolish nonsense saved me from wandering further in the wilderness of a career search and some loosen and broken promise seen from the life of friends who were Master graduates. From some perspectives, I can say I felt overwhelmed, and just like Dr. Yohannan once said, "While I stand there as in my own lost world for so long watching the golden wheat swaying in the warm breeze, I come to understand from what I look for from this world in term of psychological harvest, but this harvest can somehow turn out to be tremendously free for the taking if I understand what the Lord tells me (Mathew 9:37-8; John 4:35-38) in the first place."

In those days of ups and downs in my career as a healthcare professional, I found the expansion of hope lying beyond duty and purpose from a job, which my justification falls under the value of belief instead of educating others. This expansion of hope profoundly became a means by which I propelled myself to move forward my agenda and to get my message across to the multitudes that happened to jump up and down in the raging river of doubt and hopelessness in spite of their sickness. I had never forgotten the beginning stages of my career builder was similar to that of a game in the football field with little to none in term of team spirit or partnership. Those who love football and know how it should be played might laugh at the silly role I have. As far as I was concerned, I truly didn't know what kind of position I was in. I was not sure that I was a guard or a cornerback. If I were a quarterback or running back, surely I should throw the ball down field so my wide receivers to catch the pass and score. At least we should seek a field goal. However, in terms of rule of engagement, I was not in the mode of attack, and I also missed the strategy of defense. On a broader sense, I felt myself chasing the wind and running after something that could turn into a long-term distraction to blur my vision all along the way.

Seeing that what I was going against was mostly related to school and career, when in fact they shouldn't have been problems, was frustrating enough. I strongly believed that if I couldn't pull myself together to bridge the difference between what was done and what was needed in society, then I would need to make a major decision about my direction. Gradually, I saw my best interest was to look for what was best for my life and to all the lives closely associated with mine. A good virtue that I had learned was to stick with the values I believed. Another value was to remain low key or to go easy with what gave me hard time so I could find balance in my stressful life. Sometimes – and it might sound like a cliché – that approach kept me motivated and encouraged me to defend what I believed. On a broader scale, I was humbled and honored to say that when everything in this world began to fall apart and my world also started to shake loose, I found the faithful arms of friends kept me from drifting further.

As Albert Einstein once said, "Science without religion was lame, and religion without science was blind." Life could be a big mess in the absence of both science and religion. I felt ridiculously amused that I was being taught by those people who were ignorant of life's complexity. I also felt compelled to learn from those who viewed life to be formed in the presence of wisdom, which is known as "the juice of brain," so that they can seize opportunity to be rich or become popular. One reason for all the pretenses or excuses was that there was never been a precise wisdom or intelligence other than the One who creates the intelligence Himself. With humans, as soon as theory and creativity was applied in practically, the vision would show its imperfection and often be followed by chaos and people whining when problems arose. Indeed, we human beings were usually left without rational proof. Oftentimes, most of us could be quite spiritual for a while, but we were more prone to reject the religious proclamation because the religious truth contained no beginning while the base of spiritual sense lain in the highest law of the mind and supernatural existence itself. And from the standpoint of science, human flesh happened to have no base or intelligence, and our body could not contain the spirit or soul, if it was separated from his or her Maker. We could be a mistaken assumption that there would not be an entity or reality from the death of a fleshy body if we claim the nonexistence of any infinite spirit or immortality. We could be naive to deny a conviction for our ethical problems and spiritual inappropriateness if we live with no religious standards. We could be crazy enough to reject science or medical treatment as the therapy for our psychosocial or physiological imbalance. Certainly the final judgment after death revealed the states, phases and statutes of faith that should differ from the belief of flesh. Though human beings were still divisive in their basic understanding of their religion or confirmation of their faith, most people learned that God exists by seeing the deliverance of the abundant life and infinite love to those who put their faith in the eternal principle or truth.

In the fearful world, struggle was a must to overcome any kind of conflict. From time to time, we humans, by our nature, liked to downplay our expectations when we saw our personality was greater than the issue of our difference, and our benefits could be bigger than the problem we created. When we allowed that kind of perception get into our mind and to invalidate our actions, we not only tended to be wrestling with error in the time of confusion and frustration but instead, we tended to push it against our ill faith, doubt or nonsense belief. To a point, we might permit that perception to run against any intelligence, substance and matter. Sometimes drama of any kind was not about pain or suffering, but all about the sense of belief and commitment in doing whatever was necessary to come back from the great tribulation. Perhaps some of us could be more problematic than others while a few of us could be as much trouble and risk as others when we faced pain, sickness, sin, choice and even death. If we could be truthful with ourselves and acknowledged our limitations or shortcomings, then we surely could avoid any error or unfair accusation made to justify our belief. Oftentimes, I learned life should not be all about one's ugly past or a personal attack in the present, and literally no one needed to have bad exchange in words or the unnecessary pain to remind them of what they should believe in or how they should live.

There was a universal expression of denying the spiritual truth. There was also the mortal sense or false belief of the flesh in existence of matter. Through the material sense, many individuals were in the radar of devil and his manipulation of the truth. If science had an incentive to prove the existence of an evil spirit or curse of Satan in the life of the mortals, then it also could find the omnipresence of spirituality or spiritual power over any wicked mind. Life indeed can have two sides, like a coin. There is no absolutes in one or another unless we find the focus on religious faith could help to solve problems for which the basic reasoning from the scientific method or any of our conventional wisdom couldn't.

In a broader sense, secular humanism and materialism could pose a threat to traditional religion and lifestyles. For decades, Christianity and the evangelistic approach dominated the West and gradually spread across countries in Asia and South Africa. There were times when the natives in those countries understood and acknowledged divine love and healing coming into their lives, and they begin to reject their traditional religions of Buddhism, Hinduism, some tribal gods or some radical worshiping forms. There were cases when demons were cast away by taking authority from prayer and also when Asians were easily trapped by the grassroots of their religious lifestyle and the Gospel from Western culture, but many found their new life and joy by knowing Christ. Even there were times when humanism became the natural enemy to theistic religion such as Taoism, Maoism or Marxism just to name a few and it creates secularist movements such as nationalist, socialist and communist views to overturn divinity. Their views could be based on the scientific materialism to project individual or secular ideology to manipulate life and thought of its citizens by their political powers. Their ideas took root by denying the presence of God with the supremacy of secularism reigns high. They provide solutions in term of worldly and scientific methods to develop initiatives for health, peace, and prosperity without the intervention of any supernatural beings, not mentioning God because they themselves were once the representation of god in some forms. All these form into a culture which the concept of individual drives, desires, and beliefs was under the attack of the flesh because the pop culture was to promote the ideas of anti-Christian and the notion of rejecting God so that no alternative could be given to the desperate and besides, millions of eyes were blind from destructive cults.

In one form or another, the notion of individualism arising from the secular point of view could be a "no-brainer" approach. Despite the fact that human mind could be well-pleased by their achievements in term of successful exploration of the underworld of ocean, the remote area of jungle, and the darkest areas of the earth, this knowledge is far from complete in comparison to the intelligence of God. Because of a competitive nature and bondage to sin, humans tend to be relatively remote from God. One reason for that was because a long-term or genuine relationship requires the sense of humility and commitment to willingly serve something larger than one's own will. Another reason was because we were obligated to admit Christ as our Savior and to willingly give up our attitudes for sin as a new ransom for our transgression so that a new blood of forgiveness and transformation could form. Only in that fashion could revivals of the individual or traditional religions be manifested. By the same token, many Christian believers might find hostility and intimidation of some kind when they let go of their favorite idol or deity and when they attempt to share their faith. There never is a time more difficult than when someone experiences resistance during the circumstances he or she faces. For most of the time, the average person could see a light coming out of their desperate conditions from mysterious or unknown beings to face their fear, insecurity, doubt or troubles. For the least of the time, most people could relate their triumph over a deadly experience with the connection of a religious faith when they see an end in their own ability to break off from personal passion or search for their purpose in life. Quite a few actually believe in beating the odds with logical reason to reach their goals or add values to other people's life. Therefore, humans saw nothing new in the challenges they face except the notion of when and what could be turned around to make a way for hope. Once they pass the levels of their self-imposed limits, they will go forward to deal with their roadblocks or setback.

Human perception always can trick the mind where religion and beliefs were concerned. The trick, whether processed psychologically or perceived by the mind, could be horrendous if it was accompanied by an evil spirit. Oftentimes, we could see this kind of wicked or vicious game lead to destructive results. Once this wickedness teams up with the illusion of material sense, it often turned out to be no different than hammering nails in our coffin because it cripples our mindsets, weakens our energies, and enhances our cognitive disability. One big problem we then face is an increased likelihood of being tempted by the devil. A second problem was because our intentions tended to be driven by a powerful ego or superego, and those intentions could lead to a strong tendency to do things in our own way and are manifested in the sense of pride or overconfidence instead of a commitment to servanthood or sacrifice for humility. A third problem was we were less likely to use some unconventional way to enhance value or meaning of life. We can forget our conservative values and allow a different sets of ideas or issues to get in our way. For that very reason, secular humanism stands in the way of progress, as that kind of mentality tends to result in conflict. Sometimes this kind of secularism causes people to embrace human reason or philosophy and reject religious faith or the presence of God.

Indeed, there was a difference in the story for those who choose to live by their decisions and for those who take no responsibility for their own decisions. That could be quite compelling to see what people could be up against their agendas and beliefs before they started to blame other people or some obstacle that they ran against. Certainly there was never been any cut and dry process other than the redirection of our ignorance to focus on small details and to restart the process. There should not be a reward for the risk that people took unless our world was totally black and white with transparency in its business transaction. Oftentimes, we tend to be immune or infected by the subconscious "blame game" that played trick in our conscience and belief. Whether we choose to admit the issue of arrogance, pride and selfishness within our problems or not, we had a hard time honestly answering and directly focusing on the problem. That was the reason why I believe that we create a culture that indirectly rejects or condemns wrongdoings before they get out of control. Due to our reluctance and denial to be corrected by mistakes, we turn ourselves over to the hands of evil who eventually plays trick on matter. Depending on the nature and condition of the error, our affluence invited ruin. Gradually, it turns into a form of sin, guilt and transgression that goes along with lies and abuse. Due to our inability to capture the sense of correctness from the beginning, we were not any different from someone who slept on the roadsides or went hungry. This kind of emotional breakdown and intellectual desperation reflected the culture and attitude of the lost world that could be directly tied to the death of spiritual beliefs.

Whenever remembering a time that we were intimidated by the threat of hardships or failures that were impossible for us to overcome, we felt defeated and came to live in the shadow of darkness. Indeed, each of us faces the mountain of sickness, debt, financial crisis, depression, strife, relationship issue, and addictions of some kinds during every moment of our life. There was no doubt that we could break down when standing in front of the obstacle and the unknown. That so many of us would complain when facing difficulties was natural. Yet, some of us would speak or point to the mountain of our troubles without knowing how ineffective that could be without a plan to execute. To some extent, though the mountain of our problems could be impossible to move, but that doesn't mean we had to keep speaking to and about it without thinking or acting in a manner to help move it out of our way; otherwise, we are not different from some loser who carried suicidal thoughts.

There can be no change or improvement in our situation if we keep the same attitude of being unproductive. From the parable of David and Goliath, we see that nothing happens and changes when our faith is hijacked. The reason David, who was chosen for the mission, could defeat Goliath the Giant was because he knew what needed to be said to his adversary and when he needed to pray to God. David didn't let his obstacle stand between himself and God. He also didn't fear or back down from what the rest of the world was telling him about the impossibility of defeating Goliath. He put God and His promise before man and then carried out his assignment. Because of his unbeatable wisdom and fearless attitude, David overcomes unexpected hardships and successfully accomplishes his mission (I Samuel 17:1-58).

We'll always find that God will fight for us and with us if we lay our problems at His feet. Oftentimes, we tend to be in the flight-or-fight mode and our mentality was also put on autopilot when the storms of problems hit us. When people in Israel cover in fear facing the threat of the Giant Goliath from Philistine, David confronts the discouraging insults and fearful threats from his enemy by running straight to the battle in obedience to his Father's instructions. Because of his firm and unshaken belief in God's promise, David not only proves that he knew God historically, theologically, and experimentally, but he also demonstrates that he was a man after God's heart (Psalm 119). By acknowledging the kind of situation he had and the source of strength he gets, David realizes that fear was a physically and intellectually destructive weakness and it won't help him to defeat his enemy since he throws himself into the battle. David also sees fear as a lack of faith and a disobedience to the command God had given to his people (Deuteronomy 1:21; 31:8) but in spite of the danger he faces, he was so excited to know that he could play a significant part in making a difference that life had offered him at the time.

From the standpoint of a Christian or spiritual believers, does it mean the favor of God happens every time when we speak to our mountain of problem? Given the fact that many of us, Christians, experience storms constantly despite following Christ's footsteps, does it mean the miracles of God happen every time when pray? "Not necessary" and "absolutely not" would be the answer. But the alternative and truth were that whenever storm and mountain set in our life, they allow God to intervene in the process and to work in our advantage. Indeed there was a time for us, and especially Christians, to pray for whatsoever we face and there was also a time for us to speak through the mountain and to therefore command the problem. No matter how big the obstacle was and how frustrated we could be with our circumstance, we need to maintain our faith by talking straight to the obstacle or difficulties with our God-given intelligence. If we don't keep trying, there was always another mountain on the top of mountain that wants to knock us down and to keep us out from its reach. It was a part of us that does let it go without making another move no matter what it might be. Finally, it was always one of those restless climbs that really count and make all the difference.

People of faith need to speak with the mighty power of the Son of God when facing a mountain to climb. We need to pray persistently, wait patiently, and listen carefully before we complain about how big or horrible the obstacle is. Indeed, nothing happens to our situation until God speaks. But as soon as He does, there would be no legal authority or any power of this world that could block us to get through the unseen realm. God's supernatural could reveal and would happen anytime we declared God's favor over the mountain by demanding and commanding them to be moved out of our way, and so they would do accordingly. With God's grace and favor on our side, we could overcome all odds against us. With a mountain-moving faith, we could narrow and close the gap of impossibilities that allowed us to reach the unreached and to thus change the nightmare or harsh reality into a beautiful dream that works on our behalf.

Indeed, the reality of contradictory senses and the fear of mortal thought can't be eliminated overnight. One great truth in the science of being was the reinforcement of faith, and it shouldn't be treated as the tentative psychic for any moral or spiritual decay. Throughout the Scriptures, one could see that Moses led his people to not only worship God in spirit, but he also drew a blueprint of faith for them to follow the omnipotent supremacy. David, on the other hand, attested his faith by uplifting the law of Sinai and by honoring the tradition of burned sacrifice when God answered his prayer requests. Just like the previous two, Joseph overcomes his anguish and affliction by surrendering his faith to the completion of God's work. Due to Joseph's tentative fortitude, he not only could save his people from the drought, but he could also save the life of millions who happen to be untouchable or unreachable. This was due to the initiative of personal faith and confidence that eventually saved us from self-deception, sin, anxiety and anger.

No one should live a spiritual life without considering its relationship to the physical life. At some point in our lives, we experienced the difficulty of getting what we want from living in flesh. The problem of living in flesh was that it requires us to continue providing the body with food, drink, clothes, sleep and work to meet our basic needs. But it also required us to supply the body with dreams, desires, emotions and feelings. True Christians, who believed and understood the death of Jesus as both the perfect atonement for their sin and complete forgiveness for their transgressions, realized that they no longer lived in blasphemy or suffered the curse that this world induced once they surrender their life to Christ.

Born-again Christians, who realized the justification and purification process could be done by the grace of God, also realized that they not only should rejoice in their sufferings from the sinful world, but they also should rejoice in the abundant blessings from the Almighty God.

To live a spiritual life requires an extraordinary and comprehensive sacrifice. Throughout the Old and New Testaments, one should find the demand for all Christ's followers was to fully and completely carry his Cross. Genuine Christians need to give up their sinful desires of the heart, the lust for beauty, the love for sexual impurity, the curse of vengeance, the worship of idols or foreign gods, the indecent acts of homosexuality, and the depraved wickedness of pride, deceit, malice, arrogance, greed, jealousy and hatred. Perhaps one big challenge to all Christians was not to make an excuse or to pass judgment on someone for what was not right. Another indispensable challenge was to never show contempt for the poor, jealousy of the wealthy, intolerance of the less fortunate, and disapproval of the condemned. There was no reason for anyone to fight over nothingness, and there was no incentive for anyone to not live their physical life without the guidance and leadership from the anointing. What separates the life of substantial possession from the spiritual one was allowance, provision and acknowledgment with little to no demand of the Lord.

Perhaps some of us were living a very strong spiritual life on Sunday but leading a physical life with a poor spirit for the rest of week. So, how should we find comfort in this imbalance? To some extent, to lead a spiritual life requires the sacrifice of a physical life. If you believe that God completely owns your life, then you should surrender your life and put all your possessions – including but not limited to your heart, soul, thought, time, effort, talents and even money – to God. If you realized or acknowledged the genuine relationship coming from the sense of commitment, then you should honor the principle of God by obeying his commandments. To get the blessings, we were obligated to follow the commandments or catch up with our commitment so that God would give us the life overflowing with milk and honey as that from the Promised Land. To some extent, it was unlikely that we could be blessed with everything coming from His will, desire and love.

On the other hand, to live a spiritual life with sufficient blessing requires the same hard effort in our physical lives. This blessing doesn't come handily if we don't have the courage for living the kind of life that few of us can imagine. First and foremost, we need to be mature enough to take responsibility for anything that comes our way. This requires our full and complete attention toward what had been done and how it had been done without questioning why had been done the way it is. For instance, a lot of us might be very anxious, worry and even freak out when we sit before a job interview, give a public speech, or take a school test. Many of us might wonder what we were going to do in addition to what we had prepared. By the time we were in the process, we still believed that our preparations seemed to be insufficient, and even after we finished, we tended to feel that we give our best until we've seen the result. Secondly, we need to be up close to accept anything that would be unexpected. This required our intrepid and audacity to break off any destructive relationships. For instance, many of us were having a hard time showing our kids how to move on to the right track, to help our loved ones to overcome their addictions and illnesses, and to figure out a way of how to be prosperous from our work or businesses. We jump from one side of the line to the other to catch up with what seemed to work and to cut back what doesn't work. Days go by without knowing that we might be stepping out of line. By the time we figure out how messy the situation is, we probably could tell ourselves we'd be better off by leaving them the way they were than to attempt changing them into something that was not going to work. Third, we need to spend valuable time overcoming social barriers from our lengthy or lousy preparations. This requires our commitment to share a similar heritage beyond the culture, languages, customs and lifestyles other than our own. For instance, we hear or give a sermon for every Sunday and Wednesday to people in church. We share with people about the gospels and blessings from God and teach them how to love one another as Jesus loves us because the Scriptures tell us that God would provide a way for his children when we faithfully follow his commandments. As soon as we were not in the church or house of worship, we see our lives to be no way near what we preach or hear. We then were not only disappointed or angry, but we tended to break down because we somehow felt that we were neither wealthy and successful nor happier and blessed than those who didn't know about God.

Yet, we can be wrong when we put up with what this world told us and doubted what God does for us. In general, we had to pay close attention to what was happening in and around our lives, especially when we had to make some big decision. We could be foolish enough to think that we had nothing to lose if we enjoyed living by our flesh on the days we were not in church. We might be insane and sinful to think of living a life we plan without considering how God and religion could play out in it. If we think we actually had a better life by leaving God out of the picture while we're not in the church, then we'd better hope that the rest of our life would stay the same; otherwise, we would face problems greater and harder than we could imagine. If we happened to feel ashamed of the condition of our physical life and even to a point that we were still poorer and less fortunate than our church fellows, and nothing was better than our peers or colleagues who were not, we should realize that we indeed were under the grace of God and were living under his blessing. Imagine if God happened to give us more than we could earn – we might be too wealthy and too successful that we could no longer serve, testify and honor Him.

No one experiences anything more or worse than it already has been. We all have our own problems, and in one way or another, the problems we face would not go away instantly. Oftentimes I believe that if we human beings could see what was coming, we would not have our hands and thoughts all over the place. And if we believe in or knew what was coming in our way, we would not confuse ourselves with what other people were doing in simulating our situations. One big difference that helped to hopefully separate us from others was the nature, condition and attitude that we had regarding the problems we faced. Perhaps some of us might think how could you say something you had no idea about? How could you know that was nothing if you haven't experienced this and that? Assuming some of us were having a difficult time communicating with our kids, parents, spouses or loved ones, certainly we would not start the conversation by commenting on the sensitive issue of parenting or any relationship problems especially when we deny or fail to set our tone in a proactive way. One disappointment was to see people sitting on the sideline or on the defensive and they've forgotten that they still were a part of the solutions. Imagine that many of us were having a difficult time with finances and employment. The control of spending not only became a crucial element in every household, but it also became a factor in corporate hiring. One legitimate answer or expectation that most people want to have was how to get or create a job so that they could move on with their life. Assuming that a few of us were having problems with our health, struggling with addictions, drugs, cancers, diabetes, depression, obesity and infertility. We held on to our grievances and sufferings that spare us no time for any second thought. How could we not react if some people told us that we were not trying hard enough? If we believed to be logically correct what other people told us, then we could be even harder on ourselves for what we think as right in the beginning. But if we believe in what other people tell us to be principally incorrect, then we might torture ourselves from a bottomless pit of nothing into a deep water of something that we might have no true answer for what it could become. In other words, we could create larger problems if we don't clean up our baggage before those problems turn into bigger messes.

In almost every culture, there were two kinds of human beings when dealing with the substance, life and intelligence of man: those who choose to love and those who choose not to love. These two approaches were the expression of perception, demonstration of principle, and a description of interpersonal affection. When people were not loved, they tended to feel fear, anxiety, anger and insecurity, and they tended to behave bizarrely, egotistically and with indifference, and suffered from a discordance with God. Oftentimes, people tended to speak of the value of love but few really took it into their hearts and wondered how they could reach beyond the boundary of the material world. To the material world, any sense of unreal could be a threat to intuition, faith, performance and reality. If the value of love made no sense to the conceptual mind and if no love were physically expressed, then joy was an air bubble to true happiness, and hope was just lip service to the sense of truth.

What does love really mean in terms of matter? How does love relate to the substance, life, and performance? Indeed, love was the expression of yearning, care and concern. It was the affection from the inner heart and the promotion from any transitory thoughts without looking for anything in return. Imagine that many of us tried to draw our own expectation and agenda on what or how love should function on a regular basis. At some point of time, we realize that love was a means for sympathy to the sick, empathy to the less fortunate, and assistance to the needed instead to be an end for them. Almost across every continents and ages, love provides the possibility to break through barriers of communications, differences in cultures, and setbacks in race, gender and religion. More or less, love should be the standard for any human spirit to create the common ground that allows the majority of people to work together for common goods.

There was no guarantee of any kind of happy ending in any relationships or of any promising result when we stood up for what was right. From time to time, the cry of heart and the moaning for help could be more serious than the mission of any new exploration. They could be as important as the humanitarian aid for nonprofits and the establishment for any spiritual or religious revival in our time. Response to the lost souls continues to be the highest privilege any Christians could do to follow Christ's footsteps. Response to the poor and the needed continues to be the greatest mission so far any human beings could do to enhance the well-beings of our world. Taking good care of our loved ones continues to be the greatest responsibility any individuals could do to evolve in our human history and modern civilization. But none of these could really matter that much not until we found them to be the purpose and answer for something bigger than life itself.

Recalling the time when my life seemed doomed by the imbalance between my struggling business and my ailing father, I now see darkness and tragedy to be a great threat, as life dragged me away from my faith and belief. Many times, I found myself walking barefoot and dressed poorly – even going rogue by my standard – in my principles and my awareness. I had never been more lost and desperate in my life than at that time because I was almost shaken loose by something that attacked me, something with no form, no shape, and no boundary. Before I'm going to melt in front of the iron furnace of evil, I had to hold on to what I get without wondering how to stop the bleeding at any point. In those chilly walks of more than a year of continual struggle and trial and error, I finally brought my business up from a low-key door salesperson to the event speaker or health promoter. I found my passion again and enjoyment in what I do each day because I believe the road to my financial recovery or prosperity could be long, tough, but worthy in term of health restoration.

Norman Vincent Peale once stated and as I quoted that one of the greatest moments in anybody's growth or developing experience was when he no longer tried to hide from himself but determined to get acquainted with himself as he really is. All of us have had goals we wanted to achieve. But none of us would have it all figured out until we chose to step away from our ego and unless we decided to become who we really are. For me, that kind of active engagement turned out to be the awesome moments that helped me to rebuild my character and rebuild my confidence in overcoming excuses arising from my previous employment and academic training. Before I thought that everything in my life was going to be all right, I found that my problems were the representation of intimidation, temptation and mistrust from the devil's curses because God the Almighty had not and would not give us the spirit of fear, but of power and of love and of sound mind (II Timothy 1:7) so that we could be ready to overcome any materialistic causes and mortal beings.

I had no love for troublemaking. I might indeed be busted by the triad of error, bondage and sickness. I truly did not understand how I got them off. I believe in accountability and I understand what needs to be done in defeating my darkness. The definition and choice were clear for those who wish to enjoy in the richly furnished mansions and luxuries of life without taking on the tough challenges, and certainly they might not move away from their material view or secular world view. For those who experience the hostile challenge and daunting drama of this life can find enormous joy to build their confidence, trust and passion in their businesses and religions from the freedom, liberty and choice given by the Creator and our country. People should know that this life was given for all souls with a dream of creativity, a taking of opportunity, and a mind of God's fearfulness and obedience regardless of what our status can be.

Despite of political and philosophical differences in our time, criteria indeed were changed in the base of our perception of life. Criteria could be defined as sets of standardized or measurable goals from a working process. Pope John Paul II once claimed that "everyone who got where he is had to begin where he was." Every one of us had a past and none of us should be hindered or bothered by it. In fact, we should set our goals for every simple task or every daily encounter. The problem of our time was seen in the issues of equality, religions and race. All of us have a responsibility to step out of our own comfort zone and are encouraged to do what was right for our community. Just like a family, all of us directly or indirectly were affected by what was going wrong inside. Perhaps one of the most honest and truthful questions we needed to ask ourselves should be the level of our commitment and the degree of our priority. Instead of isolating ourselves or squeezing others out of the equation, we shouldn't blame anyone for their different philosophical views. With resources available and opportunities equal, one of the ideas or problems circulating our minds seemed to stumble at where we came from. Perhaps, few of us still had a tough time to project ourselves outside our own box, and some of us even forget or fail to learn about where we were. If we truly don't know where we are, I am not so sure that we would know where we're heading without overstepping anybody's line or doing all the possible things from what we have to hopefully get to where we are.

During the past 18 months while I was stuck in my hardships and dilemmas, I learned quite a few things that not so many people expected to have. In those vital moments of survival, I truly acknowledged that the stronger my fear, the harder I fight, the deeper I might sink and eventually the smarter I would become. With a constant spark of faith and confidence, I tried to live my life without compromising my principles too much and also tried to follow through on my intentions even when times were tough. At the end of day, I was hopeful to see those valuable lessons could provide and remind me of the sanity to not run around telling others of the mistakes or afflictions because they could add up to more than I could possibly handle. In those days, I could truly tell people tens and hundreds of stories that could relate to my endless search for wisdom and accountability in a world of hopelessness. I lose counts in how many times and trips to doctor's offices and hospitals became a routine and a necessity when my dad battled for his urinary incontinence, colicky flank pain, unstoppable convulsive hiccups, breathing distress, inconclusive tachycardia, and baseline hypotension, not mentioning the monthly follow-ups and routine screenings.

Without a doubt, pain and sickness were a part of life and seeking the appropriate treatment was the priority. Without composure, experience and knowledge, our life could easily turn out to be worse and more chaotic than we can imagine. In those restless days and nights, my family and I were fortunate to put our life back into a circle and pull them out piece by piece because God had his special way to show us what they tended to be. Sometimes I didn't quite understand what His message was for me, but I was thrilled to see that God always sends the right person for the right job and at the right time so that I could easily go with His flow. In those disturbing relationships between career and business development, I also realized the basics of need and care in the formation of solid trust. By living out the truth that I proclaimed it to be, I began to see honest appraisal and acceptance from patients, friends, prospects and even strangers. Perhaps, those were just the act of mercy from the Lord. Nonetheless, I become submissive to God because his way was always the highway and he was the only God who could straighten out anything just like the way he makes them.

In those moments of ups and downs, I learned quite a few lessons that I'll forever be grateful for. I came to my senses about how to properly take care of others without burning myself out, how to patiently wait for result without knowing what it could be, how to speak what shouldn't be meant at the time, why to do things in a certain way even though it could be silly or ridiculous but was the right thing to do, and finally how to appropriately keep my mouth shut at due time. During those moments of emotional roller coaster, my family and I ran from something into nothing because of the invisible hands of touch and healing came from the Almighty God. I remember clearly that Christ the Lord had never allowed Satan to get into our throats without giving us a time to breathe the air of his mercy. Every time we breathed and recharged ourselves, we found God looking out for us. His good stewardship stands at the consciousness of the perishing and despairing hearts waiting to receive his wounded and lost children. No matter how compelling and costly my situations could be, I felt that God was with me all those days to help me sail through the impossible storm that my financial and intellectual life didn't allow me to. I felt like being trapped in those Halloween-like imprisonments of mentality, but somehow I found a light of inspiration, intuition, and energy from the supernatural. It left me no time for argument and no time for second guesses. As I caught up with his words, I vividly was redirected by His supernatural wisdom to land a career and an unconventional practice in human health.

For the past 36 months after dad came home, I'd found what was once funny and worry-free in my life no longer was there. I had nothing to give but decided to give it freely. Somehow I agreed to trade them for compassion and enthusiasm. For more than a decade from my undergraduate, I've gone from someone who was unheard of to be someone who could have a reference to. I was glad to change from a "nobody" to be "somebody" whom other people can rely on. I used to stand up for education and career, but now I love to go beyond them in search of my purpose in life. I even willingly go behind what I love because I know what I want in life and how much it means to me to have them. Whenever I looked back at it, I truly believed what I did is really mattered for now. Never being a quitter, I never found myself having a good reason to give up on anything, small or large. I believe my best engagement to the challenge was the proactive performance without thinking about the worst result possible other than the absence of my involvement. I believe that anyone could be unwise to give up their freedom-loving spirit and their dreamer-dreaming vision, not mentioning the distinct character and fearless attitude in reminder of life could be ended in one way or another, but the task shouldn't.

Life indeed was hard. At some point, we might see the environment we were in or people in it could be bad for us. If we happen to be clueless about where we are going, every road can lead us there. Friends might have tried to knock us down. The negatives might try to run over us. Their opinions might try to drown us. Just like all of us, we're got to decide what we do and we need to do unto whom we love. We won't question for the ones whom we love and for the things that we care about. I truly convince that there was something about attitude and this kind of attitude, especially the positive one, does make a big difference in everything we do. When life was hard as it could be, I learned to believe in myself and to not give up for any reason. I also decided to surround myself with people who won't let me down. Gradually, I found my own rhythm to get my life back into my game. Up to this date, I firmly believe that if we don't believe in what we do, then we'll have tough time to convince ourselves or allow others to put their trust in us. If we're not going to win from what we do, then the rest could and would be history. If it happens to be history, then everything could happen and if it happens to be a bad one, it could be a little bit too late unless we could afford to get it started all over again.

We can't keep filling up the barrels if they aren't empty. We have to know our focus should not be on how and why we should put up with something that shouldn't be there; instead, the question should focus on what kind of thing or matter that needed to put together. If there was no incentive for its existence, then we shouldn't promote any ridiculous shielding for error and excuse that could be regretful or unhelpful for future development. From a broader sense, life was and would always be indifferent about matter, and we should disrobe our ignorance from moral deception. We should not be too open or aggravated by a glamour of life that bares no fruits for our intellectual and spiritual growths. We should be ashamed of our actions if they violate our conscience because the senseless matter or the erring mortal mind could be no different from someone who's overdosed on drugs. There would be no change in reality because error could contradict or mislead for the truth. We can't resolve our problems unless we start to behave differently. We can't change what other people think about us unless we help them to find the right solution to their problem. But we could change the outcome of situation if we do the right thing, speak the correct voice, stand on the right issue, and make the good move. It was a fundamental difference in terms of doing nothing by holding people back versus doing the right thing to pass it on. Life would not move very far if we always put ourselves on guard. We should welcome the age of problem-solving skills, encourage any endeavor that doesn't promote narcissism but promotes the entrepreneurship. I believe the call of our life is for filling anything where there was a need to make an impact to somebody's life. I happen to see the call for unity is to offer greatness or commonality for all not until there was no space or chance available for anyone to do so.

Chapter 7: Life was full of surprises...

For my thoughts were not your thoughts, neither were your ways my ways, saith the Lord. For as the heavens were higher than the earth, so were my ways higher than your ways, and my thoughts than your thoughts (Isaiah 55:8-9).

Living in the 21ˢᵗ century, we may find ourselves getting so busy with our personal lives that we were not even aware of at the time we're always filling up every of our spare moment with activity. We could be running on a road, working out in a gym, or even preparing some wonderful meal, yet we don't seem to know why we're doing these things and who were we doing these things for. Time and time again, we run here and there, yet did we know where we were heading? We found ourselves working hard 24/7 to move ahead in life, yet were we doing these so to reach the summit of success or to set aside personal losses? On the day that we don't work, we happen to take our kids for their extra-curricular activities or take a friend to see doctor, yet are we feeling fulfilled from being over-scheduled, tired or stressed out? With so much either unclear or escaping our understanding, was it any wonder that we were no longer listened to our inner voice that rested within our mind's heart?

There was nothing so special about our ordinary life because we live in a culture that encourages the little extra step to form extraordinary experience. While we were in school, we were taught that we would enjoy many benefits if we studied hard. For countless days and nights, we studied really hard, we recited and memorized all details with little to no rest, and we even picked our brains out with little to no complaint because we believed the great promises and treasures hidden from learning. We might be afraid that we could no longer be the best students, classmates or performers among our family and friends. There were times that we even constantly reminded ourselves to read and study more so that we would not fall behind. We turned ourselves into some kind of competition because we don't want to be called the average or C-kid. Deep down in our heart, I was not so sure that we've ever realized the hardest thing to overcome in study was not about the digest of information but rather, the process of useful information after each test or exam.

There was nothing incomprehensible in life. While we were at our jobs, we were told that there were rewards or good compensation if we worked hard. From time to time, we worked our sweat off to ensure a procedure was carried out efficiently. We tried not to go overboard when facing difficulties. We tried not to lose control when dealing with our problems. We tried not to lose sight of big problem lying ahead of us. We tended to forget the little details putting in front of us. We put up with all the distress and under duress when our boss or supervisors push us to cover extra shift. We tried not to cut corner when assignments were timely restricted. We turned ourselves over to the physical battle because we didn't want to see our hard work turning into nothing. But deep down inside us, we knew better than anyone that if we ourselves don't work hard, we certainly would not get the result we expected.

There was nothing ever seen before. Being grown-ups could be fun, but it also could be quite confusing sometimes. In these post-modern days, not a lot of grown-ups know what they really want. Especially in this technology-driven age, many of us were driven by accessibility and portability from laptops, iPhones, iPads, tablets, text messaging, Wechat and Skype instead of face-to-face communication. In the United States alone, every day we are always in a hurry due to our culture and tradition. We like everything to be instant. We take instant coffee. We eat microwaved food. We take pride in drive-thru for almost anything and that includes fast foods, banking, or online shopping. We use more paper cups, disposed plastic containers or bags than one-third of the world population combined. We consume more tons of processed foods than the manufacturers of all developing countries combined. We reproduce more overweight or obese people than other industrialized countries had. We live a more highly stressed lifestyle than other industrialized countries. We face more challenging issues in term of race, homosexuality, equality, religious belief, and political difference than what we could imagine.

There was nothing more insulting to our intelligence than the one creates us. Indeed, we all have to-do-lists in our calendar. Some of those lists prioritize over worldly things while others were repetitive and unaccomplished years after years. Some people develop their to-do-lists as a hobby while others make them as a habit. Regardless of what we do with our to-do-lists, we somehow found that for some reason we actually had a hard time to complete them. One reason for not completing our to-do-lists was because most of us were driven away by frustration, discouragement, lack of motivation, or no plan for success. We also could be easily distracted by lack of result, loss of support, a fear of the unknown and worry.

As we grow older, we always carry in us something that we are scared of. Many of us find that we no longer can swim more than 10 laps without getting leg cramps, walk more than a mile without suffering exhaustion, dance more than three hours without having ankle pain, and swing more than nine holes without having wrist and joint pains. Some of us felt that we no longer could sleep in late as we are used to be, drink as heavily as we want, and eat more spicy foods as we like. And even more of us realize that we no longer could climb to higher places, work longer hours, and yet we took care of our kids or grandkids more often than we're used to be. We tended to take more time and energy to complete similar tasks or assignments than when we were younger. But deep down in our hearts, we knew better than anyone that we remained hopeful as long as we held on to our beliefs.

There was nothing more complex and complicated than life. Oftentimes, we might think that we planned well for things we do. But as long as we go step by step following our plan, we find it might not always be ideal. That included but was not limited to what we could see or touch from what we battle in this physical world but also to the spiritual realm. Certainly not a lot of things could be as simple as what they seemed, but we can't think that all things were alike. For instance, when we looked at our loved ones, we might see all of their good qualities. When we bought a product, we tended to look for better quality, good price or product review. When we ate, we tended to pick the tasty foods or at least the authentic styles that satisfy our taste buds. When we befriended others, we tended to choose the ones closest to our type, class or style. When we cared for our loved ones, we tended to provide them with the best care we had. But had we ever thought that we couldn't keep taking care of people and matters as we always had or wanted, at least to some extent, we couldn't continue to live for others alone because if we kept making other people happy or tend satisfying everybody, we could eventually please no one.

Life was ever-changing. From the Stone Age to this era of modern technology, many uncertainties existed concerning the association between perceptual senses and emotions. In many studies, scientists and sociologists strive for a balance between feeling independent and living for a purpose. Emotionally, no one could say life was easy, especially when they stumbled or fell, eyes opened or closed, rich or poor, sick or well. Practically speaking, we all learn that we were actually experiencing many of the same feelings – fear, anxiety, anger, frustration, stress, loss and distortion. We were constantly reacting on what we like or dislike, what we do right or wrong, how we handle our past, and why we love doing things that sometimes we could be clueless about.

Looking back at the past few years, I found God's footprints all over me and to those who came to associate with me. Ever since my dad had survived from stroke or TIA six years ago, I gradually saw the reflection of God's love and protection. I also saw that my dad's cup overflowed with God's grace. Many times I tried to figure out what that means to live beyond the culturally and traditionally accepted ways. I began to realize the culture, customs, lifestyle and discipline from spiritual peace and biblical sin. I intend to carry out commandments since my early inception and covenant with the Lord. I no longer cry out from my heart when face tribulation, affliction, pain and injury. When I look at my dad since his bedridden status, I found that I was truly blessed to hold his hands every day, and I also happened to realize how precious and valuable life could be with him around all these days. Though daddy was able to move around every now and then, but the ways he speaks and talks indeed show the presence of his heart and soul where family was all about. Every time I stood by my dad's side, I saw his passion and love remain steadfast and consistent in the belief that home was still the finest place for one to come back to, to stay connected with, and to give back to.

That was not surprised to learn we were cautious about engaging in the pivotal point of my dad's life. We could be warm and fuzzy about what really means to be surviving especially when we see what we do tends to be a part of processes that happen to be greater than the issue of ownership. This was true for my dad during the aftermath of series of severe infections that nearly took his life not just once but more than twice, as he struggled to recover from the physical challenges of his neurological and physiological limitations.

One day while I was at work, I received a message from my sister saying my dad was rushing to the local hospital because dad had been in persistent abdominal pain with constant nausea and vomiting for the past few hours. By the time I get to the hospital, I found dad had been scheduled for a stay because he was diagnosed with gallstones. I stared at the ceiling of the emergency room where I seem to see the reflection of my shadiness along with my loathed words from his previous hospitalization. I had a difficult time slowing my pounding heart when I tried to control my feelings of shock, worry, fear and frustration.

By the late evening, my dad was moved into a room where he was resting and waiting to be seen by other physician staff and specialist. Looking at his appearance, I tried to convince myself that he was going to be all right. I happened to realize that my family and I had been down this road few times for the last few years and we lived through so many pain and tribulation together. We sang, spoke, laughed and cried together to the point where we forgot the time was flying under our feet. We couldn't change what had been a part of our past nor could we see what was awaiting us in the future. Our hearts had been broken by torment and our emotions were ripped apart by sicknesses. We had been torn apart by pain and struck down by despair. We saw that death should not be measured by the sense of giving up a life or the idea of putting an end for a life because at some point that could be very easy to do, but that also could be stupid enough because it gave no value or justification for whatsoever. On the contrary, we happened to find that life was not easy to find someone to live with but rather to find someone to live without in terms of love and care.

Perhaps what we saw from each of dad's hospital admissions reflected a true story of itself. I was not so sure that we could see things the same way they always present. I don't believe that we could value anything less than the way they present. With all due respect, we could say or second guess anything at what we see, but a fact was still a fact. From time to time, one thing we as human beings can't take or deny to accept was anything less than the truth. If without the truth, I don't truly believe that we could continue to be persistent in what we think and believe in what to be right any more.

The first few days immediately after the removal of gallstones from the ERCP (Endoscopic Retrograde Cholangiopancreatography) procedure, I learned that a small plastic bag and stents were placed in the attachment for a short period of time to prevent stone formation in the near future. In addition to that, dad continued to be treated for the infection that brought him into the hospital in the first place. Meanwhile he was constantly monitored from lab results that reflect the effectiveness of antibiotics and medications coming off the intravenous fluids.

Remembering one night I stay with my dad in the hospital and we get into some fight over the things that the medical staff expect him to not do. Because of his feisty nature, dad became a challenge for both the nurse and tech who took care of him. I forget what gets into his mind and it seemed that I miss out for quite some time since he was severely ill, yet my dad and I were actually having a real conversation that night.

"...I knew that you won't believe me even I tell you."

"Dad, what were you talking about and why were you telling me this?" I say.

"I don't think you've ever remembered if I stop telling you now."

"Dad, why do you still go over something so painful?"

"Son, people were looking for something outside in and they seldom share their true experience."

"So, Dad, you're not convinced that I'll be ever learnt about this."

Dad shook his head. "I understand why you need to know about the story. If you have, maybe this would convince you to believe the facts."

"You don't really mean it...you're scaring me, Dad!"

"I'm actually saving you, son. I see your anxiety, suspicion, and anger whenever you look at me like that."

"Please Dad...I was not mad at you. I just wonder what was left. Somehow I do believe we had to get started with what we had now ok."

"Forget the illness. I'm not talking about death."

"But...I had never thought about that. I just want to be with you, Dad."

"I understand something when I was down here few days ago. There was nothing left. I think that I'm going to be all right."

"Dad! You were scaring me and what were you talking about?"

"Son, I was talking about the dream."

"What dream?"

"I had a dream last night. In that dream I see two big ugly muscular men and they carry me through a bridge. There was a river flowing underneath the bridge. I was not sure where the place was and perhaps some kind of jungle, mountain or I don't know...but it was so terrible."

"Dad! It was all right...Let it go."

"No, no son! You don't understand. I see I was chased by groups of wolves or witches. It was so scary because they were hungry, ugly and very dangerous. They want to take me out..."

"Dad...please calm yourself down and no one was going to hurt you, OK?"

"How do you know? It was easy for you to say when you're not the one being chased and hunted down. You don't know when and what it means to be alive." Dad's face was contorted in fury, his nostrils flared up, his eyes sparkled with ferocity and he was shaken up.

"Right...but we know where we stand?" I said.

"I used to believe in fairy tales, and it isn't good enough because I'm not haunted; otherwise, I might fall into the river, beat to death, or eat alive by those monsters." Dad says

"Dad, I was so glad you don't walk through those horrible dark woods and shady valleys."

"Believe it or not, I had but somehow I'm fortunately enough to be brought back to life from the mercy of another two mighty men who happen to dress in white gown and they hold small magic star key in hands."

"Life was all about timing, Dad!"

"Life could be nothing compares to this. No one really understand what it means, not until they go thru horrible experience like mine."

"I could imagine that perfectly, Dad."

"I don't think you knew when my blood was boiled, my breaths shielded off, and my body was hardly moved." Dad rubbed his eyes.

"Dad, you don't give up and you know that we all did lose track of ourselves some time for a while. But you know that you want to leave it here." I patted his shoulders. "I've always loved you, and I totally trust you."

"Son, I knew that you tried to understand all these, but you'd had to live through it."

"I can understand something of what you felt now. I had seen that before."

"It wouldn't be the same...It took years for me to finally realize one thing that I had not truly lived for myself, not until someone and something attempt to take it away from me."

"You had no idea how happy I'm to see you coming back...Dad... everything will be OK, I promise."

For weeks, tests and evaluations of my dad were repeatedly performed by skilled professionals. These skilled professionals or clinicians were no different from anyone in the pursuit of good results. The reason why students studied hard was not just because they wanted to pass a test but because they expected to see high score from a test. Just like any businessperson or executives, the reason they worked hard was not because they wanted to obtain profit but because they wanted to accomplish great results from their goal-setting plans. A professional athlete plays hard not because he wants to be secure in his earnings but because he aims to win a championship. A musician practices either by himself or interacts with other soloist, pianist and conductor not because he wants to win great applause from audiences but because he wishes to express masterful rhythms that could resonate with other in term of emotions and feelings. Similar to what happened to my dad, all the evaluations and laboratory studies provided clinical values toward treatment plans and furnished the greatest protection against an injured organ or any dysfunctional systems.

With that in mind, I realized my greatest inner strength was to support dad all the way. I had never came to my senses that dad could come out of his darkness. By the time I understood what I needed to live out of my comfort zone, I'd gotten myself into something that I had never thought about. Day by day, I think that I might have started with the wrong feet but somehow I moved one step closer to something I did not know. Indeed I had started somewhere. I was doing great by following direction, but soon enough before I found what the true direction had been, I came to understand that I had been sidetracked for so long and it eventually endangered me and the ones around me.

As I kept track of the improvement from labs and daily treatments, I had never thought that the good results that my dad received turned out to be not so good. I had been informed that the reason dad was having abnormal high systemic infection came from the advanced imaging study that revealed not only the multiple stones over the gall bladder, but a big stone formation moving into the common bile duct that causes blockage and toxicity in the gastrointestinal (GI) system. This could eventually lead to jaundice, hepatitis and other serious complications. Dad was recommended to immediately undergo surgical intervention to treat the pathological condition and to also reduce the risk for complications. In the meantime, a consultation to the general surgeon was scheduled, paperwork was done, and date for the surgery was set up.

While we're getting ready for the procedure, we had never thought about something that was unplanned. I recall that morning was beautiful, at least at the time I left the hospital to clock in for work while dad stayed in his room with my sister. During the middle of that busy work day, I received a call from the nurse taking care of my dad at the moment. She informed me that my dad was suddenly coughing up blood with breathing distress. She was wondering that dad had been tested for tuberculosis (TB) lately or if was he on any kind of blood thinners or any anticoagulants. Nothing came to my mind. One thing I could possibly relate to the bleeding was the gastroesophageal reflux disease (GERD) that was a digestive disorder dad had for years, and it could trigger the vomiting of blood to some extent. I got another call from the nurse, and she told me the physician had ordered blood work and chest x-ray, which came back with negative finding, and so they decide to move forward with the procedure.

Finally, dad was moved downstairs for his pre-operative procedure. Soon after all the preparation was done, family and friends were escorted to the designated waiting room where they would be briefed by the surgeon and medical staff afterward. For most of us, that was the longest wait in their life, was where life and death were only narrowly separated. For a few others, that was a place and time where mixed feelings came in play. At some point in our lives, there comes a place where we have to experience that kind of life, live through it, let it go, and then move on. For our family, that was one of the shortest times of waiting since we were told that the anesthesiologist declined to sign off and decided to hold off for the surgery because my dad was coughing up blood and had breathing issues earlier that day. Then I was briefed that the anesthesiologist didn't want to move forward with the procedure because of complications and risks of the surgery outweighed its benefit, and eventually my dad may end up in the ICU.

As I stayed with dad that night, a strange feeling overcome me. Despite the fact that I had been briefed that my dad was diagnosed with a mild congested heart failure (CHF), I didn't truly believe that my strange and mixed feelings came from that finding. Instead, it seemed that I was in the middle of or just about to encounter something that I couldn't describe. From some perspective, my sixth sense was telling me that something was going to happen soon, and I could feel like that I was running against something, but I just had no clue of what it might be. Strangely enough, I was not anticipating anything, and I didn't believe that I even planned for anything other than wait to see what it happens. Until then, I had to say life was truly meant something that turned out to be slightly ugly during this hospitalization of my dad.

Sometimes we might think that we plan for everything, but sometimes we forget that life had a separate plan for us. As for my dad, I'm not so sure that we made plans for him and even if we had, I don't believe that it was a complete and perfect one. That evening, I sat in front of a computer but I didn't have my eyes on it. When I lay on a big sofa, my body seemed not to rest. I had some peace in mind when seeing my dad rests comfortably in his bed, but my mind still was flying high and strange enough, I felt like drunkard. With those mixed feelings, I found myself falling into a strange world that vividly showed through the life of a sick elderly man. Also in those mixed feelings, I seemed to have reminded of the aftermath of a prophetic life for which dad was recovered from the illness.

In that awkward time, I seemed to hear some strange but familiar voices speaking to me. Indeed, I didn't see anyone. I learned there was something that my dad himself had to be firstly overcome by himself before any new blessing could set in. Subconsciously, I didn't know what it was, but the feeling was so overwhelmingly strong that it suppressed all my thoughts and wisdom to a point that I could no longer think straight.

"Son! Wake up," said the voice.

"Who...is it you, Dad?" I speak while rubbing my eyes.

"Are you awake, son?"

"Yes, I am, Dad. Are you all right?" As I turned around to look at the bed, I saw my dad was actually sleeping well and snoring loudly.

"Son! Don't worry...He is fine," the strange voice said.

"Who...and what were you doing here?"

"You can't see me," the voice continued, "but you knew who I am."

"Who are you?"

"Don't be afraid and look it was me, your Lord."

"I remember you....you were still the one who had talked with me all through these days, aren't you? What do you want from me?"

"Look son, if history could teach us anything today, that was how we're going to deal with it and move forward."

"With life the way it was and how could I know that this thing...I mean this thing might not happen the other way around?"

"You should know that Jesus Christ was the same yesterday, today and forever. In the world of ever changing, the Lord Jesus still heals the sick today."

"How can I know His plan was good for my dad?"

"The plan had been in place, but your dad himself had to walk out of the shadow of this sickness."

"I was not followed..."

"In general, most people feel agony and lament in this kind of situation...but the grace of God lies in the sake of his loving kindness, mercy and righteousness."

"Did my dad know what he was getting himself into, and should he be expecting something else?"

"The love of this life should not be overshadowed by the lust for the flesh. Everyone had his/her time and when the time comes, he/she would see the sign."

"How do we know that it was our time? I'm confused."

"Son! Listen to me...Whatsoever and whenever you abide in your prayers, your request would be abided in heaven, and if you keep God's commandments carefully, they would become life when you found them... They also would turn out to be health to the flesh when you need them."

"I will keep your Words as long as I live," I said but didn't quite understand him fully. "You tell me every stumbling block and every stampede, which I had, should remind me of your footprint once I decided to follow you. In every pain and sickness, which I got, reflect your grace. In every fall and every rise, which I experienced, reveal your love. But when I need you the most, it seems that I only catch air instead. Many times I know the presence of your hands, but I found it to be impossible to hold on to them. I have repeatedly asked you why this life had to be me and why I had to have so many stumbling blocks."

"All these happen for a reason because I had planned an extraordinary life for you...I would make you wise and would show you where to go."

"My eyes were clear, but my vision was indeed blurred."

"I would guide you and watch over you," said the voice. "I would stand by your side and lead you."

As I put forth my hands and head into the direction of the voice, I gradually saw the face and the image of the Lord. In the meantime, my mouth stunned, my body stiffened, and the voice came to me just like a thunder blowing on to my head.

"For your dad, there will be a waiting period when he'll learn that his body needs time to cool off. By the third day, dad will be recovered just the way he should."

With a twinkle of light, the voice went off and the image slowly disappeared. All of a sudden, I felt I had lost something dearly. By the time when I took a close look around the room, though, I locked myself in but still found no one and then I knew that I had completely lost it.

For the next two days, my mind seemed to hop around quite a lot. Appointments for surgery were repeatedly canceled because both the surgeon and anesthesiologist wanted to see the clearing off of symptoms from the cardiopulmonary conditions. And so, my dad continued to be evaluated and treated by the internist until his condition was clear and safe for the procedure.

Looking at my life, I felt an unspeakable frustration. Oftentimes I lived by sets of boundaries being drawn in term of setting rules, but I had never thought of addressing my personal issues could lead to the kind of relationship that yields for submission to God's plan. I knew that I had nothing to boast about except limitations and weaknesses. While I pondered on what this process could lead me to, I felt a strong, forceful and non-resistant element growing inside of me, and I felt as if the implantation of Holy Spirit growing at an extent to what was happening to my dad's body before and during the surgery.

Whether I saw one day's delay or a three-day's wait, I felt the existence of an unknown plan that surpassed our thought process. We think that the day was near, but it does not mean an end. It reminded me of the many boundaries that were broken by means of our conception, denial and tradition. It meant well when we count the works we had done, but the works alone can't lead us to the salvation. We believed that life was a total reflection of what we represented, pursued and possessed. We took pride in what stores in our earthly house. We value more in what holds treasure in our financial world. We concern about what had been hidden behind those beautiful walls. Deep down in my mind, I repetitively questioned when was the last time that we checked in to see how valid and significant was our faith to sharpen our personal life?

To certain extent, we didn't see the shred of light until we found the conviction. This kind of conviction could be in form of system, image and word. Without the right expression, no real conviction could be meant unless we see the word. Perhaps every word could mean different thing but there was only one thing that separates all others and that was His Words. As before, we could be drawn by some separated lines or boundaries, and those lines could underline the execution of orders, the law of inheritance, and the concept of belief or faith.

The sets of boundaries reminded me that we should possess conservative principles and a vitalistic philosophy. Regardless of how the delay of a prophetic word could affect the disease process, I felt that there was nothing more detrimental than the damaged organ or bodily system. This surgery somehow reflected the setting of an attempted repair or recovery. In the meantime, it could lead to the impartation of Holy Spirit, as I followed commandments saying that "remove not the ancient landmarks, which thy fathers had set (Proverb 22:28; Proverb 23:10; Deuteronomy 19:14)." With spiritual application, landmarks, similar to sets of boundaries, show ownership.

This ownership could be seen in term of beliefs. In most of today's churches, one probably sees that some preachers generally give sermons about what people love to hear. They focus more on topics or parables that are more acceptable to an empty soul. These preachers were less likely to touch on the sensitive issues or doctrines that represent their beliefs in accordance with the biblical truth. Some pastors liked to emphasize that God loves everyone and so everyone was going to heaven. Some of them fail to preach the message of the Cross. Many of them were less likely willing to link salvation with going to heaven. In fact, it was not a matter of how we go to heaven if we believe that there was a life after death. Salvation should not be done by works but our works help to bring out God's grace. Indeed salvation can't be done by joining a particular church, going to church, and being baptized but rather through Jesus Christ, the true son of God, and His holy blood by dying on the Cross to pay for our sins in full (James 2:19). Besides, going to heaven should not be confused with doing good deeds or work alone, but instead we had to be reborn of water and of the Spirit (John 3:5).

Secondly, these ownerships could be seen in term of faith. In today's society, cynicism plays a great effect on religion, as Christians are shaken up with their true identity or beliefs. Some Christians were tone dead when speak about their faith. Some tend to forget that we were not down in this world and we had to live apart from this world in term of gambling, adultery and addictions while the anti-Christ points out that everyone was alike and everyone was going to heaven regardless. By faith, Christians realize that salvation was a free gift from God, and we need Jesus to make us a true catcher of man, woman and child. We need to reach out to the lost world, to spread His Words, and to guide people for Christ.

Third, ownership could be seen in term of sickness and death. According to the Masonic term and Jewish law, landmarks designate inheritance. Inheritance could come in the form of a supreme being and the immortality of soul. By believing in metaphysics or in something beyond the physical realm and the material world, human existence became a mystery in spite of scientific breakthroughs and life in the postmodern world. It superseded the spiritual side to human being in the form of immanence and transcendence. Indeed, mankind was physical. For instance, when a man dies, his soul returns to his Creator, and his spirit was either going to heaven or ending up in hell. Death indeed was a separation of soul from the physical body as dust belongs to the dust, but the spiritual part belongs to deity. Man was subjected to death because of sin and fornication, but God promises a resurrection to an eternal life for those who repent for sins, worship God and accept Christ as personal savior or Messiah and also accept his holy blood as the sacrifice even to those who had no relationships with the Father and Jesus Christ. This inheritance ensures the first resurrection for immortality taking place when Christ returns to establish God's Kingdom on this earth.

By the third day, a Saturday morning, I brought my dad to the surgery. I followed dad to the surgical center and prior to the procedure, I even spoke with both the operating room (OR) nurse and the general surgeon after all the assessments were finished. Looking at my dad's facial expression at the time, he was quite calm and at ease. For some reason, dad seemed to not know anything despite his physical conditions. Somehow he revealed to have figured out a lot of thing even though we dare not tell him everything. In fact, it doesn't mean that we want to hide things from him but instead, we were afraid that if we tell him everything, dad might not be able to take them, not mentioning the fact that he was not ready to endure them at once. Despite the potentially high complications with his chronic illness, I was confident that he'd agree to our decision.

With surgery performed in the room a couple blocks from where I sat, I seemed to feel the palpitation of life extending via some mysterious medium. Strange enough, when the reality hits me, I don't believe that we had rights to change our fates unless we could find clues to figure out our next move. Oftentimes, there was a small possibility or probability that we might be able to plan ahead for future events. More than 90% of happenings among and around us were the collectives or exponential derivatives in term of metaphysical sense. These include in the many myths or mysteries we experience in our daily lives that often are described in terms of destiny. We need to significantly figure out what deeply run inside our mind, how and who we think we were, and what we could be.

I thought of life and breath at a man's fingertips until briefed by the surgeon who informs me that the procedure went well with dad. Within a split second, I saw a miracle stretching out of the thin air. I can't wait to grasp his hands and rub his face as dad began to slowly recover from his surgery. With a close look at the laparoscopic cholecystectomy, I had nothing to say against the procedure itself but instead felt joyful for the elderly who survived the procedure. A laparoscopic cholecystectomy indeed was very common in North America and especially in the United States, the removal of gall bladder did not associate with any impairment of digestion in most people but in the meantime, it helped to prevent the formation of gallstones and to thus reduce the incident for gallstone attack. The truth of the matter was that daddy was blessed to get over with the surgery at the age of over ninety two. Though the physical scars from the incision marks with five small delicate holes over the abdominal regions could be seen, I hoped that my dad was able to overcome the emotional scars he bore.

For the next few days or week after the surgery, dad stayed at the hospital and monitored closely until he was safe to be discharged for home. As the days went by, the smile on the elderly ill disappeared when family and friends visited him. He instead worries constantly, was anxious, and even angry sometimes. He thought that he missed out and was singled out from all activities from home. At some point, dad seemed to deny the fact that the body required a longer period of time to recover as one ages and he had not understood why he was still being monitored.

Indeed, life was phenomenal. No one could say what life could be when it was ongoing. At least to a few, we were living in lies and among cheaters. We were wrestling with fear, compromise, trade-off and identity crisis. We were growing up among mockers, snobs and traitors. We face a similar challenge that doubt and denial not only become a part of our emotional burdens, but they also root into our veins, leading to painful illnesses. To our family, we saw our heads beating against a wall greater than all of the physical sicknesses combined. Over a period of time, we found that it wasn't so frightening to see the impact of an imminent death that reconnects a family to its backbone. I had never thought that, because of my dad's health conditions, brought all my siblings and relatives together to take care of him until the end. If the caring for a chronically or terminally ill senior could be dangerous, I would respectfully say that the only fear for anyone to undertake that solemn duty was to not see our loved ones recovering from sickness and disease. If we were obligated in giving up our lives or energy to cover for his wellness, then our fear for the caring should not be restricted in sacrifice but rather, it was toward the physical, psychological and emotional demands. I gradually saw the dreadful part of life rested not in the combination of disease and sickness but rather, revealed the contemplation of sin and loss of faith that could disqualify us from entering heaven.

During those mixed emotions, my family and I felt time flying at our fingertips, and we saw the cohesiveness of prophecy. Believe it or not, we had never held such strong feelings that His love for dad was steadfast and His promise for better healing remained unchanged. Perhaps, we might have stumbled a lot over our denial and suspicion from the moment that we were told and encountered. We had not lost sight of seeing our God persistent with His Words and besides, the manifestation of his love was also delivered at the best time and at the right place. We had not thought of the fact that my dad had survived a stroke seven years ago since he was once thought to be at the end of his life. We had not been forgotten the doctors' reports that my dad was in good health in comparison to his peer in the same age and that once he recovered, his life would be extraordinary.

Since the infection was slowly winding down, approximately a week after the surgery, my dad was finally discharged from the hospital. This life was indeed full of surprises but none would amaze me more or give me more security than what I had in God, the Master and Lord of Surprises, especially when I could feel his presence at my side. Looking at the sunlight shines through the top of our head, we began to feel a new life leading our path and we were on our way home...

Chapter 8: God had plans

In their hearts humans plan their course, but the LORD establishes their steps. (Proverbs 16:9)

For some reason, many of us believe after suffering from some dreadful event or a deadly disease that a better life awaits us. Some of us see the deadly disease or dreadful event as a natural part of life and would not be bothered by its challenge. Others see it as a reflection of special gift, and they view it as a hard ball falling into their court so that they had to play at their best.

Born in 1921 to a middle-class family from Guang Dong, China, my dad was moved to and grew up in Phnom Penh, Cambodia, where he was raised by his two older sisters who loved him very much, in part because he was the youngest of nine siblings. Dad didn't do well in most of his academic studies. Homework and exams were two of his worst enemies that would constantly freeze up his brain. While a teenager, he developed a great interest in business and slowly developing his talents and skills in domestic and foreign trades. Right after he was married in his late twenties, dad started to run his own business along with trades in china, porcelain and ceramic wares that required him to travel all over Cambodia and surrounding countries in Southeast Asia.

For as long as I could remember, dad was talented and multitasked. By not following my grandfather's footstep in traditional Chinese medicine, my dad not only was successful in his grocery store and bookstore businesses, but he also was a good chef in a casino near Mountain Phnom Aural. He worked very hard every day to bring in money to raise his family and eight children. He loved to put his family first and himself second.

I never learned what dad did to keep his family alive and together when the Cambodian Civil War broke out in 1975. I did later learn that the war was the reflection of inhuman leaders, their political revolution, extremist ideology, and ethnic animosity that eventually led to the massacre of its citizens. Under the totalitarian regime and senseless utopian policies of Pol-Pot, the Khmer Rouge induced massive political havoc and a genocide that kill about 1.5 million out of 8 million Kampucheans across Cambodia, a small country in Southeast Asia, the center of the once ancient kingdom of the Khmer, and the birthplace of Angkor Wat temple with the largest religious and Buddhist monuments in the world.

In retrospect, the beginning of my life was when my family had to separate into two groups to escape the war. I don't know how long my family spent fleeing from government persecution, religion oppression, and the ban on foreign languages since Pol-Pot and his armies marched into Phnom Penh, the capitol of Cambodia, and took control of the country. Businesses were closed, religion was banned, and education was blocked. In those days, all things were in chaos, houses were on fire, mourning could be heard all over the place, and dead bodies could be seen all over the city and suburbs because monks, doctors, healthcare workers, business people, educators, former government officials, and average citizens were forced to leave their workplaces, homes and the streets. Along with millions of Kampucheans or Cambodians who fled to neighboring countries, such as Laos or Thailand, our family also was forced to leave our house and to move away from the city to places we'd never been.

In the beginning of our exile, I remember riding a family-owned truck loaded with food, medication, and money. We were able to load up with medicine because my oldest sister was a nurse and midwife. I don't know how long we had been wandered around the city and into the countryside because I was just a toddler at the time. I didn't really know what was happening except that I was told to follow my family closely until one day our truck ran out of gas and money was no longer used for exchange. Gradually, our food was ate up, and our medicine was either dispersed or used up. Then we started to walk barefooted over the rocky road through the countryside and into villages that were filled with wet mud, red dirt, and sharp thorns. I have never forgotten those ugly, skinny and long faces that scared me into crying a lot along my way. I have been told that our family also was forced into slave labor for some time during that period. We saw many people executed by the dictatorship. Some people died from overwork. Others died from starvation or malnutrition. Quite a lot of Cambodians were indeed lost from illness, widespread disease, malaria or toxic conditions in the war zone. Many were killed and shot due to their objection or refusal to follow orders from the commanding officer of the Khmer Rouge. And almost everywhere, bodies exploded from mines leftover from a previous battlefield in a secluded forest or side road from the woods, river banks along the border between Cambodia and Vietnam. Still many were seen to be slaughtered by knives, beheaded with axes, or buried alive from big holes they'd just dug for themselves and others. I also have been told that many times my sisters and mom had to stay hungry for more than two days without foods except drinking water from ponds or some forest trees. Later I learned the reason my family members were willing to stay hungry was because they give their foods to me and my young sister. There were times my sisters and mom had to pick up rotten food from the road or mountainside to eat. We ate tree bark, roots or branches of plants, juicy fruit or berries found in the wilderness so that we could survive from famine and thus stay alive.

Perhaps seeking a peaceful place became a primal force that led us to overcome tribulation and sickness during the war. I had no idea what my family did that was any different from other victims, but I am certain the pains still were incredible and the anguishes indescribable. During my youth, my dad used to remind my siblings and me that our life and freedom were bought by blood and death. We were fortunate enough to live through the havoc of a bloody warlord and a revolutionary maniac because we had an unfinished mission to be a living proof of what God wants our lives to be.

At some point in our lives, many of us see some of our loved ones heading down the wrong side of the road but don't realize that they need time to find their way again. Life was not easy, but it could be joyful, as all of our family members reunited in Southern Vietnam. But this so-called new life, compared to those victims at war, gave us an advantage to see how fortunate we were to be alive. Though slightly different from when Moses led his people out of Egypt into the Promised Land, our escape revealed that though our life could be hard, we were indeed living in the grace period that God put forth for us.

During the early 1980s, the Vietnamese government had started its economic reform by following the Chinese model, a socialist ideology. The Vietnamese government seized wealth, property and landholdings under the policy of combating private property that began in 1979. Gradually, the government replaced private-owned corporations and businesses with state-trading network or joint state-private enterprises under the policy of inventory inspection. Many merchants and landowners were tossed into the streets and were shipped off to some new economic or recovery regions. Due to the scarcity of food and the failure of heavy industry from state investment, socialism took hold of agricultural policies that eventually drove the state to own everything. During those times, a high deficit in trade balance occurred because foreign aid, mainly from the United States, China and the Soviet Union, was cut back. Though the level of industrialization remained the same, the Vietnamese economy and life depended significantly on agriculture or related sectors. The situation became very bad and turned into a debt crisis.

This so-called Vietnamese Economic crisis in the 1980s marked the time when the global economy began to shift dramatically from inflation to recession. The crisis marked high inflation, low productivity, low-quality export standards, energy shortages, and food supply shortages. Eventually it led to a multi-directional foreign policy that focused on the economic, social and political reforms known as the renovation policies, which were implemented until the late 1980s.

During the early 1980s, times were very rough, and like many in Vietnam, my family had to sell everything that we owned just to survive. Many Cambodian Chinese or those having a Kampuchean background living in Vietnam at that time were segregated in Saigon and/or many provinces in southern Vietnam. To some extent, even families, which included Chinese or Cambodians, needed to live separately or spread out so that they would not be caught by the Vietnamese government or authorities at night. Many traded in all their money, gold and valuable goods to buy just a chance of returning to mainland China. Some used small wooden fishing boats while many made larger boats with engines to flee from Vietnam to start a new life elsewhere. For my family, we traded in all we had, became impoverished under the policy of inventory inspection, and eventually were forced to head to a small village or some sort of camp as refugees to start a new, peaceful life under the large-scale agricultural collectivization.

Life in the village wasn't easy, especially for those of us used to live in the city. Every morning my dad led a few of my siblings to work in the sugarcane fields. Each day we tended those stout, jointed fibrous stalks among grasses until they were cut and sent to the factory for the production of sugar. After the sugarcane was harvested, the leftover root, trash and stalk were burned in a fire so that the field could be recultivated for the next round of planting. In the afternoons, my dad went out to the marketplace to sell groceries with my mom. For years, we lived this kind of lifestyle, but we were happy to have peace and comfort at a certain extent. Despite being a teenager and laboring on the farm, I was proud to be brought up and schooled mostly in the Christian church, even though my parents were not Christian. As I grew older and had to spend most of my time helping on the farm with very limited machinery, I still ran, sang, played and even danced in the sugarcane field. Many times I bled, cut by the sugarcane stalks. I ate and rested in the muggy air and mosquito-filled environment. We sweated working under the sun and showered by working in the rain. Though life was hard, we were happy. While I learned to grow sugarcane trees, I also made use of my time to read and write. For most of my teenage years, I was fortunate to have a good time with my younger sister to learn through the church, self-study, and home school because our family was poor.

For some reason, I truly believe that life's challenges were not designed to cripple me but rather to help build my true self. Poverty, on the other hand, might tend to cripple our mind and weaken our energy, but it can't shake up our beliefs. I remembered during the good season when there was no war that my family and especially my dad liked to feed me with big meal because they were afraid of having me grown up malnourished since I was the youngest male in the family. However, while my family were forced to live in the village during the Vietnamese economic crisis or turmoil in 1980-81, I'd never forgotten that even two ounces of pork had to feed six people for three days, not mentioning the mixture of vegetables, rootlets and vines were widely used to fill our empty stomach at a time we could not afford to buy meat or seafood and when the food supply was limited.

Indeed, every one of us needs a home and wants a family that helps to cover our emotional and physical tolls. At some point, I definitely hated my life and all the terrible changes I faced. I always thought time was a horrible thief who happened to steal all my past by leaving me some broken and disconnected memories. I didn't know what I had done to deserve such a trick from life, not to mention the overcoming of war and hunger to find a place, of which was a terrible small village to be precise, to live in the foreign soil. From a broader perspective, I believe that, whether rich or poor, every one of us should have a home and all of us deserve to have a nice family. I am not so sure the home and family that I had at the time really mean something special because they seemed to lack of some kind of deeper significance or meaning. Though my home and family were not broken, they seemed different from traditional ones.

Apart from those poor quality of life, years later my family and I were blessed to have a second chance to head to another foreign country where we gradually rediscovered the genuine meaning of life, liberty and pursuit of happiness. Certainly relocation was a big part of life with my family, and at the time I never thought of it as a great idea, but somehow it did fall under the Master's design. By the time we got to the United States in the early 1990s and lived through all those ups and downs as many immigrants had, we gradually realized that my family and I were not much different from the ancient Hebrews, who were God's chosen people. They were once enslaved and then wandered forty years over the wilderness until they were brought into the Promised Land. Similar to the biblical Hebrews, we found trial, tribulation, suffering, hunger and anguish to be indescribable.

Over the years, I realized that endurance and overcoming in due and difficult times were a valuable lesson. Remembering what dad had once taught me – though people age and change, at all times they should be willing to dare to deal with their setbacks. Initially, I didn't fully understand what that meant. As time went on, I understood that it truly took great courage to grow up, be responsible, and become who I could be. Obedience and honesty could be difficult to achieve when one lacked maturity. I believe commitment to our religious faith and cherishing our loved ones tended to be the most difficult virtue we can face because we don't want to be shaken loose by the sense of responsibility. I also came to my senses that taking responsibility for a higher standard without worrying about other people's expectation could be challenging enough, but day by day, I saw that what I chose and what I did truly reflected who I was going to become.

I remember one Tuesday night when dad was rushed to the emergency room after his breathing was compromised, as he had a difficulty getting mucus or foods out of his body because he could not cough. Looking at his distended belly, I felt that the devil played a big joke onto the elderly ill's life with unknown disease or sicknesses. After evaluations, lab tests and imaging studies, the attending physician from the emergency room told my sister and I that our dad would be admitted for pneumonia due to his advanced age. Looking around the hospital, everything was new. The feeling was strange, and the environment was clean. The floor nurse and patient care unit staff were very friendly, and they worked very hard to care for the sick. They greeted us with a smile and communicated with us very quick because their nurse station was two or three rooms down from where we stayed.

In less than a day, dad's condition grew worse. The pulmonologist ordered a Bipap ventilator to help him breathe because his saturated oxygen kept dropping below normal. IV fluid, antibiotics and other medications were given as schedule for the first two to three days. When alert, dad knew where he was and understood his condition. During the time when he was not connected by the oxygen mask, dad enjoyed his time talking to his daughters and grandchildren and listening to their prayers. The hospital staff from the internal medicine closely monitored dad's condition was until late one Friday afternoon when the doctor informed me that she needed to transfer dad to the intensive care unit because his lungs were more compromised than before and his heart rate was running too fast.

For the next twenty-four hours in the ICU, our room became busier than the regular patient room had been. While dad was treated for pneumonia, we found that the heart monitor stayed on the top of his bed and oxygen was connected by a mask into the nose through a plastic valve that was hooked into the Bipap ventilator along with the high flow from the air-oxygen blender connecting into the wall. The oxygen was set at 80% and 50 liters. A breathing treatment was scheduled for every four hours. EKG screening, blood tests, and blood pressure medication were used to treat arrhythmia and to thus help prevent stroke. Throughout the first week, dad had seesawed in his cardiopulmonary functions, but overall his body improved slightly. Soon the pulmonologist and respiratory therapist begin trying to wean dad of the treatments. Still, every day was a nightmare because dad is, in some fashion, failed in his treatments.

I remembered one interesting story that my sisters tell me during the first weekend dad stays at the ICU. I had been told that in a dream, dad was visited by angels and taken into heaven.

"Who are you and why are you taking me?" dad asked the angels.

"Do not be frightened, Son! Follow us," the angels said.

"Where are you taking me?"

"You'll know," said one of the angels.

In his dream, dad told us that they flew over dark clouds and through clear skies. There were times that he felt deep pressure and breathing distress. There were times that he felt chills in his body and aches in his spine. There were times that he had to hold on to something to keep his body balanced. There were times that he didn't know what to expect from prayers. Sometimes they just circled steep hills. Sometimes they faced some strange humidity or air pressure. Dad didn't recognize where he was heading to because he had a hard time keeping his eyes open at all times.

"How do you know that you were taking the right person?" dad asked them.

"Trust your Lord with all your heart and soul" said one of the angels.

"I see...but where were we heading?"

"Open your eyes and see for yourself," the angel said.

"Wow, this is amazing; is it yours?"

"This belongs to my Master," said one of the angels, "and what were you planning to do one day?"

"You mean...here in this garden? If I may, I'd like to plant flowers. I mean all kinds of flowers."

"We'll let the Master know but right now, you can't go up there to see Him."

"What do you mean?" dad asked.

"Calm down and you'll know one day, Son! No one should be worried, and when the time comes, you'll be received into His house."

"So you were saying I don't need to do anything now," dad said.

"We were told to bring you here for a tour, but you are not allowed to go up there yet."

"May I see your Master by any chance?"

"This was neither the time nor the place for the Master to see you, and as He said when the time was right, you'll be brought and received into His house," one of the angels explained.

"How should I know the time was right if you don't tell me?"

"No one knows what time could be right, except the Master. Do not worry what could be in the way, for He shall reveal to you."

Dad wandered about the garden and around the place known to him as Heaven. The place was quite different from that which he was exposed to a few years ago. He didn't see people eating, making noise, or working inside the garden. Dad was told those people were enjoying fresh fruits or something fruit-like, and dad wasn't given a chance to taste it.

Back in reality, dad was happy and loved because he became more alert and had more fun with daughters and grandkids around. Though still bedridden, the physicians began to wean him off the ventilator. They had him on the high-flow being set at 60 percent and 50 liters. Regular tube feeding was set to maintain adequate nutrition. The breathing treatment was reduced to once every eight hours. Chest X-rays, lab work, and advanced imaging studies performed to rule out pulmonary edema in term of cardiopulmonary problem.

I soon found that life was playing a fool out of me. Every time I walked down the same hallway and saw those familiar medical personnel and hospital staff, I somehow came up with different thoughts. Though my mind was clear, my thoughts were mixed and perplexed whenever I found patients staying nearby my dad's room happen to be either gone or transferred. When I witnessed the status of my dad's health in each of the evenings I stayed with him, I almost came to tears but tried to remain strong by holding on to my faith because I believed in the promise from the Bible. I shouted out His holy name, and I also cried out loud to the Lord at a time when dad was sleeping because I didn't want him to see through the weak part of my true self. Though I was backed by my family and my church, I realize how fragile human life could be once reality set in. I understood the high death ratio for the elderly from the complications of pneumonia, pulmonary edema, or stroke as opposed to cancer or brain disorders. Sometimes I even had some unorthodox thinking that if we human beings had an option or right to choose what kind of disease, illness or no sickness that we could have to face a death-related issue, then I think life would be absolutely inexpensive and less stressful notwithstanding the pain, suffering, guilt, remorse and even burden passing on to our loved ones and also to those who we leave behind.

What seemed to us as bitterness and tribulation at the time turn out to be some kind of comfort and blessing. I remembered dad used to teach us the most significant reason why we remained together as a family was because we should always love one another and that we should not do anything to hurt one another. Regardless of how bad a situation got, we should not fight inside the house and every competition should be done outside. Looking at what dad had overcame during the past few days, we felt inexplicable joy for the improvement. We believed in what was holding inside him when he behaves slightly weird. When we talk to him at that time, dad was more likely to be confused than coherent. Dad was in and out of his own alertness to a point that the physicians also thought that to be normal for an elderly person during an infection.

In retrospect, I believe life had shown us some signs, but I guess that we failed to recognize them. For example, one weekend two of my sisters stayed the night with dad so that I could catch up with my sleep because I had been with him for the entire week. My sisters told me that they spent the time chatting, praying, singing and consoling dad. From time to time, they saw dad holding up three fingers. At some point, they thought dad was pointing at something or he was using those three fingers to scratch his body because he felt an itch and some red or bluish spots from the IV and blood extraction. My sisters tried to ask dad what the three fingers meant, but he refused or failed to explain it to them. Perhaps dad wanted to tell my sisters what the fingers really meant, but he was too weak to fully express it in detail. My sisters failed to connect the dots, to see the relationship in between, and they also forget to ask the rest of the family what that could mean to dad and our family as a whole.

One of the regrettable aspects of life was the tendency to let go of opportunities to learn what you don't know. Certainly no one should be blamed for things they don't know because no one knew everything.

Personally I don't blame my sisters for not telling me what had happened to dad during the time I wasn't there, but instead I was disappointed at myself because I believed that I've been tricked by this life. I had never imagined that trickery turned out to be something that eventually stretched beyond my life to a point that I wanted to surrender to learn more about the sign language or something similar to that fashion so that I don't need to pay a high price for something I did not know.

Despite nothing worst had truly happened during the time I was not with my dad, the lack of understanding to the sign language or the raising of dad's three fingers eventually caused us to forever remember. I recall the early Monday morning when the pulmonologist came in to evaluate dad and reported to me that he was unresponsive to his treatments and wondered whether our family had come up with a plan of what we expected the hospital and staff would do for him. I told him that our family was waiting for the rest of the family members coming in from out of town. Then later the day, the nurse practitioner talked with me about the proposal from the hospital, and she called upon me to have a family meeting with the physicians, administrator and hospital staffs. The meeting eventually was set for Wednesday afternoon. From some perspective, the meeting reminded me of what we had seven years ago when dad was on life support and intensive care for stroke or TIA.

Life remained relatively the same for the next two days – dad continued to have his regular care, medications and oxygen therapies continued as scheduled, children and grandkids visited dad as they were used to be doing. As previously scheduled, at least one person stayed with dad in the daytime in addition to visitors from friends and church members. In the evening, I stayed with dad until the next day. On Tuesday night, I continued to talk with dad, pray with him, and sing for him even though he was less responsive and depressed at the time. Even at the time when the nurse, technician or therapist needed an additional hand, I always helped them as they instructed me how to do. For the entire night, dad's health conditions were relatively stable even though he tended to be less responsive to treatment until around 5 a.m., dad seemed to behave a little bizarrely, and I told the nurse to call the doctor requesting new medications to raise his blood pressure. After the medication was given intravenously, his blood pressure level went up slightly, but about an hour later, it drops again along with decreasing saturated oxygen level. At that moment, I came to my senses that dad might be in his last hours. By good faith, I still continued to pray for him, and in the meantime, I waited patiently for the attending physician to come in for the evaluation.

Around 10 a.m., the pulmonologist came in, read the data, and received a report from the nurse. He looked at the numbers in term of ECG (heart rate), NIBP (non-invasive blood pressure), SP02 (oxygen saturation), and RR (respiration rate) on the ICU monitor. He told me that my dad was not going to make it through the day, and he probably would last two to three hours because all the functions in his heart and lungs were failing. He asked me to confirm whether my family still wanted the hospital staff to resuscitate dad at his last minute. After considering all the data, weighing all the pros and cons, and taking advice from an experienced medical doctor, I told the physician to not resuscitate dad and to let nature take its course. While I called home to inform my family members to come in to see dad for the last time before he leaves forever; I also asked the doctor for other measure to help keeping him for hopefully one to two days before other siblings arrive from out of state. A few minutes later, the nurse practitioner came into the room to advise me the proposal for providing dad hospice care in the same room where he was staying. She said the hospice care could allow dad to die with dignity by buying some time for the rest of my family to see him.

For the first time in my life, I had not seen anyone like dad who had gone through so much pain, sickness, disease and agony but still maintained his calmness despite the fact that he could not speak at the time. In his eyes, I could read from his lip of what he tended to say, and I almost could touch the depth of his heart in what he felt. While I looked at the associate pastor, the senior pastor's wife, few of my siblings, and nephew who were all in the room with dad, I felt that he was blessed to have good people around. Though dad might not fully know what had been done to him, I continued to encourage my siblings to talk with dad because I truly believed that he could still hear and understand. Indeed, we know that we couldn't afford to reverse the course by risking anything. And yet I believed that dad had made the best bet. There should not be any bigger risk for us to take because dad revealed the biggest risk, greatest achievement, and best gift this life had to offer.

Around 2 p.m., my siblings and I headed to complete the paperwork with an independent company that would help to transfer dad into hospice care. The process was not easy and took an emotional toll. We had never thought of the specifics and complexities relating to the expectation for dad. With some mixed emotions, I couldn't imagine what could be given to those who were similar to dad, so they could stay comfortable at the time of death. I had never prepared for anything like that before and I don't believe that I would be fully prepared for something like that. Definitely my siblings and I had never thought of such an occasion for us to come for a consent of making an unprecedented decision for dad. After we set our difference aside by giving dad all the respect, love and care he deserved to have, we were on our way to see him.

At some point of our lives, there always was something that couldn't be fully planned out. Perhaps we felt to be all right to organize our life or living conditions neatly, but in reality we couldn't always have them completed. We might find to be in our best interest to plan our living conditions out. We might also happen to be in good position to bring out our very best and good heart to those we cared deeply. By the time my siblings and I came back from the administrative paperwork or registration for hospice care, I saw my dad lying in his bed with the same group of people around him. As soon as I reached his bedside, I told him to not worry about anything because my siblings and I had completed the paperwork and he'd be in better hands. I told dad to stay strong and wait for other siblings to arrive to see him. I had never thought that whatever I told him at that moment eventually would lead him into another peaceful state. Even today, I still can't believe that was truly the last time ever for me to physically be close with dad. In less than three minutes, we all witnessed dad closing his eyes completely with a good smile, and he gave up his last breath, freely and silently. At the twinkle of an eye, I saw my dad surrendering his life willingly and completely. Dad gave up his last breath on earth and took his first breath in heaven. All of a sudden, I remembered all that had happened since early that morning. From the time that the pulmonologist warned me of his expected leaving to the actual time he left, dad revealed himself as a brave man and firm believer who knew what he was expecting to get. Besides, he had been waiting and giving us additional time to learn about God's grace and to also feel the touch in real time that God placed in the last minute of his life.

Then my sister Helen suddenly told us that his passing marked the third day from the time when she saw the sign of three fingers. It truly revealed that dad was indeed a strong man who knew how to endure his agony by not putting his children in a bad situation or an emotional breakdown. For all these times, I firmly believed that dad himself truly had it all figured out from the beginning even though he was mostly silent for the last day or two, but deep down in his heart and soul, he remained very clear and calm because he knew that he was about to move on.

At that very moment, I acknowledged life as a reflection seen in shattered glass. As I took a last gaze at the ceiling and a close look at my father in the reflecting mirror, I gradually realized that when we had a vision or purpose in life, we won't be misled by distractions. We could control our own environment instead of being manipulated by people or the circumstance. If our vision could be set by His will, we not only could be more passionate about our destiny or purpose, but we also could set as a priority with the leading of our family to purpose and eventually inspire others to run with us in the quest for a larger purpose in life. In the parable of Elijah, he changes his environment that was once controlled by King Ahab. Because of the favor, wisdom and vision came from God, and knowing that God was going to punish Ahab for the sin of worshipping Baal, Elijah found a personal and conditional promise after he prayed to God in faith specifically. He eventually not only was free from the King's control, but he made the King listening to him and allowed him to lead the people of Israel (I Kings 18:41-46). Similar to Elijah on some smaller scale, my dad had led me and my family to successfully escape from the political storm of Pol-Pot's genocide and the lightning-like attack and persecution from the Vietnamese post-war economic depression. My dad happened to be a visionary man who not only set high standards for himself in terms of reaching his peaceful life, but he also raised the bar to help his family and children having a better future when he decides to move us all to the States.

I gradually found that a nearly dead person often says extremely weird things or behaves very strangely, sometimes indifferent or becoming absolutely unrecognizable. Perhaps every individual had a different grace period, but by the time that final moment arrived, all of us were going to act in some similar fashion. I believe that we humans had some kind of premonition, the natural intellect to learn, or the ability to envisage the coming of death so that we could yield our soul to first move into another state and then allow our body to have some kind of transition, whether in peace or struggling. Due to that special connection at the last minute of dad's life, I finally saw the world through God's face because I learned a big truth from a scripture that said, "For I knew the plans I had for you, declares the Lord, plans for welfare and not for evil, to give you a future and a hope" (Jeremiah 29:11). Definitely, I feel the peace of mind when I saw my dad left peacefully, comfortably, and also with dignity because I knew that my dad had found his true refuge and final rest in His arms. I truly believed that this time dad would be taken to meet his true Master, welcomed to His mansion, and thus live in His Kingdom forever...

Chapter 9: What to do
at the crossroads?

"No matter how hard times may get, always hold your head up and be strong; show them you're not as weak as they think you are." – Dr. Seuss

Every one of us has had problems in life. Every problem had its own cause and effect. Whether the problem was large or small depended on how we perceived it and also to a large extent on our personality. Generally speaking, all things happened for a reason. No matter who you are, what you do for living, or where you go, things would happen that do not make sense — unexpected things that make our life seem as though we had a "rendezvous" with destiny or fate. Whether you believe in the limitations of matter or in something beyond your own control, you would probably come to a point where you believed that there was an entity or supernatural power in control of all happenings with or without your permission or participation in the process. With faith, we could live life without testing the truth. With a heart, we could make few excuses by having more time to allow ourselves back into something that we were less capable of.

Life indeed was about making a choice at every step of the way because a life without choice was not worth living. In every community, there were some people who liked to manipulate or be manipulated without giving any justification whatsoever. Others liked to make excuses for being victimized or being disabled by events or situations that didn't meet their expectations. In some cultures, there were people who like to defame others or induce conflicts. Perhaps to a certain extent, we could live with drama or keep up with trauma and disaster that happened to cripple other human beings for a good reason, but we tended to be difficult in accepting others with excuses that were relatively insensitive or irrelevant to the subject of suffering, not to mention the lack of sympathy or tolerance from those who took advantage of the abusive system. Sometimes that was not about how good we could praise people from overcoming their affliction but about how bad we could boycott people for something they should not be entitled to. People remained hopeful that lines should be drawn appropriately and choices should be made clear so that we could move forward in term of description, classification and determination.

No one could force you to do anything that you don't want to do. Most occurrences or happenings in this material world were conditional or at least close to that in some fashion. In this world, there was a difference in the court of law for the crime you might or might not have committed. There also was a big difference in the court of spiritual law for the sin you were guilty of. Whether you were actually indicted in the eyes of the law or not, you always could be convicted. Whether your problem was related to abuse, lies, addictions, drugs, sex, illness or violence, it was always advantageous for you to acknowledge their existence as an interference or disruption to life. To be stress-free, you need to know one or two of the best choices in life was to seek professional help, counseling or therapy as soon as possible before your situations got worse or matters changed their course over time. And instead of running away from the reality or disregarding the truth, you should work through your problem or situations with no assumption that they might fade away over time.

Every one of us had a life to live. Every life was a journey. Every journey began with a process. Every process had a turning point. Everyone and almost all of us go through life with ups and downs. Before we can find the silver lining for our destination, we hopefully could remain calm upon mishaps or calamity. Despite different encounters and experiences, we need to acknowledge the presence of problems standing in the way between wisdom and confusion. To some people, these difficulties were not much different from anything they had not seen in their lifetimes, and they believed that nothing could block them from moving forward. To a few others, difficulties could be real threats to advancement and improvement leading to a better life. These people anticipate great changes coming out of tough challenges. Still, to many individuals, difficulties tended to cut loose of their confidence and success. These people could be so overwhelmed by defeats and errors that they could become mentally unavailable and emotionally unstable by slipping their feet all over the mud of their wrongdoings. From some perspectives, we might find some kind of abstract or obscurity being embedded in the philosophy of why we spend time chasing things and also in the rationale of why we were afraid of being cut loose from things we run after. I happened to believe or in other words, I was almost certain that pain was inevitable in life, but suffering could be optional.

If you want to save yourself from difficulties and sufferings, do you know how good you could be and where could you start? As Dr. Seuss wrote, don't cry because it's over but smile because it happened. Sometimes we could understand that expectation could be way over the roof even though life might be not going well. In the record book of some individuals, there was never been a problem until some issue arrives or personalities conflict. As change took place, the concept of overcoming problem or personal difficulties become a discrete thing. Perhaps the discrepancy between the best and the norm was the degree of confidence and the level of experience. It was not the celebration of getting by or the great attempt of how skillful people could get around with the twist and turn of not being tossed upside down. It was not the idea of not seeing what was running up but it was the little thought piles together that was truly worth for a second thought to what we were running against with. In spite of bruises and bumps from the counted and uncounted lessons, I remained hopeful that many people could slow down from what they were doing and reconsider the safety and comfort from which they could change to make life a little easier than it was.

Not everyone responds to difficulties in the same way. The notion of getting out of your comfort zone could be one thing and the idea of staying out of trouble became another thing. There were few stages of psychological response to those who were caught up or stuck in the midst of difficulties. No matter how intelligent and skillful you could be with your problem-solving abilities, you need to remain informed. In general, stages of eliciting distress to difficulty or problems include, but not limited to the sense of unbelief, hesitation, intimidation and fear. It was not unheard of to find that many people could be confident enough to step on to their difficulties as some kind of nail or stone on the road without being tripped. I remained hopeful that a few people had little to no reservations from calling their problems out, though their problems could be different from what stood between their obstacles and crossroads. Disturbing reports and acknowledgment of the reality of the underlying problems could be overwhelming or possibly misleading. Personal balance, corporate management, and governmental guideline to address standards for problem-solving could reach to a point that matches with the mandate to meet up challenges. To provide appropriate accommodation for declining mentality was necessary to strengthen recovery and to thus reduce any risk-taking action. It was crucial that all of us could be aware of and realize what and when to call upon our situations or conditions as a crossroads.

Fundamentally speaking, we should be good to address problems and to deal with them accordingly. It was encouraging to see the anticipation of difficulties turned into passion that could make use of resources available to approach them. For instance, if you believe that there was actually a crossroad standing in the way of how you choose to differentiate problems and how you manage to overcome difficulties, you should know whatever you do matters most to not only the party involved, but it also matters to the substance of thing or event relatively covers. If you suspect or question about the presence of crossroads within any aspect of difficulties or problems, you should better investigate but not pontificate on the generalized ideas. We should see one extraordinary element to rise against tough challenge in the political fallouts, geothermal problems, acts of violence, toxic rhetoric of hate, financial meltdowns, broken family, strained or broken relationships, career or educational issues was to embrace difference, to share in grief, to comfort for the lost, to reach out to the weak or poor, and to finally pray God for the blessing.

Not surprisingly we see that the vast majority could be divisive on certain issues. Looking at the dynamic of social conflicts, religious beliefs, political agendas, public relations, social networks and private communications, we probably see the ideas of conservatism, liberalism and extremism were practiced even in a culture of tolerance. To a certain extent, no one should be blamed for the practice of the occult and the violence of a narrow-minded individual or organization. No one should be fully responsible for the intellectual and moral decays unless people could move together to reshape a healthy environment for those who lock themselves in a deadly dark corner and for those who expect to come off from the unrestrained or overindulgent institution. Nobody should think of their legal rights to complain of anything unless they knew a better way to correct a setback or backlash of any kind. Nobody should allow their wisdom to interfere with other people's choices unless they see greater harm from not acting out. Nothing was more vital than getting down to the people's business when we were called to serve on behalf of others, and that I believe to be the highest call for humanity in terms of safety, peace, freedom and health. Nothing was reasonable and worthy to tackle on the worldwide issue other than to address the disoriented mind, the deviated behavior, the messy infrastructure, and the biased principle or policy. If we were going to put up with one person to finger point at another people's mistrust or wrongdoings, and if we were digging into the wound of another human being, we should come up with a better idea or reason to explain our acts or justified fallacy.

What makes one person morally right and politically correct might not necessarily make him or her to be better than another. Human beings were not statistics. One remarkable responsibility or conviction was that we need to get down to the bottom of thing or matter to ensure common sense and mutual respect. People might feel inadequate or any preparation when they were dealing with problems of risking other people's life, endangering the safety of a group, and jeopardizing the health of community. That was never been easy for anyone to learn the virtue of individual tolerance might not be enough to cover problems from human tragedy, mindless violence, human trafficking, racial profiling, heinous murder, and brutal vandalism. People need to take a proactive approach to step back from their conservative voices or beliefs and to remain as neutral as possible before they measure or access the bottom of story, not to mention the difficulty of trying to resolve conflicts from any biased comment or to reduce standoff from any violent acts.

In fact, all of us have had a difficult time fully controlling our behaviors. Generally speaking, our behaviors arose from a relationship between our true self and society. Each of our actions was closely related to our attitude and value we hold. We constantly reflected upon what we said, how we thought, and why we acted. Whether it was good or bad, our actions draw us close to what we want and encourage us to keep on taking and serving our community. A lot of times we found ourselves to be affected by emotions because we couldn't solve the problem that we faced. There even was a time when we found ourselves falling into the love and hate relationships because we couldn't help to overcome our own mistake.

That was not easy to live up to the promise when conditions were tough. We hear people talking about challenges that they experience with their spouse, children, parents, employers, co-workers, family members, friends or loved ones. Plans were not just affected by disaster and tragedy but also diverted by unexpected happenings. We could see frustrations and angers when aroused by the sense of disbelief. We would not easily find peace or consent during the dispute of our difference unless we all could work together to help people who were stranded in storm, stuck in hunger or thirst, strangled in the financial crisis, terrified by the deadly diseases, and beaten up by lies, cheating, and criticism. We should be clear that we won't go very far unless we keep working on and taking care of the issue before that issue could be wired up pretty bad to a point that not many of us could take anymore. No one likely would offer any bailouts to others unless there was a security deposit of good policy or strategy in place. No one should condemn the wrongful if the process of investigation was ongoing, and no one should discredit the less successful if people were still improving their performance.

Perhaps we were feeling good to bring up the talking points so that the involved parties could be fully aware of boundaries being drawn and thus make some justification in between. For instance, parents knew that they needed a lot of time and effort to tell their children not to play video games before they haven't completed homework assignments. Whenever you, the parents, catch your kids playing video games, you probably want to stop them right away and redirect them to something else. But as soon as you were not around, your children were going back to the game they hadn't finished. Up to this date, more and more grownups and married adults – especially men – just like kids, were addicted to video or computer games to a point that they don't want to do any outdoor activities, they don't like to work, and they don't even do anything around the house. The same thing could happen to those adults who had been told of bad food choices and unhealthy lifestyles could endanger themselves with obesity issues unless they were committed to change their eating habits and choices. I have seen and have been told by many adults who regret the choices they made. They share with me that if they listened carefully to their parents, counselors and pastors at the time, then they wouldn't need to go back to school in their forties and fifties trying to finish up their college while they happened to struggle between work and care for their family and kids. By and large, incidents happened when we trade in our own goods for some loose feeling or pleasure during the time we deny remarks for own goods. Bad results occurred when we exploited our freedom to willfully reject references that could make the fallout more dramatic and even tragic than we could imagine. We should understand that there were a lot of things we need to take care of before we conclude how terrible someone could be and how horrible the condition could become. One undying truth was that we needed to consider things for a little longer than what we could handle. Another great wisdom in life was how could we make use of the circumstance to overcome our shortcomings and in the meantime allow us to achieve the best result possible?

We might see many people were contaminated by editorials or intoxicated by commentaries, as their mindset or thoughts suffered from a viral infection of material ideas. No one should be intimidated by the heart. No one should be threatened by different tones and volumes from those open communications, direct dialogues, and civilized debates. Mentality was an important element that could shake up the degree of motivation and the level of confidence. Such character became a karma or persona that allowed policymakers and management teams to check off performance in terms of economy, education, politics, sports and business. If leaders won't step up their extraordinary measures to protect Christians on religious faith, discrimination and abuses, they should reconsider the aftermath of religious disaster. If governments don't buckle down on their legislation and policies to better address corruption, violence, crime, human rights, foreign affairs, national defense and the deficit, they had better be ready to honestly accept the fallout or catastrophic situation from their leadership crisis. If elected officials tend to push agendas by their lobbying groups instead of serving their constituents and communities, they would realize that justice won't be well served until their principle and core values live up to that of the reality. If the poor and weak won't stand up for what they believe to be right and if they don't turn the negatives into positives or opportunities, they won't deliver any effective message for many followers to honor life the best way that it should. If all of us fail to become a living proof for whom we were and what we could be, we could hardly make an impact to those who we love, not to mention the lack of connection with the lost, the wounded, and the almighty. Obviously we see that our mind power and true understanding of the situation, without leaning to either the left or the right, could help to sustain vitality and creditability over conviction.

Have you learned anything about yourself while you happened to be in the spotlight of the camera, the echo from surrounding walls, the walking zombie suffering from hunger or sickness, the roaring of the storm, the shaking loose of a tsunami, the stress from conflicts, the institutional change from transitions of power, the stranding from a blizzard or a landslide? If either natural disasters or personal difficulties fail to make you aware of the problems and issues in your life, I am not sure what kinds of things could catch your eyes to see the difference. If you think that nothing could stop you from all the walls you build with your actions, I am not so certain what would when it was just you and the circumstances standing in the crossroads. If you think that you could not be moved by the loss of your loved one or your dearly possessions, I could be speechless at the audacity you manage to keep yourselves on top of the very moment. If you claim whatever happens to Mary or Johnny had very little chance of affecting you, I respectfully say that you should not say "never" because one day you'll find yourself trying to catch up with your own breath.

History seems to repeat itself, and so do events or matters. Although the features vary among those who plan, operate and access the system, we need to look beyond the subject at the time with a sense of maturity. To some extent, we might be unable to change what was behind the transaction, but the road to recovery could be expected when we put resources together to work for common goals. We might find all right and not uncommon to not have all the answers to the problems we faced at the time, but one key play in each of those critical trials was not to solve the differences among us but the problems ahead of us. We shouldn't forget who we were and we shouldn't go back to who we are. But one thing we could correct ourselves and one way we could help those around us was to do what we really could with little hesitation, judgment, fear and criticism. Besides, we should not waste time by worrying about what and who should be there. Similarly, we need to set aside work and projects that don't bring in good results so that we instead could deliver plans proven for success from what we know.

Most problems were rooted the same and all crossroads were alike, though they might seem to be different at a time. What varies between yours and mine tend not to be the ways they were set up but rather, the measures we came up with. Though we could all set sail in the same open sea of problems that this world imposes, the degree and scale of difficulties were different between what you experienced and how I felt, not to mention the fact of how we deal with them differently. Despite how devastating the problems could be in times of disaster, war and violence, nothing could separate us from providing comfort to the lost and wounded. Despite how desperate the situations could be in times of a tragic event, deadly disease, and depressive economy, nothing could stop us from reaching out to the hopeless and less fortunate. Perhaps the world we lived in today was different from what it used to be. Perhaps our busy and stressful lifestyles had put up some roadblocks to prevent us from living a happy, loving and God-fearing life. These roadblocks could be hidden or closely related to technology, the seeking of attention via social media, and the no-face-time from texting. These roadblocks could give us more baggage than our parents or even grandparents had in terms of sharing quality time with our loved ones. One of the greatest virtues in the go-getting American spirit was not the possibility of succeeding in one's dreams but the ability to accept the objective pursuits, good or bad, just as they are. Whether we like it or not, bad things exist in our almost perfect society, and bad things do happen to good people, and they include but are not limited to Christians. Indeed, we could be upsetting to see few good people and things going before us without giving us an opportunity to either say goodbye or to figure out what they are. One precious thing that we all share in common was to behold the ones who live beside and among us by telling them how fortunate and blessed we are. We should never be questionable to think of the power that tends to divide us should not be equal or greater than the power that unites or unifies us. In some constructive thoughts, we remain hopeful in reminding people of the dreams, legacies and expectations from the loss, and we shouldn't allow them to die in vain by our "do nothing" mentality or careless attitudes.

Perhaps the one healing that anyone could draw from their distresses and breakdowns was to find comfort of some kind. It was never too early for anyone to not seek professional consultation and counseling for the pain and suffering they go through, the harsh criticism in the line of duty that they were not deserved of, and the strong conviction of corruption or wrongful allegation that they had no knowledge of. It was never too late for anyone to not pursue their spiritual revival or sanctification for their fornications, transgressions, extortions, idolatries, adulteries, perjuries and crimes. Many people see good day from the beautiful life uphill and they found the platform for their talents to make great adjustment for the life they anticipated. But not many of them could anticipate enough at how they could cover the pivotal moment of those people, especially in the Third World countries who were deserted, trapped, run down, and living without the necessities of life and the simplest means of convenience that most Americans take for granted.

We should feel a significance to acknowledge crossroads in our life. Perhaps the vast majority sees only obstacles standing in their way, and when they were tired of removing them or being told how to remove them, they became hardheaded. That was quite interesting to see how many people keep their temperature down to learn through the process. We should understand that many of us like to raise our voices or change our tones or even possess a bad attitude when all happenings turned out to be not what we anticipate or want. There was never been any better time or being happy in life when our to-do-lists were checked off from the schedule and our wishes were granted. One reason for that situation was it allowed us to look back at what we had done. Perhaps it was all right to see mistakes and silliness that we make along the way, but with open-mindedness and courage, we could continue to learn new things, as we move along. Another reason for that condition was it gave us an opportunity to step up and step out of our comfort zone to meet old challenges, to break off from our bad habit, and to strive for new results. Forgetting about the status quo, there never has been any miserable state other than the failed attempt to make our life worthy to live. There were no successful people who do not trip, fall, get up, and start all over if they had to. Life indeed would not knock us down; we only need to decide when or if we need to get back up. Some people might take a little longer time than others to pull themselves up and thus get over their failure or error. Most people, however, know that one of their best chances to possibly beat all odds was to know how, where and when to get up after each fall. No state or country in this world could be strong and rich without going through a hard and possibly, series of brutal battles, both politically and economically. No leaders, politicians and educators could become well-known and powerful overnight if they didn't experience toughness and hardship throughout their early encounter or career. Regardless of how it could be, perhaps one difference that separated them and the norm was their willingness to accept criticism, to take a hard fall, and to not give up with each and every practical opportunity they have.

That could be a blessing for those who learn or know how to take advantage of their personal difficulties. People could claim how discouraging their life could be and make all sorts of excuses for how disgraceful it was if they failed to make good use of the opportunity they had. Life could be more detrimental when people found they were on the wrong side of life if they don't give some deep thought to what they have. Perhaps people should reconsider what they had and how they made use of their thought before they were all tangled up with problems. No one deserves to know anything less than you. No one should worry about anything other than the ones that they were working with and the ones they love. If people decided to let their problems or shortcomings dictate what they could do and how they acted or should act at the time, their life could be a mystery before they could quit. They could far more be over at any given point of life before they realized that their reluctance or lack of commitment to things greater than themselves could turn into chaos. But if they could listen closely to what was actually happening and if they could disregard what was occurring before they found themselves choked up by what other people, friends and co-workers tell them of what was not. If other people really happened to be in their shoes, they wouldn't give you advice on things that they had no clue of or to tell you what wasn't working.

If you could just slow down a little bit and open your ears, then you might be able to hear what the Almighty God is telling you. Humbly speaking, I do believe that a peaceful mind could allow us to think thoroughly and cautiously about what we had and communicate well with our innate intelligence. Practically speaking, all things happened for a reason and yet love and success, for instance, also could happen by chance. No matter how hard you had tried, sometimes you might think that you were no way near to where you were and what you do if you truly believe that you can achieve more things in life than you could possibly imagine. Personally, I always was grateful for the very moment I received divine contact with my life and thankful to the Lord's presence that guided me through the thick and thin of my life. As long as I could remember, it was His grace reaching out to my life. I always could recall that God told me to slow down when the time was not right or when my life was in a mess; He taught me to grow when I was not right or happened to be wrongfully led by all kinds of wisdom other than His; He signaled me to go ahead when the time was right or my work was on target; and He gave me chances to laugh out loud when I happened to be well-trained and wise enough to be on my own way. Everything was a blessing, and that included but was not limited to the bad experiences, and all the warm touches on my unimaginable and seemingly impossible journey.

Opportunity could appear anywhere, and it could come to anyone. Whether or not anyone of us could actually see an opportunity at any given time or condition, we were still moving in some sort of direction that represented our personality, character or adjustment in between or within the system. Humbly speaking, the optimists see an opportunity in every difficult or painful moment while the pessimists see pain or problem in every opportunity. We should know time was not the real factor, but time could definitely bring in a difference from one person to another in term of results. We should find the kind of perception in term of behavior or action that underlines the true difference from all within. We could respectfully disagree or legally point out the real, obvious and practical error or controversy, but we should not make false accusations at the time when an improvement was made within the window of opportunity. Perhaps people could be easy to say what seemed to be unimportant or insignificant, but please don't project that to anyone either by chance or by excuses. Otherwise, we could drive people to make use of the idea of individualism or differences in term of principles, standards and priorities to achieve result that eventually separates all those between us.

Knowing what we serve was indeed important, but knowing who we serve is even more so. Most of us don't live with a conscious awareness, and we were obviously living by our own emotions or whatsoever helped to guide our decisions at a time. We were no doubt changing our beliefs on behalf of what we felt or see but not necessarily based on what we experienced and how we thought. No one likes to be judged, and no one really wants to do things that somebody told or expects them to. What truly catches us between the crossfire of our controversy and the backlash of our decision was not "if" and "when" that many of us perceive the need to do so. That instead was if it was the right and smart move to keep us from addressing the issue of "if" and "when" that we needed to live life without worrying about the possibility of any second opportunity. If there was indeed a second chance or any more second opportunities to serve others well, we probably wouldn't be so emotional or negative about it. One reason for that was the finding of rhythm or the rediscovery of passion. Another reason for that was the style of our act or the relay of our passion. Therefore, how could we motivate or change other people's mind with a second chance depend on our personality, intellect and speech. Either way, our extraordinary and possibly imminent priority should focus on the great need of individuals who had the rightful incentives or plans for making meaningful contribution to the group's efforts and thus enlightening others to think and act accordingly. Another priority was to make an impact on those who were and could be out of touch from the rest of the world.

Perhaps not many people could actually see where the problem came from, but many somehow could feel what kind of problem they were getting. On any occasion and almost anywhere, many of us might have had a short-term memory in patronizing or being accused of what they had done wrong. Whether a word or events could be constructive or destructive, many people could be off the hook for what they said yet could also understand that decent people won't embrace a vengeful practice or vicious attack as a way of either getting ahead or getting even with others. In this modern day and post-religion age, we might feel difficult to find mass murder not by any biological warfare or political means but rather by the perverseness of verbal criticism of personality, symbolism, rhetoric, or figures of speech. There was a filing of motion in the legal proceedings for issues that disrupted the life of a community and the will of its citizen. For the education purpose, we saw a contrast of principle violation being taken in between the fundamentalist and the lunatic in the concept of whether it was appropriate or politically correct to have criticism and accusation without overstepping boundaries. Above and beyond, the overhaul effect was not on how powerful or harmful any speculation could become, but it was the credibility of facts. And at the end of the day, it tended to be the little voice inside of us that might wake us all up to acknowledge that our end roads could become God's crossroads.

Labels may not be important to some people, but they indeed can play a major role in people's lives. Whether we fully pay attention to our surroundings or not, we do, from time to time, "label" attempt to put some kind of "label" onto and almost in everything we know. Correct and good labels were no different from favorite dresses or suits that people wear. Wrong labels were similar to the nightmare or infection that could come back to keep a person from moving their life forward. Instead of closing up all the opportunities or shutting people out from voicing their opinion, we should open more doors or windows for people who aren't afraid to stand up for what they believe to be right and live up to what they claim to be right or fair. Our thoughts and perspectives in life should come from the accumulated experience in people, things and substances. Those sets of values continuously formulate and shape the kind of life we live in and also highlight the direction of our path. Regardless of how labels might play out some time in our life, I do hope that every one of us should have at least one thing in common that allows us to be passionate about. Hopefully, it could become something that we could proudly endorse or sponsor others to either team up or follow in footstep besides our dearly inspiration.

To have somebody who always could make us laugh and stay positive at our side was important even when life gets rough. As a matter of fact, we'd like to surround ourselves with positive, kind, uplifting and like-mind people who we care deeply about. No one truly likes to listen when other people give harsh remarks, hate speech, or racist comments on matters that were not going to help them live a healthy, successful and prosperous life. No one disagrees with what most people tend to believe about what makes us special and unique – lying in the power of God, the impact from family, the essence of health, the pursuit of happiness, the teaching of Golden Rule, and the free spirit of working hard. One big reason for that was the fundamental belief and principle of diligence that allow people living their dreams. Another reason was the experience coming from all dimensions of life along with the freedom to choose from what they had.

When speaking of positive thoughts, we should understand that the positive attitude helped paving ways for a better life. No matter what kinds of backgrounds we had, each and all of us had the ability to turn our lives to follow the path that we expected. That was up to our discretion to capture the opportunity and make use of available resources to produce the greatest results. Good motives and planning could help one to achieve. Wrong and malicious motives not only could limit the possibility of success but could surely scale down any rebounding confidence and thus narrow our mentality to be defeated.

Loving others should come from the bottom of the heart without requiring anything in return. Despite the fact that many people seemed very easy to talk about love, they indeed took a lot of thought and courage to truly express what love really meant. Some people found difficulty to understand others before they could love others. Some people think that they were all right to earn the love from other people before they could give it back to others. In fact, true love didn't come around very often, perhaps once or twice in a lifetime. Many people found that they need to hold their love separated from others. Still, many people think that was acceptable to not give their love, not to mention true love, to others unless circumstances or conditions told them to do so. With little to no hard feeling to those who happened to think selfishness was right, I felt hard to imagine what kind of life and future might hold if we took away the ability and passion from those who put their thoughtfulness in volunteer services, community services, habitat for humanity, charity works, and fundraising events. Indeed, respecting others should come from a non-judgmental state of mind. Despite the person or groups who happen to serve or work with us could be inferior to us in term of physical, intellectual and socioeconomic status, there could be one or two things that they could offer better than anyone we could possibly know. With that perspective in mind, we might see or come to appreciate the fact that our world should not be limited in black and white but could be a mixture or combination of colors that

245

reveal the best picture ever seen. If the bel boys, bus boys, cleanup crews, cab drivers, bartenders, customer service representatives, flight attendants, Coast Guard, and emergency rescue workers could do nothing except their works, then what good could they be compared to someone who gives a hand, a smile, a cheer, a hug, a lift, and a shoulder pat during those downs of life? Don't people deserve love just because of who they were and what they do? Should people deserve to live better and to treat others nicer just because of what and who God created them to be?

All of us might live our life with a vision and a dream. Whether some of us really knew or were informed of what we beheld, we somehow continue to carry out our vision and dream piece by piece with little to no regrets. Perhaps we indeed could have something that we could work on to restore or replace for the loss of our confidence. Some people were born to continue their family legacy. Some others were born to be a true legend of their own. As kids, most of us were used to count off the good little things or results we had, and we tended to either brag about them or keep them as treasure. As we began to grow older, we kept on doing the same thing by grouping them into types and subtypes based on our basic reasoning of what they should be. For instance, when we were a kid, we tended to find out or make sure that our dolls shouldn't look like what Mary had. We hated to play with Johnny because he looked ugly and ate our cookies. As we reached our prime age, we rejoiced over what we cherished, and we celebrated life by overcoming difficulties, suffering and pain. We held on to the substance of things and people that provide us with the greatest value and benefit. When we passed our prime age, we called off what drove us away from fear of nothing as we were young. When emptiness or loneliness hit us, we more likely became more interested in what held us back from our past. What really frightened us off wasn't from those we expected but the details and life that held us back from all we were longed for. Some people did enjoy and had a good time with what they were working on. While some people chased rabbits that were not real, some others might lose count of the valuable things they were after. In spite of all that could be added up for success, physically, materially, and substantially, hopefully we won't need to repeat the drama or what's standing in our way. If a vision and a dream were only designed for our fleshy nature, we probably knew that we would do anything to keep that alive without questioning what was really rustling around our minds. If we get a second chance to catch up with the loosen piece of our dream and/or vision, we'll know how to avoid doing the cut and chase. We'll know what to expect with little to no limits other than the sense of humility to serve well with others without losing our passion to serve God and his Kingdom at the same time.

Perhaps one of the most disturbing things in life was our inability to find our own vision and dream. Indeed, we live to learn that we might have a bigger role in other thing else because we want our lives to be valuable when searching for our own purpose in life. Sometimes we should know how we chose to live was not really mattered much in comparison to how we could believe in ourselves to do things that we were supposed to do. You could be confused more or happen to fight harder with the kind of life and the level of responsibility that stretches out in front of you, but you would not be bothered by the kind of commitment when life demands it. Imagining the fact that you could be more stressful by sitting around with nothing to do than putting them back to where they belong. You would be more pitiful and miserable if you knew that you could be excluded or that you'd disqualified yourself from what could possibly make a difference in where you are. Certainly there was no guarantee in what you do, but there was no limit in what you could do either. Whatever you do or willingly choose to do might not bring back the history, legacy and dream that your life had, but it at least marks the work you do in response to the need at the time. The work you do and contributions you make could be trivial and even worthless to mention though you indeed were doing the right thing. You should be proud of yourself for the service you perform without any regrets by comparing yourself to those wealthy, talented and famous individuals whose works sometimes were less likely sprung from their hearts or passion. Whether you decide to be more committed to your vision and dream or you choose to let go of them, you should know better than anyone that your life could depend on it, your reputation was on the line, and further your experience would be incredible and sensational. No matter how burned out or frustrated you might be, you'll never be an annoyance to God, and you won't wither if you stretch out your hands to willingly accept His empowerment. No matter how little and insignificant you think you are, you'll never be so if you surrender your life to the entity that was far reaching than your wisdom and also to the mission that was greater than both of your life and experience combined. Regardless of how and whether you put your religious faith into the practicum of daily life or not, you'll never be too old to be an instrument and a testimonial for the work of His Kingdom, and you'll find the deliverance, decree and apprehension that God has for you beyond the chivalry in Hinduism or the reincarnated spirit of Buddhism as I had learned.

Do you think that you were persecuted to a degree that your freedom or security was jeopardized? Do you realize that your acknowledgment of safety and your confidence in the divine mind could be robbed of its spiritual innocence or giving from those you love? From several perspectives, the spirit of initiative helped to determine the possibility of success regardless of backgrounds and the mentality of freewill, determinism or open-mindedness in Christianity. In today's lifestyle, we could have a difficult time imagining that anyone could be less serious or not too caught up with their life. Indeed, you should be ambitious with your career and yet loving to your family at the same time. You should be diligent in your work and yet possess a thirst for knowledge. You should know your limits and yet make your way through challenges in your life. You should be drawn to friends and people with intelligence and confidence but not too full of themselves, and that was to say they likely stood for something or were with similar interest and passion in life. Politically correct, you should fall for people who were smart, self-sufficient, and share good common sense or ethical and moral values but not someone who tends to be irrational, pushy, vindictive, judgmental or quick to conclude anything. You should be drawn to people with sharp wit, good heart or limited resources, but they shouldn't deserve anything more if their lives were driven by corruptions, vanity, sarcasms and manipulations with little love or no empathy to those wounded, fell and lost. You should be disappointed by the nagging feeling and painful experience from the brokenness of a relationship, the addiction of drugs, the abuse of sex, the tyranny of violence, and the mocking from the atheist that literally could ruin all that you were associated with; however, you would never imagine the destruction of life and all it stands when manifestations of human trafficking, legal abortion, racial rhetoric, and irrational dictatorship were acceptable in ripping the hope of innocence and the freedom or equality from the suffered.

There was nothing more important than keeping your hope alive by realizing that help was on the way even if you were in the pit of death. Hardships indeed could be stressful, and sufferings could be horrifying, but there was nothing more dangerous and terrible than suicidal thoughts and desperate acts. It could be understood that some of us believe that we live to experience the best, the most beautiful, the most comfortable, and the greatest love this life offers. Not so many of us think that we live to experience the torture, to undertake the impossible, and to taste the bitterness. In fact, life can be a mess, reality is harsh, and our experience of life can even be worse some time. Even at our worst, few of us agree or are willing to accept what tends to be the byproduct of somebody's failed policy, misleading principles, corrupt thoughts, irresponsible errors, and wrongful accusations, not to mention the loss of public faith or confidence. From the parable of Jesus Christ's walking on the water, one can see that Christ the Lord was looking for someone who was an ordinary person to do the extraordinary. Peter, one of Christ's twelve disciples, is unsuccessful stepping out of the boat when he was asked to. Peter failed miserably and terribly in advancing God's calling because he knew that Jesus was there to pick him up. Peter, who was not much different from any one of us, failed in public faith because he lacked spiritual stability to meet life's challenges. Spiritually, intuitively and physically, most of us fear to step out of our comfort zone and we tended to be insecure when we had to further think out of the box and especially when we need to act unprecedentedly or non-traditionally. The problem we face in our life today tends not to be how deep the valley of hardships could be or how shallow the water of difficulties could become, it was always about how we carry out the kind of attitude to overcome those unimagined moments or incomprehensive situations. Regardless of political, religious and philosophical differences, we should not just live up to what was expected, but we should also be ready to live up to what was unexpected or at least we need to stay on course within the mean of something even though it was untouchable sometimes.

There is nothing more precious in life than acknowledging the sources of our limitations. Everyday people experienced problems in their physical, financial, spiritual and political arenas. People lived in a state of war against poverty, disease, oppression, abuse and violence. People fought hard to survive within their means regardless if it was for their work, skills, education, religions or politics, they see fairness as a framework of social justices, equality as a fundamental human right, competition as an opportunity for excellence, and stability as a presentation of peace and security for themselves, their loved ones, and the society. From time to time, most of us were compromising each other in sustaining a relationship or some kind of business. Because of that, some people like to compromise to close deals or to get things done by returning favors that they might not truly want to give. Many enjoy the results from the fruits of their hard work or labors while others favor prosperity from the technological advancement, social networking, or risky investment. The spirit was encouraging and the mentality was strong as more and more people aim for higher objectives that give little room for error or any hesitation for correction but rather, greater chance for advancement.

People could garner a better idea of how productive they could be by using some hypothetical and analytical methods to test the equation of success. People can find a high level of energy in their intellectual or physical competition when they knew that they had to work hard to win. And along the way, the sense of creativity and the kind of positive energy could outcast personalities when the hard work reflects a burning desire. If people were unable to trade in their creativity or talent for some fraction of productivity, then they might be not ready to roll with the functionality of corporate world or have the infrastructure needed in a political showdown. If people were unwilling to take up challenges or muscle up with their situations, they might end up with more problems than they anticipated and over time they might face tougher decisions than they had ever imagined. There was a time when a personal win might not be so important than the team approach or organizational goals. There also was a time when complicated rules, budget shortfalls, and hoops to jump through approached some unbearable levels and the sense of chaos and the loss of confidence continued to be skyrocketing.

If we could treat each new problem or episode with a strategy, we'd find new idea and new solution emerge. If we could replace the most critical illness with principled values and consistent standard of care, we should come to a point learning the appropriate therapy was a significant part for health recovery. If we could place our common sense to overlook the standard operating procedures, we'd see good result from recordkeeping or exiting strategy to correct any lapse we might have. For instance, when you were in the hospital, you should not get too upset with the nurses or other staff. Perhaps you or your loved ones were in pain and needed immediate medical attention at the time. You thought that you were being left out or your schedule of care happened to be late when the medical staff tried explaining to you what was happening. Sometimes you might get angry or frustrated with your therapists because you think that they were not helpful for your condition. You talked to their supervisors or management team even though your therapists had done nothing wrong to jeopardize the care. You thought that they were overpaid and you deserved better. One thing most of us seemed to be forgotten during our emotional toll was a good result in general should come steady. If we could truly read other people's minds, we would know where we should be heading, not waste time, or make an unnecessary expenditure of resources. Further, if we could go back to read between lines in the Holy Scripture, we probably could see result and expectation might not be aligned at the same time and they should not be restricted to a single form of interpretation or one side of the story as well.

There were a lot of mockers and pretenders in life. Whether you were a fundamentalist or an ideologue, conservative or liberal, religious or agnostic, intelligent or average, rich or poor, you were always in the middle of something, and you were a part of what was in and around your social circle. Most of the time we remain hopeful that our thought and act continued to be the best presentation of who we were. When we spend time completing over our vanishing illusions, some escapists control their fear and focus on their mind for things with foreshadowing futures. In the beginning when people found something good with God, they did not see courage under fire. When they move into the middle of a mess or a hardship, they put faith on trial. Most of the time when we race through the way of material possessions, we seem to be shortsighted by the partial view standing in front of us. When we celebrate success, happiness and commitment to service from the abundant life, we can feel little to no resistance from people around us; however, we might face great setbacks or tremendous resistance even from people who we didn't know when came down to the issue of getting help or sharing responsibility for reducing environmental pollution, toxic substance, chemical waste, drug or weapon smuggling, violence or human trafficking, just to name a few major issues of the day.

Even with a goodwill or kindness being set in place, we tended to not imagine what kinds of people were put into proper use for certain assignments, and we might forget to pass our good virtue on to the next generation. When many of us suffered from temptation, persecution and addiction, few of us really knew how to encourage others to stand up with their battles without being too much vented of their own. When some of us were proud of our own heritage or way of managing our problems, we might see that some people were making fun of or slapping on our strategy. When people were confronting with their financial difficulties, career or business downturn, imagine how many of them were immediately turning to coaches, mentors or latest gadgets for problem-solving and advice. When people expanded their territory by energizing or broadening their base, they should have weighed in on all options to minimize setbacks. Given the fact that many of us experienced isolation, disenfranchisement, and sarcasm even from our supporters and buddies, many people might still feel that some of us were not so good and generous to welcome others with good faith, pleasant experience, or stress-free life. There were times when some people wouldn't let go of their hands to scratch another person's back because they hated their gut or the way they behaved. There also were times when some people just couldn't give up their ridicules or gossip when others were still struggling to get some balance from the process. Still, there were times when people couldn't stop beating a dead horse when they saw an opportunity to attack others for a weakness, mistake, or failure regardless of how sensitive an issue could be or how funny a thing could become. For whatever that was worth, the sense of self sufficiency tended to be harder to achieve, and whenever you choose to close the door or narrow your social circle, the world seemed to close with you, as the negativity seemed to not shut you out. For whatsoever happens to our ego and confidence, the wheel of jokes and lies go around and around until some of us started to figure out the spices of life can't be fully completed in the absence of salt and pepper. If people could relate them to what Christ the Lord demonstrates in his teaching and ministry, they probably envision the principle of love that bears all loads and the concept of faith that removes all blocks so that He approximates human hood with priesthood and also unites men with God.

According to William James, the art of being wise means knowing what to overlook. Obviously all mankind should overlook the facts and then comment on the issue of agendas, principles and deeds regardless of ethnicity, religion and class. Nothing should ever hold man from his future and nobody should be intimidated by the threat of freedom, liberty and equality because they were the endowments and basic human rights gifted from the Almighty God. Politically correct, people should not complain of how bad is a regime or policy, which could come from some pathetic, corrupted and deregulating systems, could eventually damage their lives. People could be moved by the desires for economic development despite what came from conservative or liberal governing. Whether it came from the post-modern science or technology, nobody knew what could happen and at least they knew a change did not come from a chronological order. People needed to learn that if there was a change, our world was not going to be the same and our very characters also need to become a fairly balanced representation from multiculturalism, but not the movement from some radicals or ideologues.

Perhaps, however we were used to do business in the good old days needed to be left behind. As the world of business dealt with the problem of a declining economy, corporate leaders and entrepreneurs worked tirelessly and became extra cautious to ensure a balanced budget. It tended to be the real crunch time for finding the revolutionary idea to provide new employment and stable economy. As our lifestyles began to march on with a high demand for technological breakthroughs, constant innovation and luxury replacement should not be the solution for infrastructure spending and frivolous projects that would not be cost-effective. As high education began to play a vital role in career-building or job-related performance, the sense of corruption and ethical violation took a big toll and hit every walk of life. Along the line of intellectual advancement, the issues of high school dropouts, teen pregnancies, family illiteracy, violence, abortion and addictions gained social acceptance and went beyond the principle and responsibility from parents, classrooms and governments. As morality and spiritual redemption continue to reach all time high, roadblocks in our society turn out to be a reminder of our lower self. Those roadblocks might not truly reflect all the error and mistake we had from any irrational and cynical views, but they could bring us some hidden truths from the negative events we encountered. Connecting to our true nature requires a good backup plan before everything was going to be ended up in the air. Comparing to all the ways apply to any business or relationships we had, we must be aware that the limited abilities of the mind could lead to misconceptions about matters and events, but that could transform us for a misrepresentation to a spiritual life.

History was constantly evolving and new records were made by what we do, whether good or bad. As human beings, we had the ability to decide what we stood for and how we will go from where we are. We should not embrace the greatest void in our life to be our greatest values. We should encourage the overcoming of childhood deprivations to be the goal of adult dreams and aspirations. We should promote the high spirit of difference in talents or creativity from any diverse group instead of putting all fences up because of those differences. We should inspire others to become big brothers and sisters for their family, schools, church and community. Let us not lose sight of what brings us closer to our commonality in terms of a hope for good job, a desire for good education, a plan for better future, and action from a smarter government. Let us never lose hope of what we could do to change the reality of the unknown by developing strategies that yield good results because decisions and roleplays would be out of hands if we lose control of ourselves. In reality, no one could coil a hard-boiled egg. As a human being, we don't and we can't fix everybody. Whatsoever we decide or choose to do today would play a role in tomorrow's outcomes. What happened yesterday always would be a souvenir for today's gathering and continues to be a treasure for tomorrow's journey. Nobody could truly know what a future holds. Our future should not be decided by the run over a short distance but should be focused on the race for a great purpose in life and for the fight of a better life. Regardless of how terrible and desperate our current situation could be, no one should lose sight of what they could do. Certainly no one could take away the privilege of how you dream, and you should not be afraid of being judged by someone because it was always you to be judged at your own crossroads or at each intercepted point of your life. And at the end of day, it was you who were going to honestly answer to your true self, and it was you who were responsible for all the remarks you make, footprints you have, and lives you touch.

How many roadblocks did you identify and how many crossroads did you find? Some people like to run their own life. Some others like to run with life. Still, others like to run against life. I know many people had challenged experiences with their previous relationships but that should not stop them from getting themselves back onto the horse again because discovery never sleeps. I know our world might be different from what we were grown up with, but that did not mean we couldn't work through with our world. I am confident that we can move away from our ego and one day all of us would turn our differences into something that we could enjoy and be passionate about. No one knows how long we can stay on holding our horses for life, but let's see how the trail takes us and hopefully one day we no longer need to say we just tag along but instead, we should proudly say that we own our life completely.

How long had we prayed and how many times had we been prayed? No matter how different or difficult our world could be, I believe we all did pray and even aggressively prayed for something that might harden our heart at the time. Though what we prayed for vary from one another, but the purpose of our prayers somehow might be relatively the same except our motives. For instance, our prayer lists could include but were not limited to wealth, health, love, power and fame, not to mention some ridiculous prayers of getting even or ahead of someone who we didn't like. For me, I remembered my prayer to God was very simple when I first was accepted to Gordon College to study my remediation courses in comparison to my friends or freshman class. I did not ask God to help me passed all my classes, provided me all kinds of scholarships and gave me beautiful girlfriends. What I prayed for at the time might not be what many people nowadays dared to challenge themselves with. Even when I looked back at what my prayer lists were, I even laughed at myself for being silly enough. But I am truly grateful that God saw through my simplicity in the request and hunger for excellence and so He put me through trial and error, and even some disturbing relationship with God as a way of training me. Besides, I am forever grateful because of my prayer was to have great knowledge and durable popularity so that I could use that experience to help others overcoming what seem to be impossible whether it was in medicine, dentistry, nursing, education, business, auto mechanics, architecture, art, cooking or theological seminary studies.

A time comes when each of us reaches a crossroads. Whether our crossroads could turn out to be a good turning point remained to be seen by how we acted on behalf of our acknowledgment of this crossroads. Personally, *mes carrefour* become my benchmarks so that I could transform my mind and revolutionize my ideas to match up with my future encounter or any unexpected journey. Looking back at more than two decades ago, I once traded in my citizenship rights to be an alien of another foreign country and after growing tired of living from both the social and communist governments, I also willingly cashed in for a freedom that I don't truly know of any benefits to possessing. Though poor and undereducated at a time, I'm now thankful to be raised from a strong conservative family that taught me to not label anything, judge anyone, or condemn anybody. I wanted to be educated so badly that eventually I slept only 3-4 hours a night so that I could have time to catch up with all of my homework assignments and studies. I yearned for being successful but somehow was not quite there yet. I was a freak for quite some time when I think that I could run over anything based on my youth, talents, strength and wisdom until I overheard some voices whispering deeply in my ears saying, "this is the way, walk ye in it, when ye turn to the right hand, and when ye turn to the left" (Isaiah 30:21). Because of that strange voice, many times I found myself to be out of trouble from the life I lived, and as I remembered in the quote from a beautiful gospel song written, "When the oceans rise and thunders roar, I will soar with you above the storm. Father, you are King over the flood, I will be still, know you were God." Though I dreamed of having a high profile life, that dream costed me a decade of learning and choosing the wrong path instead of living. I had been soul searching for a clearer and larger purpose in life but somehow I fell in the trap of wrecked ideas and frivolous life. For a little more than seven years, I felt blessed that my dad had survived from multiple episodes of diseases and sicknesses accompanied by risks and complications that more than once threatened to take his life away. Indeed, my dad's life was a working miracle from the Almighty until he was called home after living for an additional seven years, a grace period given to him. For more than five years ago, I felt encouraged when I saw my struggling business continue to thrive and survive from what was once started during the most challenging time of the Great Recession in the modern day. Indeed, I might have been crippled in many situations, tripped in numerous occasions, and beaten up really bad in many tribulations, but if I counted up all my setbacks and failures coming from my pride and self-center that could give compliment to my desires and achievements, I would hold no hostility against anything or anyone other than my hijacked faith. Despite conflict, rejection, defeat, transgression and sins in life, I had not lost my passion in search of a lasting purpose. Though I had seen my loss and grief over the years, I still held on to God's promise. Though I saw a gap or big hole in human relationships, I was so glad to learn from His steadfast love even when I failed Him.

To a certain degree, I had been grateful to find myself calm in many of my lonesome days when I was only half-awaken. I'm blessed to have had an extraordinary opportunity to think and meditate on the shower of grace that allowed me to hold a reasonable conversation with my Creator during my painstaking life. Perhaps I did have a breathtaking moment over what I had and anyone I knew, but I had not really cherished the moment. Indeed, my financial hardships helped me to foresee the glory or riches from God's Kingdom. My intellectual guilt helped to rip me of my naked innocence to run from His teachings. My mindful attitude helped to pull me out of my nutshell to care for something larger than my own life. My clear mind kept my emotions from being torn or broken down from any catastrophe or disaster. My temperament saved me from rewinding my terrible past. My resilient spirit ignited my passion for a greater avocation and service to humanity where restoring health and bridging the healthcare gap though doing so meant facing a stigma as painful as disease itself. Between religion and practical life, I somehow found that there was a space or separation between the two. In that space was our ability to form a philosophy or belief to lead our lifestyle and thus live our life. And also that practical life revealed our growth, ability, determination and freedom to choose and to also pursue happiness, liberty and purpose in life.

I can't remember when I turned from a worry-free teenager into a responsible, mature man. I won't forget the last time I got so mad and really upset – I needed a friend so bad, but my friend or so-called "buddies" had cut me loose and couldn't be there for me. I could barely recognize myself the first time that I put on an old heart from a young naïve mind. I had never dared to forget when was the right time that I let go my search for a better life without looking back at my miserable past. I can't imagine when would be the best time that I could reap the fruit of my labor without breaking up more hearts and tearing more souls apart. I truly believe that our culture was obsessed with success. Whether success should be defined in term of intellectual, spiritual or financial growths, we were constantly changed and redefined by our experience. I firmly believed our ultimate success should not be restricted in physical and material achievements of this world but rather, our faith and eternal security that rested in Christ alone. We were indeed made for life with God, and I realized that our peace of mind or real happiness could be found in life when our purpose was achieved with, in and through Christ because in reality, we never knew what could happen next. I was not proud of what I had because I was just a poor kid who had never been inherited any wealth or talents, but I happened to believe that my standards, principles, beliefs and faith were once again under the watch of many who believed that we could bring the joy of our life to others. Indeed, this life should reflect the will and determination of many who wish to earn a fruitful life and to thus win something bigger than themselves, for their community, for their family, for their loved ones, for life as a whole, and even the life after death.

The world was full of magic, and the magic occurs in the things that we might pay little attention to, never think of, or don't even believe in. Oftentimes I did not recognize a miracle even when I saw it. I always thought that some of God's miraculous healing or miracle should be instantaneous. I do not fully understand why some of His miracles must go through stages with the progression of time so that the blessing or healing process could be completed. For instance, there was a time when I cried many nights during my sleep. I knew that I had been stripped of myself during those drunken years. Slowly I found there should be time that I needed to stop from being addicted or indulging in my own way of life. I also realized there should be a point that I needed to criticize my failure for not disciplining myself enough. By and large, I saw what we all could be scared of eventually do happen in real time. When social values shift across distance and time, cultures moved along with them. When culture or perception begins to change over time, attitudes emerge to keep humanity blindfolded to the sense of right and wrong. When we realized the sense of magic going away from the time we let our ego flying high, nothing seemed to be mattered anymore. We would not have the strength to believe in the signs that could change our life. The same feeling still exists today when people are in love but tend to not know or admit about love. Some people don't want to be committed in love, and some even tend to put an end to the dating scene because they were afraid to get hurt. The pattern of trust and belief in the supernatural or higher power dies when we were more likely and easily heart-broken than cherished what holds deep inside of our heart. Whether or not you've had a life that could be as struggling and challenging as that of mine, you should not fall for anything and lose focus on being your own best; instead, find balance and work through your belief system so that your future would be better than your past. I truly believe that though we couldn't change the choice we made in the past, but we can change the choice for the future because we all have our moment in life and at some point, we need a moment to figure out what if. Don't blame "fate" because we could find fate relating to the other side of life. Don't make excuses for time, money or talents because we allowed "them" to get in our way. Besides, confusion could be a suicide for anything such as love, relationships, health and success. When we have doubt, we need to get it out as soon as possible before our life could be messed up. Whatever happened in between the obstacles and our perceptions, there would be a time that we no longer could lie anymore and couldn't keep our loved ones in the darkness all the time because life needed to move forward from any pointless drama.

Indeed, we should always work hard to achieve the life we dream of. We can't get there if we do not believe in the goodness of people and if we fail to trust in the Lord. To this very day, I can smile in front of mirror when I look at my past. From time to time, I see how all my failings, shortcomings, hardships and setbacks drowned me. I say to myself that I had never thought I could do it. One thing that I will never forget was how God saw and found me in the first place. Since the inception of faith and re-baptism in spirit, I found that I no longer needed protection or some kind of cover-up to control my sense of fear, denial and frustration because I knew that God had a plan for my life. I rejoice each day to experience the shower of blessing by following my dad's footsteps. Though I see my current life was simple and quiet, I tend to like it more by enjoying myself close to my nature. From time to time, I find out that people seemed to be in such a hurry or overscheduled themselves, but I truly believe that there was upon a time in our life, we should need to slow down and that we maintain to work hard toward our goal. By and large, it's the reason I actually can retain my composure during various changes in my life, and I also happen to come a long way to overcome all kinds of people who tried to bring me down and all the negatives that seemed to knock me off were only because I had found the supernatural who happen to have the most superb wisdom on earth and the greatest peace of mind from this world to help me overcome my hunger, thirst and emptiness. As I looked back at those bumps in my life, I believed my intention was not to hurt anyone even though I couldn't think of anything I wanted in life because I don't want to get confused and perplexed anymore. I realize those bumps indeed caused a major pileup some time and they placed me at a crucial intersection or turning point, and they further made me strong as I moved forward. While I took a close look at my dad's great smile and at his overcoming of grief, I feel blessed because our Lord had put a few good men and women into the life of my family so that we could get back on to our feet comfortably. But not surprisingly, as far as I could remember and also when I looked at my dad for one last time by laying him down into the ground, I came to my senses to learn one last truth that his faith, devotion, courage and passion were truly commemorated, his legacy was absolutely inspiring, and his fatherhood was incredibly fascinating and yet profoundly well done. Meanwhile, I also learned that I have another dad who happened to be greatly loved, kind, devoted, unselfish and more capable than my biological father, and this spiritual dad, God, was there and will be there for me at all time.

Time and culture could indeed change. We've grown up in a world where our parents or even our grandparents could hardly imagine the movement of science and the revolution of technology. As the world continues to evolve vis-à-vis high technology, life was gradually getting better. Today, though we live in an era in which every business transaction and every level of communication could be done within a tap or click of fingertips coming off the electronic devices, we find the way of our connection or communication remained relatively slow in comparison to what God put inside our heart and into our mind. We could choose to live in an environment that no longer required any face time interaction between the parties involved, personally, institutionally or society as a whole. Indeed, we live in this high technology time when our grandparents could hardly imagine how far a dollar could stretch to cover our expense. We could choose to live and continue to press on when we had no idea how far we could push our personal agendas and thoughts into other people's lives. Whether some of us believe in the law of inertia or not, we probably saw that the physical force of "our want" was still unchangeable in relative to the terms of gravity that supported the nature of "our need." Sometimes I believe that we tended to run away from something we didn't know and whether or not we're in fear or doubt, we, from time to time, tend to run away, avoid or put little concern from all those that we thought to be of less value in relative to our need or want. Whether we care about this life or not, the law of attraction still applies in terms of desire, objective pursuit, and physical appearance in spite of great evolutions from history, science and technology. Whether we believe or not, our life was not much different from that of the tide or wave. The tide or wave could move silently or with loud noise, but it indeed did rise and fall within motion. Even at a time when the tide chose to not move at all, but life moves on. Whether we like it or not, pharmaceuticals have become an increasingly dominant in modern medicine and continue to play an indispensable role in our lives, especially when the medical community aggressively pushes its agenda into the wellness of others. Whether we agree with or reject any specific philosophy, we were and continued to face interpersonal problems, political conflicts, cultural setbacks, and relationship issues. Whether we make it an exceptional agenda or not, Christians and conservatives still were and continued to care more about their core values, moral percepts, and/or principles of well-being for a better life regarding their faith. Whether or not we pay close attention to what's happening in and around our life, physical laws still interact with us and in some cases, they became naturally bound to us with little regard to our nature, opinions, permissions, and decisions on their premises. Despite of all the changes in this world that might be predicted, there was only one truth that was everlasting and unchangeable regardless of all political and interpersonal conflicts. In fact, knowing God was more than knowing a religion. Understanding the signs given at a time was as important as acknowledging the truth from the Bible. Though religion in general could be different from what was given from the Bible, our life would never be the same when we figured out the eternal value from the spiritual law, as the Scriptures say that "Jesus the Lord was never changed yesterday, today, tomorrow and forever" (Hebrews 13:8) and "his plans were always good" (Jeremiah 29:11). Though hardships, tribulations and difficulties could be as sharp as blade and hit hard as a rock, we could respond to them by not thinking of defeat, refusing the fearfulness of those about us, taking strong stands in the midst of pressure, focusing on the goals but not on the storm, and finally obeying God without fear of negative consequences of any kind.

Every one of us has a story of our own to tell. We could decide to share our story with others or choose not to. Life, to some people, could be considered as a game. Sometimes people do not really care about what you play in your own game, but the important thing was that you need to know how and why you play so that you won't be confused. Whether many of us view our life as a game, story or anything else, we should keep ourselves alert at all times so that the devil can't easily make an excuse to attack and steal our belongings in the years of tribulation, trial or hardships. Relationships could be difficult and complicated like that of the roller coaster that could cause nerve breakdown. Some experience could even be more painful than others, and that requires our patience and faith so that we could bring out the best of what we cherish most in our heart. At some point in our lives, every one of us would be snapped by our weakest links. Those weakest links could include but were not limited to gambling, addictions, doubt, fear, obsession, anger, frustration, emotional tolls and just to name a few, would cause more problem than what we could be ever imagined. Every one of us hurts in one way or another, and we need some form of healing. Not everyone is as happy as what you might see. Not everyone is as good as how you think they are. Not everyone is actually living their life as adult as you may think. Not everyone is so loving and caring as you thought they should be. And not everyone wants the exact thing you want. In reality, every one of us worships something in one way or another, and sometimes it could be different because the ones we worshipped could be named differently, such as Buddha, Mother Theresa, Gandhi, Jesus, Mohammed, mountain, sea or some rock, just to name a few. One big difference between them was the way we were committed to them.

Every one of us have our own life or living in other words, and whether it's good or bad, ordinary or extraordinary, simple or complicated, they are still our own way of life. Life is a journey of experience that reflects and sums up what we live from moment to moment. Life could be somewhat miserable, but memories could be sweet. From time to time, we had to walk our own path of life and keep walking our way despite the fact that we could be lonely and frustrated enough. But if every one of us could go back to our path of life, then I truly believe that we should have a different version of how that life should be. In fact, no one assures of what can start or end our dream or plans without going through a painful story. Hopefully some of our stories could give us a successful tip for some happy ending in between. Indeed all life, regardless of race, age, status or stage of development deserves dignity as it carries a great value of its own. Racial diversity and varying characteristics were proven to be God's wisdom to form the dynamic of family and society that allowed all of us to shake off preference and thus to promote unity in term of co-existence. I truly don't know what the secrets were for living a long life and what could be the reasons behind in not sharing life together. Sometimes I honestly believe our life or living lifestyle could be very challenged or difficult to change into the way we wanted. For some reasons, I repetitively ask myself and give a considerable thought that if I didn't have the war, hunger, escape and setbacks, I could have a hard time to imagine how my life could be, not to mention the courage to face them as my mission was to strive for excellence, peace and liberty.

I realized that I have been on that bus of denial, loss, hardships and confusion, and it is very tough to get that off. But by the grace of our Almighty God, I gradually realize no condemnation should be given to those who trust Jesus and I couldn't believe the guidance, comfort, strength, freedom and happiness that I was once longed for turn out to be the love and security He promised but eventually gives that to me with a high price for me to pay at my own expense.

Indeed, knowing our purpose helps us to seek life in a different way and that also helps us to be proactive with decision making when confronting a situation. Believe or not, the genuine meaning of life is to find our unique gift that allows us to make use of our special gift or talents to achieve our calling and purpose of life itself. And the ultimate goal of life is to find out our own purpose and to rediscover our great passion so that we can live our life to the fullest. Whether we had sought our purpose in life or not, I was convinced that one day many of us would take a next step or a new beginning to connect and promote a genuine relationship with our true God. Knowing God is different from knowing a religion because religion, by definition, is a structured system of doctrine and practice or a specific fundamental set of beliefs. Religion indeed can have significant drawbacks despite the fact that it helps to shape our world, motivates us to better deal with concerns about our lives, and guides us to cultivate with respect to good and evil through interpersonal involvement and/or social engagement. Whether we were a firm believer, religious fanatic, spiritual seeker, agnostic or atheist, the abundant life only came to those who were willing to take challenges by following Jesus Christ up the mountain and to thus climb higher with God. Whether we are able to change our existing life or bring our current living lifestyle to a new level, we are fully responsible for how we are responding to what God says and reveals in our life and further, that also depends on how we are going to follow him. Whether we were the best author of our own life or not, God always gave a "wake-up" call to each and every one of us at some point, but sometimes what mattered most was how and if we choose to follow or ignore that call. By and large, our first and last story could be perfect only if we agree to allow the supernatural stepping into our very life especially when we were going through the emotions. Last but not least and regardless of what we could see or can't imagine, God was still the greatest editor of all times because he was forever with us, for us, and within us no matter what kind of storyline we have.

References

1. Arthur C. Guyton, MD and John E. Hall, PhD. Textbook of Medical Physiology (Philadelphia, PA: W.B. Saunders company, 2001).
2. Mary B. Eddy, Science and Health with key to the Scripture (The Christian Science Board Directors, 1994).
3. K.P. Yohannan, Revolution in World Missions (Carrollton, TX: GFA Books, 1986).
4. Holy Bible: King James Version (Salt Lake City, UT: Intellectual Reserve, Ins., 2000).
5. Merck Manual of Medical Information (New York, NY: Simon & Schuster, Inc., 1997).